After
the
Ecstasy,
the
Laundry

OTHER BOOKS BY JACK KORNFIELD

Living Buddhist Masters (Living Dharma)
A Still Forest Pool (with Paul Breiter)
Seeking the Heart of Wisdom (with Joseph Goldstein)
Stories of the Spirit, Stories of the Heart/Soul Food
(with Christina Feldman)
Buddha's Little Instruction Book
Teachings of the Buddha
A Path with Heart

FOR INFORMATION ABOUT INSIGHT MEDITATION WRITE TO:
Spirit Rock Center
P.O. Box 909-E
Woodacre, California 94973
Or visit: www.spiritrock.org

FOR TAPES OF LECTURES AND MEDITATIONS CONTACT:
Dharma Seed Tape Library
P.O. Box 66
Wendell Depot, Massachusetts 01380
Or visit: www.dharma.org

JACK KORNFIELD

After the Ecstasy, the Laundry

HOW THE HEART GROWS WISE ON THE SPIRITUAL PATH

BANTAM BOOKS

New York   Toronto   London   Sydney   Auckland

AFTER THE ECSTASY, THE LAUNDRY
A Bantam Book / June 2000

BOOK DESIGN BY CAROL MALCOLM RUSSO/SIGNET M DESIGN, INC.

Library of Congress Cataloging-in-Publication Data
Kornfield, Jack, 1945–
After the ecstasy, the laundry : how the heart grows wise
on the spiritual path / Jack Kornfield.
p. cm.
Includes index.
ISBN 0-553-10290-7
1. Spiritual life — Buddhism. I. Title.
BQ5660.K66 2000
294.3'444 — dc21   00-021153

Published simultaneously in the United States and Canada

Bantam Books are published by Bantam Books, a division of Random
House, Inc. Its trademark, consisting of the words "Bantam Books"
and the portrayal of a rooster, is Registered in U.S. Patent and
Trademark Office and in other countries. Marca Registrada.
Bantam Books, 1540 Broadway, New York, New York 10036.

PRINTED IN THE UNITED STATES OF AMERICA

BVG   10   9   8   7   6   5   4   3   2   1

Dedicated to
Ven. Ajahn Chah,
to his Dharma brother
Ven. Ajahn Buddhadasa,
and to
the lineage of
the Elders of the forest.

CONTENTS

PART THREE
No Enlightened Retirement

PART FOUR
Awakening in the Laundry

AN OPENING BOW

When I found myself becoming a Buddhist monk in a forest monastery of Thailand over thirty years ago, I had to learn how to bow. It was awkward at first. Each time we entered the meditation hall we would drop to our knees and three times respectfully place our head between our palms on the stone floor. It was a practice of reverence and mindfulness, a way of honoring with a bodily gesture our commitment to the monk's path of simplicity, compassion, and awareness. We would bow in the same way each time we took our seat for training with the master.

After I had been in the monastery for a week or two, one of the senior monks pulled me aside for further instruction. "In this monastery you must not only bow when entering the meditation hall and receiving teachings from the master, but also when you meet your elders." As the only Westerner, and wanting to act correctly, I asked who my elders were. "It is traditional that all who are older in ordination time, who've been monks longer than you, are your elders," I was told. It took only a moment to realize that meant everybody.

So I began to bow to them. Sometimes it was just fine—there were quite a few wise and worthy elders in the community. But sometimes it felt ridiculous. I would encounter some twenty-one-year-old monk, full of hubris, who was there only to please his parents or to eat better food than he could at home, and I had to bow because he had been ordained the week before me. Or I had to bow to a sloppy old rice farmer who had come to the monastery the season before on the farmers' retirement plan, who chewed betel nut constantly and had never meditated a day in his life. It was hard to pay reverence to these fellow forest dwellers as if they were great masters.

Yet there I was bowing, and because I was in conflict, I sought a way to make it work. Finally, as I prepared yet again for a day of bowing to my "elders," I began to look for some worthy aspect of each person I bowed to. I bowed to the wrinkles around the retired farmer's eyes, for all the difficulties he had seen and suffered through and triumphed over. I bowed to the vitality and playfulness in the young monks, the incredible possibilities each of their lives held yet ahead of them.

I began to enjoy bowing. I bowed to my elders, I bowed before I entered the dining hall and as I left. I bowed as I entered my forest hut, and I bowed at the well before taking a bath. After some time bowing became my way—it was just what I did. If it moved, I bowed to it.

It is the spirit of bowing that informs this book. The true task of spiritual life is not found in faraway places or unusual states of consciousness: It is here in the present. It asks of us a welcoming spirit to greet all that life presents to us with a wise, respectful, and kindly heart. We can bow to both beauty and suffering, to our entanglements and confusion, to our fears and to the injustices of the world. Honoring the truth in this way is the path to freedom. To bow to what *is* rather than to some ideal is not necessarily easy, but however difficult, it is one of the most useful and honorable practices.

To bow to the fact of our life's sorrows and betrayals is to accept them; and from this deep gesture we discover that all life is workable. As we learn to bow, we discover that the heart holds more freedom and compassion than we could imagine.

The Persian poet Rumi speaks of it this way:

> This being human is a guest house.
> Every morning a new arrival.
>
> A joy, a depression, a meanness,
> some momentary awareness comes
> as an unexpected visitor.
>
> Welcome and entertain them all
> Even if they're a crowd of sorrows,
> who violently sweep your house
> empty of its furniture.
>
> Still treat each guest honorably,
> He may be clearing you out
> for some new delight.
>
> The dark thought, the shame, the malice,
> meet them at the door laughing,
> and invite them in.
>
> Be grateful for whoever comes,
> because each has been sent
> as a guide from beyond.

INTRODUCTION:
Some Honest Questions

When the bird and the book disagree, always believe the bird.
JAMES AUDUBON

Enlightenment does exist. It is pos-
sible to awaken. Unbounded freedom and joy, oneness with the
Divine, awakening into a state of timeless grace—these experiences are more common than you know, and not far away. There
is one further truth, however: They don't last. Our realizations and
awakenings show us the reality of the world, and they bring transformation, but they pass.

Of course, you may have read traditional accounts of fully
enlightened sages in Asia or of wholly unblemished saints and
mystics in the West. But these ideal narratives can be misleading.
In fact, in the awakening of the heart there is no such thing as
enlightened retirement. That is not how it happens to us.

We all know that after the honeymoon comes the marriage,
after the election comes the hard task of governance. In spiritual
life it is the same: After the ecstasy comes the laundry.

Most spiritual accounts end with illumination or enlightenment. But what if we ask what happens after that? What happens when the Zen master returns home to spouse and children? What happens when the Christian mystic goes shopping? What is life like after the ecstasy? How do we live our understanding with a full heart?

To explore these questions I have spoken with a number of people who have dedicated twenty-five, thirty-five, forty years to a spiritual path, especially those who have become the Western meditation masters and abbots, the Western teachers and lamas of our generation. They told me of their initial journeys and awakenings, and then described the lessons of the years that followed, as they have sought to fulfill the true path of compassion on this earth.

Here is one account of a Western Zen master's initial satori (enlightenment experience) and its aftermath. Such accounts are rarely made public because of the danger that they will give the wrong impression, that those who experience such an awakening are somehow special. Although the experience is special, it does not happen to a special person. It happens to any of us when the conditions of letting go and opening the heart are present, when we can sense the world in a radically new way.

For this teacher, awakening came at age fifty-eight, after many years of practice with several meditation masters, while at the same time he was developing a career and raising a family.

The weeklong meditation of a Zen sesshin was always very intense for me. I would feel a deep emotional release, and strong memories would come up as if I were in a birth process—strong pains and physical catharsis. These would carry over for weeks when I went back home.

This sesshin began the same way. During the first days I struggled with powerful emotions and the release of energies coursing through my body, and each time I saw the master he would sit there like a rock, his presence steadying me like a rudder in dark turbulent seas. I felt as if I was dying or breaking apart. He urged me to sink into my koan, to let

*myself go completely into it. I couldn't tell where my life
began or left off.*

*Then a surprising sweetness began to seep in. I saw three
young birch trees out the window, and they were like my
family. I could feel myself go and stroke their smooth bark,
and I became the tree touching myself. My meditation filled
with light.*

*I had felt bliss before—big waves of it on some retreats
after my body pains opened up—but this was different. All
struggle stopped, and my mind became luminous, radiant,
vast as the sky, and filled with a most delicious scent of freedom, of awakening. I felt like the Buddha sitting effortlessly
hour after hour, held and protected by the whole universe.
I lived in a world of unending peace and unspeakable joy.*

*The great truths of life were so clear—the way grasping
is the cause of suffering; that by following the small sense of
self, this false ego, we run around like the petty landlord,
squabbling over nothing. I wept at all our unnecessary sorrows. Then for hours I could not stop smiling and laughing.
I saw how perfect it all is, how every single moment is
enlightenment if only we open to it.*

*For days I rested in this timeless utter peace, my body
floating, my mind empty. I would wake up and waves of love
and joyful energy would stream through my consciousness.
Then, insights and revelations came, one after another. I saw
how the stream of life unfolds in patterns that we create as
the flow of our karma. I saw the whole idea of spiritual
renunciation as kind of a joke, trying to make oneself let go
of ordinary life and pleasures. In fact, Nirvana is so open
and joyful, is so much more than any of the small pleasures
we grasp after. You don't renounce the world, you gain the
world.*

The description of a great awakening like this usually appears
at the end of a spiritual story. Enlightenment comes, the person
enters the stream of wise beings, and everything follows naturally

after that. In essence we are left with the impression that the awakened person lives happily ever after. But what happens if we stay with this story and ask to hear further chapters?

Some months after all this ecstasy came a depression, along with some significant betrayals in my work. I had continuing trouble with my children and family too. Oh, my teaching was fine. I could give inspired lectures, but if you talk to my wife, she'll tell you that as the time passed I became grouchy and as impatient as ever. I knew that this great spiritual vision was the truth, and it was there underneath, but I also recognized how many things didn't change at all. To be honest, my mind and personality were pretty much the same, and my neuroses too. Perhaps it's worse, because now I see them more clearly. Here were these cosmic revelations and I still needed therapy just to sort through the day-to-day mistakes and lessons of living a human life.

What are we to make of an account of awakening like this one and the story that follows? It offers us a mirror for self-understanding. Sacred traditions have always been carried in great measure by storytelling: We tell and retell the story of Noah, the Bal Shem Tov, Mohammed, St. Theresa, Milarepa, Krishna and Arjuna, the Buddha's search, the stories of Jesus. In modern times we learn from the lives of Thomas Merton, Suzuki Roshi, Anne Frank, and Martin Luther King Jr. Through other spiritual lives we can see our own possibilities and better understand how to live wisely.

People-watching is also in my lineage. My teacher Ajahn Chah knew that through our character is found both our suffering and our liberation. So he would peer at those who came to see him like a watchmaker taking off the case of a watch to see how it ticks.

By good fortune, as a spiritual "professional," circumstances have given me close contact with many figures in modern spiritual life. I have lived and taught with holy nuns and wise abbots of Christian monasteries, with Jewish mystics, with Hindu, Sufi, and Buddhist masters, and with leading figures of the Jungian and Transpersonal communities. What one can observe and hear in such company reveals much about the way the modern spiritual journey unfolds, and the difficulties even the most dedicated people encounter. Here is an example of what one might learn in such company.

Since the early 1990s, I have been involved in convening a succession of gatherings for Buddhist teachers from all the great schools. One series was hosted by the Dalai Lama at his Dharamsala palace. Here Western and Asian teachers gathered to discuss the ways Buddhist practice might be of help in the modern world, and also to address the difficulties we encountered. It was a roomful of good-hearted, compassionate Zen masters, lamas, monks, and meditation masters whose wisdom, work, and communities had brought benefit to thousands. We talked about many successes, and our joy in being part of them. But when the time came to talk honestly about our problems, it grew clear that spiritual life was not entirely harmonious; it reflected our collective struggles and individual neuroses as well. Even among such an august and dedicated company, there were major areas of prejudice and blindness.

Sylvia Wetzel, a Buddhist teacher from Germany, talked about how hard it was for women and feminine wisdom to be fully included in the Buddhist community. She pointed to the many golden Buddhas and exquisite Tibetan paintings surrounding our room, noting they were all depicting males. Then she instructed the Dalai Lama and the other lamas and masters to close their eyes and meditate with her, to imagine that they were entering the room and that it had been transformed so that they bowed to the fourteenth female incarnation of the Dalai Lama. With her were many advisors who had always been female, and surrounding them were images of Buddhas and saints, all naturally in women's bodies. Of course, it is never taught that there is anything lesser about being a man. Despite that, these men were asked to sit in the back, be silent, and after the meeting to help with the cooking. At the end of her meditation, the eyes of every man in the room reopened, slightly astonished.

Then Ani Tenzin Palmo, a Tibetan nun of English descent who had trained for twenty years, twelve of them in caves on the Tibetan border, spoke in a gentle voice describing the spiritual longing and incredible hardships of devoted women, who were allowed to live only at the periphery of the monasteries, often without teaching, food, or support. When she finished, the Dalai Lama put his head in his hands and wept. He pledged his best support to revising the place of women in his community to one of more equality. And yet in the years since, many senior teachers in every Buddhist country have continued to resist and struggle against these changes, sometimes in the name of tradition, at other times because of psychological and cultural conditioning. At the meeting with the Dalai Lama, one senior Zen abbot admitted that his painful relationship with his mother made it nearly impossible for him to guide the group of women who had become priests in his temple. Others admitted their own struggles in this area.

Our conversation turned to other forms of blindness: sectarianism and destructive power struggles between certain Buddhist masters and communities; the isolation and loneliness of the role of the teacher; the teachers who may in turn have exploited their students through misuse of power, money, and sexuality. In informal discussions we spoke also of more personal problems: Teachers described painful divorces, periods of fear and depression, conflicts with family or other community members. Meditation teachers told of stress and illness, of teenage children threatening suicide or belligerent teens wanting to stay out all night, who confront their parents with "You're a Zen master, and look how attached you are." We all have the problems that come with bodies, personalities, family, and community. We saw our common humanity.

Fortunately we also shared the astonishing gifts that spiritual practices had given us, the joy and freedom we had learned to carry with us in the difficult and changing circumstances of the world.

What was remarkable and new was the honesty with which we spoke. Our intention was inspired by the humility and compassion of the Dalai Lama himself, always eager to learn, even from his mistakes. We began to see that we could learn from one another, find ways to avoid re-creating painful mistakes, to allow our ideals to embrace our humanness. It was as if the flowering of individual wisdom and learning came more fully alive as a collective, as a whole.

The difficulties of finding a wise expression of spiritual life in modern circumstances are not limited to Eastern traditions. One mother superior, the beloved abbess of a century-old Catholic nunnery in Maine, grew up in the silence of her cloister from age seventeen until the 1960s. Then Pope John XXIII, in the spirit of reform, changed the mass from Latin to English, and opened the strict silence of the monastic orders. This was incredibly hard for those who had been sheltered in holy silence for decades, their days filled with prayer and inner reflection. They simply didn't know how to talk, and when they did, what emerged was sometimes surprisingly conflicted. Along with their love came out many hidden judgments, built-up resentments, pettiness, and fears that had been kept hidden within the container of prayer and silence. The sisters were forced to grapple with their spiritual life out loud, without any prior training in wise speech. Many fled the convent. It took some years for the community to find the same grace in human words they had felt in silence. Yet spiritual life needs both. As much as our breath comes in and out, it must integrate inner knowing and outer expression. It is not enough to touch awakening. We must find ways to live its vision fully.

Perfect enlightenment appears in many texts, but amid all the Western masters and teachers I know, such utter perfection is not apparent. Times of great wisdom, deep compassion, and a real knowing of freedom alternate with periods of fear, confusion, neurosis, and struggle. Most teachers will readily admit this truth. Unfortunately, a few Westerners have claimed to achieve a perfection and freedom with no shadow. Among their communities, things are worse: By their self-inflation they have often created the most power-centered and destructive communities among us.

The wisest express a greater humility. Abbots like Father Thomas Keating of Snowmass Monastery and Norman Fischer of the San Francisco Zen Center, for example, regularly say, "I'm learning" and "I don't know." In the spirit of Gandhi, Mother Teresa, Dorothy Day, and the Dalai Lama, they understand that spiritual perfection is not born of oneself, but of patience and love that grow through the wisdom of the larger community; that spiritual fulfillment and freedom include a compassion for all that arises in this human form.

One might ask at this point: What about the old masters in Asia? Might it not be that Western Zen masters and lamas are simply too young and undeveloped to represent real enlightenment? Many Western teachers would agree that this is true of themselves. But while there might be someone far away who appears to fit the image of perfect enlightenment, that appearance may result from a confusion between the archetypal and the human levels. In Tibet there is a saying that your guru should live at least three valleys away. These valleys are separated by huge mountains, so to see your teacher means many days of hard travel. The point is that only at this distance can you be inspired by the perfection of the guru.

When I complained to my abbot Ajahn Chah, considered by millions to be a great saint, that he didn't always act as if he were completely enlightened, he laughed and told me that was good, "because otherwise you would still be imagining that you could find the Buddha outside of yourself. And he is not here."

Indeed, many of the most appealing and highly regarded Asian masters have spoken about still being students themselves, always learning from mistakes. Some, like Zen Master Shunryu Suzuki, did not even claim enlightenment. Instead, Suzuki Roshi said, "Strictly speaking, there are no enlightened people, there is only enlightened activity." This remarkable statement tells us that enlightenment cannot be held by anyone. It simply exists in moments of freedom.

Pir Vilayat Khan, the seventy-five-year-old head of the Sufi Order in the West, confides his own belief:

> *Of so many great teachers I've met in India and Asia, if you were to bring them to America, get them a house, two cars, a spouse, three kids, a job, insurance, and taxes . . . they would all have a hard time.*

Whatever our initial vision of spiritual life, to be authentic, it must be fulfilled here and now, in the place where we live. What does a Westerner's journey look like in the midst of a complex society? How have those who have devoted twenty-five, thirty, forty years to spiritual practice learned to live? These are the questions I began to ask of those who have become Western Zen masters, lamas, rabbis, abbots, nuns, yogis, teachers, and their most senior students.

To understand spiritual life I started at the beginning. I asked what draws us to the life of the spirit and what difficulties we have to pass through on our way. I asked what gifts and awakenings have come, and what we can know about enlightenment. Then I asked what happens after the ecstasy, as we mature in the cycles of spiritual life. Is there a wisdom which includes both the ecstasy and the laundry?

PART ONE

Preparation
for Ecstasy

1

BABA YAGA AND OUR
SACRED LONGING

The moment I heard my first story
I started looking for you. . . .
—RUMI

Midway along our road of life I woke to find
myself standing alone in a dark wood.
DANTE ALIGHIERI

W hat is it that draws a person to
spiritual life? From as far back as we can remember, we can each
sense a mystery in being alive. When we are present with an infant
in the first moments after birth, or when the death of a loved one
brushes close to us, the mystery becomes tangible. It is there when
we witness a radiant sunset or find a moment's silent stillness in
the flowing seasons of our days. Connecting to the sacred is perhaps our deepest need and longing.

Awakening calls to us in a thousand ways. As the poet Rumi
sings, "Grapes want to turn to wine." There is a pull to wholeness,
to being fully alive, even when we have forgotten. The Hindus tell
us that the child in the womb sings, "Do not let me forget who I

3

am," but that the song after birth becomes, "Oh, I have forgotten already."

Still, as surely as there is a voyage away, there is a journey home.

Throughout the world we find stories of this journey, images of the longing to awaken, the steps along the path that we all follow, the voices that call, the intensity of the initiation we may meet, the courage we need. At the heart of each is the original sincerity of the seeker, who must honestly admit how small is our knowledge of the universe, how great the unknown.

The honesty the spiritual quest requires of us is addressed in the Russian initiation tales about Baba Yaga. Baba Yaga is an old woman with a wild, haglike visage who stirs her pot and knows all things. She lives deep in the forest. When we seek her out we are frightened, for she requires us to go into the dark, to ask dangerous questions, to step outside the world of logic and comfort.

When the first young seeker comes quaking up to the door of her hut, Baba Yaga demands, "Are you on your own errand or are you sent by another?" The young man, encouraged in his quest by his family, answers, "I am sent by my father." Baba Yaga promptly throws him into the pot and cooks him. The next to attempt this quest, a young woman, sees the smoldering fire and hears the cackle of Baba Yaga. Baba Yaga again demands, "Are you on your own errand or are you sent by another?" This young woman has been pulled to the woods alone to seek what she can find there. "I am on my own errand," she replies. Baba Yaga throws her in the pot and cooks her too.

Later a third visitor, again a young woman, deeply confused by the world, comes to Baba Yaga's house far into the forest. She sees the smoke and knows it is dangerous. Baba Yaga confronts her, "Are you on your own errand, or are you sent by another?" This young woman answers truthfully. "In large part I'm on my own errand, but in large part I also come because of others. And in large part I have come because you are here, and because of the forest, and something I have forgotten, and in large part I know not why I come." Baba Yaga regards her for a moment and says, "You'll do," and shows her into the hut.

Into the Woods

We don't know all the reasons that propel us on a spiritual journey, but somehow our life compels us to go. Something in us knows that we are not just here to toil at our work. There is a mysterious pull to remember. What takes us out of our homes and into the dark of Baba Yaga's forest can be a combination of events. It can be a longing from childhood, or an "accidental" encounter with a spiritual book or figure. Sometimes something in us awakens when we travel to a foreign culture and the exotic world of new rhythms, fragrances, colors, and activity catapults us out of our usual sense of reality. Sometimes it is as simple as walking in the blue-green mountains or hearing choral music so beautiful it seems inspired by the gods. Sometimes it is that mysterious transformation when we attend at the bedside of the dying and a "person" vanishes from existence, leaving only a lifeless sack of flesh awaiting burial. A thousand gates open to the spirit. Whether in the brilliance of beauty or the dark woods of confusion and sorrow, a force as sure as gravity brings us back to our heart. It happens to every one of us.

The Messengers of Suffering

The most frequent entryway to the sacred is our own suffering and dissatisfaction. Countless spiritual journeys have begun in an encounter with the difficulties of life. For Western masters, suffering in early family life is a common start: alcoholic or abusive parents, grave family illness, loss of a loved relative, or cold absentee parents and warring family members all recur in many of their stories. For one wise and respected meditation master it started with isolation and disconnection.

When I was a child, our family life had so much unhappiness. Everyone was yelling and I felt I didn't belong there. I felt like an alien. Then, about age nine I became really

interested in flying saucers. For years at night I would fan-
tasize that a UFO was going to pick me up, that I would be
abducted and taken back to another planet. I really wanted
that to escape from my alienation and loneliness. I guess that
was the beginning of my four decades of spiritual search.

We all know how much the heart longs for spiritual sustenance in times of difficulty. "Honor this longing," says Rumi.
"Those that make you return, for whatever reason, to the spirit,
be grateful to them. Worry about the others, who give you delicious comfort that keeps you from prayer."

For another spiritual teacher, physician, and healer, thirty
years of inner work also began with family sorrows.

My parents fought terribly and then divorced quite violently
when I was young. I was sent to an awful boarding school.
My family life was so painful, it left me lonely, filled with
grief, restlessness, and discontent with everything. I didn't
know how to live.

One day I saw a man in orange robes and shaved head
chanting "Hare Krishna" on the steps of the square. I naively
thought he was some wise Indian saint. He told me about
karma, reincarnation, meditation, and the possibility of
freedom. It rang true in my whole body. I was so excited, I
phoned my mother and said, "I'm leaving school. I want to
be a Hare Krishna monk." She became quite hysterical, so
we compromised to where I would learn meditation. That
opened me to another world. I learned to let go of my past
and to have compassion for myself. Meditation saved my life.

Crisis is an invitation to the spirit not only in childhood, but
whenever our life passes through suffering. For many masters, the
gateway to the spiritual opened when loss or desperation, suffering or confusion drove them to look for solace of the heart, for a
hidden wholeness. The long journey of one teacher began in
adulthood, overseas.

I was in Hong Kong. My marriage was going badly, my youngest daughter had died from sudden infant death syndrome two years earlier, and in every way I was not happy. We returned to America and at Stanford Business School I saw a sign for tai chi and signed up. That began to calm my body, but my heart remained sorrowful and confused. I separated from my wife and tried various forms of meditation to calm myself. Then a girlfriend introduced me to her meditation master, who invited me to a retreat. The room was formal and silent as we all sat hour after hour. On the second morning, suddenly I saw myself standing looking at my daughter's grave, with a shovelful of red earth being thrown on it. Tears came and a wail rose from me. The other students nearby hissed and whispered "Shut up," but the master came over and told them to be still and held me for a time. And I wept and blubbered, filled with grief all morning. That was how it began. Now, thirty years later, I am the one holding those who weep.

The encounter with suffering that leads us to seek an answer is a universal story. In the life story of the Buddha as Prince Siddhartha, the Buddha-to-be was deliberately protected from the problems of the world by his father, sequestered in beautiful palaces during his early years. Finally the young prince insisted on going out to see the world. As he rode through the kingdom with his charioteer Channa, he saw four sights which stunned him deeply. First the Buddha saw a very old person, tottering, bent over, and frail. Next he saw a man grievously ill, cared for by his friends. Then he saw a dead body. Each time he asked his charioteer, "To whom do these things happen?" Each time Channa replied, "To everyone, my lord."

These sights are called "the Heavenly Messengers," for just as they awakened the Buddha, so they remind us all to seek liberation, to seek a spiritual freedom in this life.

Can you remember the first time you saw a dead body or a person gravely ill? This first up-close encounter with sickness and death sent a shock through Siddhartha's whole being. "How can we best live in a life haunted by illness and death?" he wondered. The fourth messenger came when he saw a monk standing at the edge of the forest, a hermit who had devoted a life of simplicity to seek an end to the sorrows of the world. At this sight the Buddha realized that he too must follow this path, that he must face directly the sorrows of life and attempt to find a way beyond their grasp.

Like a modern Siddhartha, one teacher tells how her journey in the cities and countryside called her to her path.

After college I worked in a social service agency in Philadelphia trying to help a series of desperate families. No work, lots of children, squalid housing, drug problems. Some days I would come home from the agency and weep. Then with a friend I went to work in Central America—El Salvador and Guatemala. It seemed like an ocean of problems for the poor campesinos. They labored just to get enough food and medicine for their kids, and had to suffer periodic military raids. It was very hard. When I came back I entered the convent for four years, not to run away, but to find myself, to learn what I could really do to benefit this world.

The heavenly messengers come in some form to each of us, calling us to seek a wholeness missing in our lives. They come not just as our own struggles, but in the sorrows of the world. These have such a powerful effect on our hearts that any day's news could break them open. The perennial floods of Bangladesh; the hunger and warfare of Africa, Europe, Asia; the ecological crisis worldwide; the racism, poverty, and violence of our cities—they too are the messengers. They are a call. As they did for the Buddha, they demand that we awaken.

Return to Innocence

Lest it all sound difficult, there is another side to the forces that draw so many of us into the woods. A beauty calls to us, a wholeness that we know exists. The Sufis call this "the voice of the beloved." We are born into this world with the song in our ears, yet we may first come to know it by its absence.

When we live without connectedness, without an illumination of spirit, we can feel in ourselves the deep longing of a lost child, a subtle longing as though we know something essential is missing, something that dances at the edge of our vision, always with us like the air we forget until the wind blows. Yet it is this elusive spirit which holds us completely, which nourishes the heart, summoning us toward our search for what life is all about. We are pulled to return to our true nature, to our wise and knowing heart.

This sacred longing can arise first in childhood, as it did for the Zen master of a large community in Europe.

I remembered as a child having experiences of wonder and identity with the world. I felt an identity with the hills, seeing them dance, and the rivers in between. One day I imagined myself a part of a great summer storm that swept through our town. At about twelve I recognized how incredible the game of life is, how much bigger than anything I knew. Then I would forget and go back to playing soccer and playing with friends until the next time it happened, another moment of this naive sweet opening. Later I heard an Indian swami talk at the university about the world of nature and mystery, and he wept quite openly. I was so touched, as if I was hearing Jesus talk, and I began to remember again that innocent connection to my childhood. When you realize how much you've lost, you have to go looking again for those moments when your spirit first came alive.

Over the years, a practical and materialistic society can usurp the original mystery of childhood. We are sent to school early to "grow up," to "be serious," and if we don't let go of our childhood innocence, all too often the world tries to knock it out of us. A hundred years ago the American painter James McNeill Whistler encountered this attitude in his engineering class at West Point Military Academy. The students were instructed to draw a careful study of a bridge, and Whistler submitted a beautifully detailed picturesque stone arch with children fishing from its top. The lieutenant in charge ordered, "This is a military exercise. Get those children off the bridge." Whistler resubmitted the drawing with the two children now fishing from the side of the river. "I said get those children completely out of the picture," said the angry lieutenant. So Whistler's last version had the river, the bridge, and two small tombstones along its bank.

As the existentialist writer Albert Camus discovered:

> A man's life is nothing but an extended trek through the detours of art to recapture those one or two moments when his heart first opened.

The Zen tradition describes this journey in its account of the sacred ox. In ancient India, oxen were a symbol for the wondrous and powerful qualities that reside within every being, that awaken as we discover our true nature. The Zen ox-herding story begins with a scroll painting of a man wandering into the mountain thickets. The image is entitled "Seeking the Ox." Behind the man is a maze of crisscrossing roads: the old highways of ambition and fear, confusion and loss, praise and blame. For a long time this man has forgotten the flowing rivers and mountain vistas. But on the day he finally remembers, he sets out seeking the tracks of the sacred ox. In his heart he knows that even in the deepest gorges and the topmost mountains, the ox cannot be lost. In the beauty of the forest he stops to rest. And looking down, he sees the first tracks.

For one meditation teacher in her sixties, ox-seeking began in middle age, after raising three children.

When I was a girl I grew up in an intellectual environment where spiritual life was never mentioned except maybe at Christmas. It's as if my parents thought we were beyond that religion stuff. I was so jealous of my friends who went to church. Starting at seven I cut the pictures of Mary and angels and Jesus out of Christmas cards. I hid them in the bottom of my dresser drawer and made a secret altar there. I would take them out every Sunday and make up my own kind of service.

Then, at forty-three, I was traveling on business and had time to visit a famous cathedral. I went into the vast cool interior and saw the sunlight flaming through the stained glass. A choir began to sing Gregorian chants for the late afternoon service, and the altar held a beautiful Mary, just like my Christmas cards. I had to sit down. I felt seven again, my eyes filled with tears and my heart about burst. That poor little girl was spiritually starved. The next week I went to a yoga class and then signed up for a meditation retreat.

The Sacred Question

The first sighting of the tracks of the ox is described by Joseph Campbell as a call to awakening, an inner pull. With it arises a sacred question. For each of us this sacred question is different. Some of us struggle with pain, others simply want to know how best to live; some wonder what is important or what is the purpose of life. Others ask how can we love, or who are we, or how can we be free. Some of us ask the question as we hurry through our days, "Why such a rush?"

Some masters who were interviewed turned to philosophy to answer their questions, others tried the avenue of poetry and the arts. Sacred questioning is the root of much poetry. "Rhetoric is the argument you have with another," wrote Yeats, "poetry, with one-self." The call to the journey is like a half-formed poem, awaiting completion. Kabir, the Indian mystic poet, asks: "Can you tell me who has built this house of ours? And where do you hurry to before your death? Can you find the thing of true value in this world?"

Whatever the source of this profound questioning, we must follow where it leads. A Buddhist teacher found her questions growing when she finished her training in clinical psychology.

I had finished my Ph.D. in psychology and I found myself working in an adolescent unit and in suicide prevention. For years I had believed psychology had all the answers I was looking for. But as I worked, my faith began to crack. Because of the vast unalleviated suffering I encountered, the idea that psychology could give me all the answers seemed ridiculous. What could I turn to to understand this life?

One day in 1972 I visited a friend in Berkeley and as we walked she encountered a jolly bright foreign man and began a conversation with him. Later she explained he was a Tibetan lama and invited me to his teachings on dreams. I didn't understand a word of it, but at one moment when a woman questioned him about compassionate action, and I saw the way he answered, compassion was no longer just a word. He brought into his answer a manifestation of compassion that totally touched my heart. I was stunned. Up until that time I had thought of compassion as a nice Presbyterian word that had no reality; you know, a nice idea. Here it was a living force. I was completely intrigued. I wanted to know what this was. That opened the spiritual door for me.

A Chicago businesswoman, brought up in a close-knit family, lived a traditional life until her outward success became difficult and empty; then she began to question it all.

I was the middle child of five who loved each other, went to mass every day, attended Catholic girls' schools all the way along. As a girl I prayed often and fervently. I offered things

*up for the souls in purgatory, made up various harmless rit-
uals to remind myself of Jesus and how much he loved me.
Then I got married. It was the tumultuous sixties and my
marriage didn't last very long. Having entered a bigger,
wilder life, more frightening than I knew, I graduated
Chicago business school and several years of therapy at the
same time. My thirties were hell . . . battling a prolonged
and deep depression, with no idea of who I might be or what
I might hope for from life. All I could do was throw myself
into my work night and day, and in ten years I was chosen
the first woman vice president of our company at a ceremony
at the Carlton Hotel ballroom. This success was heady at
first—it made up for other losses. But eventually the charm
wore off and my life seemed supremely selfish. With the rich
getting richer and the poor sliding down the ladder, I realized I was part of the problem, and I wasn't even having fun
doing it.*

*Then two of my closest friends died. My mother was
next. I resigned from my company to care for her and found
that being present for her and my father through their shock
and denial to acceptance was the most satisfying task of my
life. I began volunteering at a hospice, and started to meditate. Wrestling with the persistent devil of emptiness
directly for the first time was like coming home. I would
never have thought it possible, but now I feel most myself
when sitting in silence, listening. And I found my heart
again after all these years; and with a lot of help from
friends, the courage to follow it.*

Calls from Beyond

Sometimes the opening of the mind and heart comes as if a call
from the gods, a pull from outside of our ordinary life. It is as if
we are compelled to enter the forest, to search out Baba Yaga, by
forces beyond our knowing. In Rumi's poem of the guest house

quoted earlier, he counsels us to be grateful for whoever comes, "because each has been sent as a guide from beyond."

In the powerful shock of near-death experiences, thousands of Americans have had a spiritual opening. In *Closer to the Light*, Dr. Melvin Morse, a physician, documents children's near-death experiences. A child awakens from nearly drowning and then going into a coma to tell her astonished doctor about a golden figure, an angel, who pulled her from under the dark water and brought her through a tunnel where she met her grandfather, who had died years before, and then the Heavenly Father. One after another children's accounts speak of "finding the light that makes us all and the light that has everything good in it." After that, they say, "You're not afraid to live through anything."

A Sufi master speaks of the motorcycle accident that he had at age nineteen.

> *I was on the critical list, with broken bones and internal ruptures. As my mind cleared I remembered that for a second after the impact I was looking down at my body and the street from a short distance above. I could see, but my being was completely nonphysical. It was peaceful and quiet; I was relieved. I knew that I had the option to return to my body or let go into this wonderful peaceful darkness. But when I looked at the scene below, what arose was an intense feeling of love for this body and for life. Love and joy made me come back. They kept telling me that in the ambulance I was crying and laughing. I felt a reality of freedom that was beyond the physical, an intense joy and happiness that has motivated my spiritual life now for thirty-five years. I love this reality; I have followed its call.*

Each call from beyond asks us to step outside of our ordinary sense of the world. For one teacher of kundalini yoga, the request came in the last stage of labor.

> *My breathing became faster and faster. My body began shaking between the contractions and filled with radiant*

light. Not just my pelvis, but my heart, my head, every part of me was trying to open. I felt like my baby and I were expanding, containing all the energy of the world. Later my doctor told me it frightened him. He tried to give me a tranquilizer to calm me down. My eyes were wide with wonder. But from that moment on I wanted to bring that energy into my life.

Although the materialistic and scientific world of our culture may try to hide us from the vast source of our life, it cannot be denied. Over and over we hear tales, large and small, of the heart, the spirit, the soul reawakening to a greater vision of reality.

Illness too can summon us forth. One Western lama's account:

I came to California and joined a commune and was living day by day. Then I came down with hepatitis and went to heal in a borrowed hut in the Santa Cruz Mountains. I was throwing up every night. My skin was yellow, and I felt at the end of my rope, physically and emotionally. I had abandoned everything and was confused about what to do next.

Then, in the middle of the night, I began to hear chanting. I woke up and looked through the drops of water on the window by the bed. I saw a fat man sitting outside, with a hand on his black hat. There were gongs and chanting going on loudly in my head. He stayed there for a long time. Finally I fell back to sleep. The next morning I woke up and looked in the mirror, and my skin was clear and I was better. I walked out in the woods for the first time in weeks, and sat down by the creek and cried.

Next I got connected with a hippie Tibetan theater group and followed them to Nepal. The 16th Karmapa, the Tibetan dharma master, came to Katmandu for the first time in thirteen years, and I and two other Westerners went to see him. He said he was expecting our visit. I was astonished. He was the man outside my window in Santa Cruz! We were

*told he could come in our dreams and through this we could
be healed of diseases.*

*He was pleased with our visit and after many days
together told us that we had all been Tibetans in a previous
life and old companions of his. One of the senior lamas
showed me a picture of our monastery. Whether it was true
or not, it felt like coming home. Now, thirty-two years later,
all three of us have become lamas ourselves.*

The calls from beyond can come in a thousand forms. So we
cannot ignore the effect of psychedelics on the lives of many modern masters. Andrew Weil, the Harvard physician who has studied the use of sacred substances worldwide, writes: "The tradition
of most ancient cultures included a positive use of psychoactive
medicines, from China to India to Greece and the Americas."
Many who have committed themselves to the spiritual journey
had the gates of perception burst open by psychedelic experiences.
In truth, a number of current spiritual teachers in the West have
at least in part traveled this route. Much danger lies in the misuse of these substances, and we all know the tragic stories of their
abuse, but still they are a part of our heritage. From Zen beats of
the 1950s to the flower children of the '60s and '70s to shamanic
journeyers of the '80s, many spiritual leaders I encountered spoke
of the effect of mind-altering explorations.

A French meditation master who had spent years in India and
Tibet at first had no idea of the spiritual path.

*I was young, an artist, living near the beach, out for the plea-
sures of life. Then my girlfriend left me and some friends
returning from Mexico dropped two tabs of LSD in my
hand, saying, "Eat this. You will never be the same again."
And I never was. I saw visions, spiritual realms, art forms
that I never could have imagined in my mind. And then I
had a huge opening in which I died and dissolved into the
floating world—agony, then ecstasy, then gone. I knew that
in the end all of life was a spiritual pilgrimage, a journey to*

return to this understanding. As soon as I could after that, I left for India.

Another teacher, who had been a student of mathematics at Columbia University in New York, recalls:

I was always interested in the laws of the mind. That's what got me interested in mathematics. One day my roommate gave me a big omelette full of psychedelic mushrooms, and after I ate it the sounds and colors intensified till I thought I'd never listened before. Somehow my heart just melted open and I knew the world from feeling it, actually loving it. I realized how love connected everything.

I walked up to the Cloisters, the old monastery in Fort Tryon Park, and the stones just sang to me. I went to visit Merton. Now I have lived in a Trappist monastery for twenty-one years, and it started that day.

A renowned Zen teacher whose psychedelic journeys began her spiritual search recognized that her initial visionary experiences were not enough. She went to Korea and Japan to look for a Zen master, and visited many temples, but no place seemed quite right. Back in Kyoto, the home of Zen, she came up with the idea of taking some LSD and going to the holiest temple of the city.

I was on my way when a force like a huge invisible hand simply stopped me in my tracks. I was amazed. It was as if the gods would not allow me to take another step farther. What could I do? I turned around and went into the temple gates that were just beside me by the side of the road. Inside there was a small man sitting cross-legged lecturing in simple English, saying the clearest things I had ever heard about the mind and the heart. It was the next step, just what I was looking for. I put my bags down and stayed for twelve years.

Most teachers realized right away that even at their best, psychedelics would prove too limited a path, providing no systematic way to live with an awakened mind and open heart. As one Buddhist teacher recounts:

Psychedelics were a part of my beginning, but I knew they were not enough. I decided to go to the Himalayas. I was invited to a fire puja performed by an old Tibetan lama outside of Dharamsala. My friend and I walked a mile through the forest of blooming rhododendron trees to a clearing beside roaring waterfalls. The snowy mountains loomed above us. Six or eight robed lamas sat around pouring butter offerings on a big bonfire, ringing bells and beating hand drums, doing chants and mudras. And in a second circle sitting round them was a ring of about sixty blackbirds. My mind just stopped. I felt I was witnessing something ancient, before humans and animals were separated. I knew I was in the presence of a great mystery, and that my path would be to work with the teachers who lived in this reality.

The call from beyond has carried many of today's teachers on adventures they might never have imagined. Pir Vilayat Khan, a master of the Sufi Order, tells how his father, Hazrat Inayat Khan, spoke from his deathbed. Pir was only ten at the time. Hazrat told his son to seek a great sage at the source of the holy Ganges and Jamuna Rivers in India.

With little money at age nineteen I traveled overland to India. It was arduous. In one town I was thrown in prison as a suspected Pakistani spy. Following the Ganges, above the enchanted village of Gangotri, I found a remarkable sage sitting in an ice cave. This sage explained that the source of both the Ganges and Jamuna Rivers was a secret, and directed me to a glacier beyond Jamnotri, high in the Himalayas.

I followed the trail. As I was walking in the snow, far away from any last humans, there were footprints in the snow. They were rather big, so I was afraid. I thought it was a bear. I followed them for quite a few hours and finally came to a large cave. There at the opening, sitting like a king, was a fantastic rishi. He made a sign to me which I thought meant I was not to come in.

So I sat in the snow cross-legged, closed my eyes, and then after some time when I opened my eyes, he was smiling. Somehow he knew I spoke English, and he said, "Why have you come so far to see who you should be?" I answered, "It's wonderful to see myself in you." Then he said, "You don't need a guru." I replied, "My guru is my father. I'm not looking for a guru." He said, "Well, then, if you're not looking for a guru, come right in."

The rishi said, "There's another cave over there for you to sit in." Then he gave me a practice which was to look into my heart with the third eye until I could feel it open like a lotus. I did this. Then he said, "Rest in the light, not the physical light nor the reflex image. Get to the real light. That's all that's important."

He wasn't the kind of person you could chat with. He was totally illuminated, resting in samadhi. He said, "The time has almost come when there will not be rishis living in caves anymore as I do. It is now the time when illuminated beings will have to be amongst people in the world."

After several days he said, "You have learned enough." I realized I had learned extraordinary self-sufficiency, detachment, and perspective. I had a wonderful feeling of peace and happiness and I didn't want to leave, but I knew I had to go back down into the world again. It was a huge step in the journey that has lasted a lifetime.

It seems impossible that there is not a spiritual stream, a current of potential awakening that, when the moment is right, is waiting for each of us.

Lama Govinda told much of his life story in *The Way of the White Clouds*. Later he added this account:

Early in my stay in India an old Tibetan pilgrim, walking over the Himalayas, saw the prayer flags of my mountain home and entered. I was away, but he gave my beloved housemother a gift to keep for her "son," and continued his yearlong walk to the holy shrines. Unable to read it or understand it, I put the Tibetan's gift, a book, away in the attic. Years later, after long studies of Tibetan Buddhism, I was a lama, but uncertain what to do next. Then I was invited to redo the original translation of The Tibetan Book of the Dead. *Unfortunately there were no copies to be found outside of Tibet. Then, three days later in my attic, I accidentally came across the old gift. It was the original Lhasa block print of* The Tibetan Book of the Dead! *I contacted Evans-Wentz and started to work immediately. The writing which followed, where I lived, my whole life's work, all of it, came about because I had been "accidentally" left this gift by an old pilgrim.*

Returning to Our Home

Many of these stories involve outward travels, but their real subject is finding our spiritual home. The purpose of recounting such exotic and somewhat magical tales is not to compare them with our own. We each have our own unique story, our own call to return. But such accounts can shock our system into remembrance, reminding us that we are each here on a great errand.

In time we must each awaken. Awakening may hide in our attic for years, waiting until we raise our children or finish our business career. But someday it will appear, to break down the gate and say, "Ready or not, here I am."

Being alive is itself an expression of mystery. The clues to our real nature are always around us. When the mind opens, the body changes, or the heart is touched, all the elements of spiritual life are revealed. Great questioning, unexpected suffering, original innocence—any of these can require us to open beyond our daily routine, to "step out of the bureaucracy of ego," as the Tibetan teacher Chogyam Trungpa counseled. Every day brings its own calls back to the spirit, some small, some large, some surprising, some ordinary.

One senior Zen practitioner was a young lawyer and father in 1969 when he encountered the books of Alan Watts on Zen. This piqued his curiosity and his spirit, reminding him there was something more to life. So he looked in the phone book under "Z" and found a number. In a few minutes he was talking to the roshi at the San Francisco Zen Center. He got the center's schedule and with encouragement from the master began to practice. Thirty years later, still avidly practicing, he says, "My life transformed from that first phone call."

Even more ordinary is the story told by another meditation master, who had been an avid sportsman thirty years ago. Golf was his favorite sport. As he played he became aware of how much his mind and spirit determined his game.

I tried to quiet myself. I was shocked to see how agitated and out of control my mind was. A friend suggested I come to her yoga and meditation class, and even though I struggled to sit, it felt like coming home.

While the clues are here for us each day, our family and education may have taught us to pretend we don't see. One Jewish woman, now a rabbi, said her family ignored any spiritual teachings. The occasional visits to their Reform temple were mostly about social responsibility and Jewish cooking. So she had to go, as Rilke writes, "toward a church in the East that our father forgot." She began seeking her path for ten years among the Native Americans. Then she was curiously pulled to visit Jerusalem, and she met the wife of an old Hasid who reminded

21

her of a hidden inheritance of thousands of years of spirit within her own tradition.

> *After visiting the Wailing Wall, the rabbi's wife, Miriam, took me to her back room. We sat and talked about her grandparents and the holy way they would light their candles, break their bread, and raise their children, how every part of their life was governed by the Torah, every act a sacred act. It was so like the Native Americans that I loved, but when she pulled out these thin pages of handwritten kabbalist script, I recognized that I myself was part of this ancient lineage, that the heritage of the spirit ran through my veins as well as my heart.*

Baba Yaga lives in our own neighborhood as well as in the forest. She is part of our own family history. We can go to India or Jerusalem—and some of the most magical stories of these masters might have us believe that this is the way a spiritual life must begin. But it also begins in a moment of gardening, in the simple act of returning home after a voyage and seeing it fresh, in the touch of an inspired piece of music, a poem's song, the flight of a bird. Every pair of eyes we look into can become the eyes of the Beloved.

For me, growing up on the East Coast meant the pleasure of seeing fireflies in the summer. But my daughter, who was born in California, had never seen one. In our travels we discovered there were fireflies in the tropical nights of Bali. After she went to bed one night, I tucked in her mosquito net, then went out and caught a few. Her eyes were closed. I put them in her net and whispered for her to wake up. They flew around inside her net until we let them out, and she was totally captivated by their luminous trails in the night. How improbable and fantastic, how unlikely to have beautiful insects with soft blinking lights—yet this is no more unlikely than our loving hearts. Our hearts shine in the same way as the fireflies, with the same light as the sun and the moon.

Within us is a secret longing to remember this light, to step out of time, to feel our true place in this dancing world. It's where we began and where we return.

Whether we wait until the last or see it this very day, the call to mystery presents itself again and again to our eyes and our hearts—as Mary Oliver has written.

When death comes
like the hungry bear in autumn;
when death comes and takes all the bright coins from his purse

to buy me, and snaps the purse shut . . .

I want to step through the door full of curiosity, wondering:
what is it going to be like, that cottage of darkness?

And therefore I look upon everything
as a brotherhood and a sisterhood, . . .

and I think of each life as a flower, as common
as a field daisy, and as singular . . .

and each body a lion of courage, and something
precious to the earth.

When it's over, I want to say: all my life
I was a bride married to amazement.
I was the bridegroom, taking the world into my arms . . .

2

THE GUARDIANS
OF THE HEART:
Angels of Light, Ocean of Tears

Security is mostly a superstition. It does not exist in nature, nor do the
children of humans as a whole experience it. Avoiding danger is no
safer in the long run than outright exposure. Life is either a
daring adventure or nothing.
HELEN KELLER

Once we are called to the inner
adventure, we begin following the tracks of the sacred ox in the
forest. As we look into the mind or heart, we discover they hold
and encompass our whole world. Outwardly our telescopes reveal
the vastness of space, with its myriad galaxies and its birthing
stars. Inwardly we begin to discover the equally vast regions of
consciousness out of which all things arise. Some say we should
be careful if we choose to follow the tracks of the sacred ox, for
the spiritual journey can bring everything in life into question.
Some even warn us before we begin.

When the Tibetan teacher Chogyam Trungpa arrived late, as
usual, to a crowded San Francisco lecture hall, he offered a refund
to anyone who did not want to stay. He warned those who were
new that a true spiritual path is arduous and demanding, involv-
ing "one insult after another." So he suggested that those with
doubts not embark. "If you haven't started, it's best not to begin."

Then he looked steadily around the room and said, "But if you have begun, it is best to finish."

An Honorable Practice

We live in disordered times, complicated, distracted, and demanding, yet to sustain a spiritual practice demands our steady attention. The first task, then, in almost any spiritual voyage, is to quiet ourselves enough to listen to the voices of our hearts, to listen to that which is beyond our daily affairs. Whether in prayer or meditation, in visualization, fasting, or song, we need to step out of our usual roles, out of the busy days on automatic pilot. We need to find a way to become receptive and open.

To recognize spiritual longing is not enough. The heart needs inspiration for renewal, it needs support to find forgiveness, to awaken freedom, to open to grace. We must find a vessel, an honorable practice to carry us on this journey, a trustworthy discipline that is able to bring us back to the present and open us to mystery—not in order to become someone else, to "fix" ourselves, but in order to see who we really are.

Great spiritual traditions offer us a hundred good ways to do this. Some practices use the breath to quiet the mind and open the heart. There are meditative disciplines of the body that transcend the grasping of our small self, and lead us to openness. There are mantras and rituals of devotion, prayers and rosaries, daily practices of sacred attention; there is the silent inquiry of the heart. In one Native American community, a youth would fast, seeking visions for days, while rolling a small stone around a larger one, without pause, like the moon around the earth, until the answer to his quest appeared.

While we might initially explore several traditions and practices, in the end we must choose one practice and follow it with our whole heart. What matters is the sincerity that we bring to the way we have chosen, a perseverance and willingness to stay with it and see what opens within us.

A true practice leads us into the silence of the forest. Wherever we begin, we have to stop and listen. There is a story from the time Bill Moyers was press secretary for President Lyndon Johnson. At a White House cabinet lunch, Moyers, who was trained as a minister, was asked to offer the grace. "Speak up, Bill," commanded Johnson, "I can't hear a damned thing." From his end of the table, Moyers answered softly, "I wasn't addressing you, Mr. President."

What can we expect as we enter the forest to listen more deeply to the quietest of speech? Whether taken through ritual, prayer, or meditation, the first steps into the forest bring us small amazements and tender revelations. When our heartfelt attention begins to separate the reality of the present from the endless waterfall of our thoughts, the world shines with a brilliant beauty. We also begin to see how much our unnoticed interior states and unrecognized beliefs control our life. We awaken to patterns of emotions and habits. We can sense the conflicts we carry from a larger perspective, from the spacious stream of the practice we have chosen. With each step we open further.

A traditional Swedish story gives a sense of the next phase of the journey. Because of the mishaps of her parents, a young princess named Aris must be betrothed to a fearful dragon. When the king and queen tell her, she becomes frightened for her life. But recovering her wits, she goes out beyond the market to seek a wise woman, who has raised twelve children and twenty-nine grandchildren, and knows the ways of dragons and men.

The wise woman tells Aris that she indeed must marry the dragon, but that there are proper ways to approach him. She then gives instructions for the wedding night. In particular, the princess is bidden to wear ten beautiful gowns, one on top of another.

The wedding takes place. A feast is held in the palace, after which the dragon carries the princess off to his bedchamber. When the dragon advances toward his bride, she stops him, saying that she must carefully remove her wedding attire before offering her heart to him. And he too, she adds (instructed by the wise woman), must properly remove his attire. To this he willingly agrees.

"As I take off each layer of my gown, you must also remove a layer." Then, taking off the first gown, the princess watches as the dragon sheds his outer layer of scaly armor. Though it is painful, the dragon has done this periodically before. But then the princess removes another gown, and then another. Each time the dragon finds he too must claw off a deeper layer of scales. By the fifth gown the dragon begins to weep copious tears at the pain. Yet the princess continues.

With each successive layer the dragon's skin becomes more tender and his form softens. He becomes lighter and lighter. When the princess removes her tenth gown, the dragon releases the last vestige of dragon form and emerges as a man, a fine prince whose eyes sparkle like a child's, released at last from the ancient spell of his dragon form. Princess Aris and her new husband are then left to the pleasures of their bridal chamber, to fulfill the last advice of the wise woman with twelve children and twenty-nine grandchildren.

As in a dream, all the figures in such a story can be found within us. We find the scaly dragon and the attending princess, the wise grandmother, the irresponsible king and queen, the hidden prince, and the unknown one who cast his enchantment long ago. What this story reveals from the start is that the journey is not about going into the light. The forces of our human history and entanglement are tenacious and powerful. The path to inner freedom requires passing through them. Receiving grace, opening to illumination, becoming wise has not been easy even for the masters. It is described as a difficult purification: cleansing, letting go, and stripping away. Suzuki Roshi called it a "general housecleaning of the mind." It is painful to cast off our own scales, and the dragons guarding the way are fierce. It requires the inspiration of angels; it requires diving into the ocean of tears.

Sometimes the end of the path shows itself early. It is as if the mystical flirts with us, entices us into the world of the spirit. One meditation teacher remembers it this way:

People talk about peak moments. At the end of my very first meditation retreat . . . well, this was a whole peak day. After a week of great pain and frustration and considerable struggle, on the final day the colors of the trees along the road seemed to sparkle with light, my heart was open like the mother of the world. I felt I could embrace the fullness of life, and everything I saw rested in a natural love. It all seemed natural and pure. I knew that this is always true, even when I have forgotten it. It didn't last, but it inspired my heart to go on.

This first beauty is important to remember. But we must also remember the weeks of pain and considerable struggle that went before, and the many years of practice that must follow. When we seek to open to the illumination of the divine, even if we know that the prince and princess will succeed in awakening, even if we can actually glimpse the sacred wedding, we cannot just go to the last page of the story and live happily ever after. We have to go through the great fear of marrying the dragon, the seeking of wise counsel, and the long process of releasing the painful habits we have clung to. It is the difficult, slow letting go that allows us to awaken from our enchantment.

Removing the Scales of the Body

Most people report that their first years of spiritual practice involve uncovering the scales of the dragon. We directly experience these layers in the body, the heart, and the mind. The first scaly layer to be revealed, whether in prayer, meditation, or devotion, is the pattern of tensions we keep in our body. All it takes is sitting quietly for the areas of contraction and holding to become apparent: the tightness in our shoulders or back or jaw or legs. For much of our lives, whenever we encounter conflict and stress, we contract in habitual ways, building up what Wilhelm Reich called "character armor."

Some traditions begin to release the physical holding in the breath and body directly through techniques like yoga, tai chi, or Sufi movement. If these practices are used wisely, to free rather than conquer the body, the tensions begin to open naturally, and the sense of holding can give way to a new flexibility.

But even in traditions without such physical practices, the body layers will show themselves and must be dealt with. In the hours of prayer, meditation, or contemplation we start to feel pain and tension build. All the holdings of years start to come to the surface. One student remembers:

At first it was my knees that hurt, and I blamed it all on the meditation. But then I felt my neck and shoulders become hot, my back more painful in places it always felt tight. The tension in my body continued to grow. At times it was even hard to breathe deeply. Memories and old pains were surfacing now. It was so unpleasant I tried to push it away. I even tried to meditate by lying down on the softest pad I could find, hoping the pain would go away. But to my surprise, even lying down, as soon as I really paid attention, all the tension was right there again, waiting for me. I fought with my body a long time, years. Only when I finally learned to let even the deepest pain be okay, and hold it with kindness, did it begin to release. Now it comes and goes. What a blessing it was to finally accept my body.

Along with the tensions of the body, there also arise layers of restlessness and resistance. This can feel like the struggle to calm down in the midst of a very busy day. At first we can scarcely stay in our seat—we have so many ideas and responsibilities. We have taken so much of the hectic energy inside us. But the practices of prayer, meditation, or devotion ask for repeated surrender, for perseverance through every form of restlessness and resistance. One teacher recalls beginning her practice of a hundred thousand bows:

When I did the traditional Tibetan devotion and bowing practice, for the first years I struggled just to stay with it. I had always kept myself busy. I never could sit still easily in my life. I was always opening the refrigerator, turning on the TV, calling a friend. It was probably both loneliness and the pain hidden in my body. I started to practice because I didn't want to run away from myself anymore. I thought that bowing and moving would be easier than sitting, but the same resistances came there too. I learned you can't escape from yourself. If you really do a practice, you just have to stay with it. You go through some rough periods, but eventually it will work out.

Fortunately, as the dragon skins are removed it is not all pain. There also comes a lightness as each wedding gown is removed, as if angels are bringing blessings to alternate with our tears. Moments of spaciousness and wonderful calm can arise, bringing an opening of the senses, a restoration of our heart's innocence. One Christian monk remembers:

In the monastery garden I was doing a simple walking meditation, back and forth, saying a prayer, and breathing gently with each step to steady myself. All of a sudden I was a two-year-old boy again, taking his first steps. It was glorious. Just the pleasure of putting my foot down, the spongy grass, the smell of the earth and the roses. All the plants and insects seemed much bigger, like when I was so young. It all felt so alive. I felt I would do anything to stay in touch with this pure heart.

Shedding the Skins of the Heart

As we struggle to open the body, we inevitably encounter the necessity of opening and healing the heart as well. The dragon skins of the heart first appear as the unconscious energies of contraction. The Sufis call these "the Nafs"; the Buddhists and Hindus speak of hindrances to the pure heart; the Christians wrestle with the seven deadly sins, such as lust and pride. All spiritual journeys require that we directly face these energies of grasping, anger, pride, fear, restlessness, and doubt—the habits that keep the heart closed.

Initially we may discover how the heart closes when we are caught in the power of our own grasping. The wanting mind or the neediness in us always wants more than we have now. It tries to use external experience to fill our spiritual need for connection. After thirty years of practice, one teacher remembers:

My parents were spiritual types, but during the sixties all my energy went into my sex drive and rock and roll. I didn't want to go to God and skip the bottom rung. For years I viewed men and sexuality as the path to my happiness.

I became a fairly successful actress. And then finally I had enough of really good sex and realized it wasn't the answer. I still wanted something. My mother had been trying to get me to a yoga retreat but I never went because I was afraid she would cramp my sexual style. And sure enough, that was what I had to deal with when I went. I had to face the wanting that was driving me. That's what my first step in yoga and meditation was about.

To release the dragon skins of grasping and wanting, we must first come to know directly how they are held in our body and the stories they tell in our mind. We must locate and name our longings. And we must discover that it is possible to release our heart from their entangling thrall.

At the other pole from desire and the wanting mind we will discover scaly armor that pushes the world away: the anger and judgment that reject how things are. New practitioners in any discipline are usually shocked by how much judgment, aversion, and hatred they discover in themselves. Each time we blame and fight with the world around us, we reject and cut off parts of ourselves.

Aleksandr Solzhenitsyn, whose books on Stalinist Russia have awakened us to the suffering of millions, writes:

> If only there were evil people out there insidiously committing evil deeds and it was only necessary to separate them from the rest of us and destroy them. But the line dividing good and evil cuts through the heart of every human being, and who among us is willing to destroy a piece of their own heart?

Like the dragon, before we can be free to love, we need to touch our own scales and come to terms with our judgmental voices. We will find layers of anger and hatred caused by betrayal and loss, we will find a thousand aversions and resistance to the way things are. Meditative awareness begins to unravel the thought-weave of judgment. We discover a critical commentary that continually evaluates us and all those around us, that keeps us in battle with life as it is. One Buddhist teacher says:

> *I never knew how judgmental I was until I meditated. There was a judgment and opinion about every little thing, inside and out—too loud, too soft, not enough, too much. Finally my teacher had me count them—hundreds of judgments in an hour. I started to laugh a little when I realized it was so clearly a habit and I didn't have to take it so seriously. But then the next year my practice changed and I hit rage. That was hard. I had used all those judgments to try to be a good boy for so long. I had no idea how much pain and anger were stored in there. For months it came out in feelings, images, thoughts, and in my body.*

A sixty-five-year-old Ursuline nun recalls a similar process.

> *We had a period of great innocence and inspiration after we first entered the novitiate. But when most of us got to our thirties a sense of betrayal set in. We had worked and prayed*

and tried to be saints for all of our youthful years and left much of ourselves behind. When we finally started to be honest with ourselves about who we actually were, some of us became very angry, and the anger went back to long before we were nuns.

Anger, like the grasping of desire or the tyranny of judgment, is a skin that we can loosen. In the story the princess and the dragon must reveal themselves, layer by layer, and both become more available, more tender. As the first scales and gowns of disguise are peeled away, we begin to learn what is underneath the contraction of anger, judgment, and wanting. Usually we discover a new layer of hurt, loneliness, fear, and grief.

This is where offering a tender heart becomes essential. This is the place of courage—the courage to hold in love the hardest pain, our deepest sorrows and greatest fears. It is here that trust and surrender are nurtured. The awakening of this spirit of mercy and kindness is like the visitation of the angels. There comes an energy to forgive, a new softening and receptivity of the heart.

My teacher Ajahn Chah put it like this:

If you haven't wept deeply, you haven't begun to meditate.

The grief and sorrow that arise when we begin to open are both personal and universal. Many teachers say they had not expected such grief to come, but the heart has its own logic. One respected Zen teacher remembers:

After the first several years of flirting with Zen, the time came for me to commit. I signed up for the winter practice period, three months of intensive training without a break. My sitting had become quite calm and spacious, and I expected this Zen-like clarity only to grow. But it was not to be. I spent the entire practice period weeping, and wept for half the following winter period as well. I grieved for all the conflict and insecurity of my early years, the hurt of lost relationships, for the ways I'd misused my body, for sorrows, for the death of my father. Only then, after two years, did my sitting open to an immense and deep silence.

The dragon skin of our unshed tears covers the sadness and longing that connect us with the realm of sorrow in all of life. Sometimes our sorrow is the result of a particular event: the death of a parent, a family history of alcohol or abuse, a major loss in our life. Other times it is the accumulation of a thousand moments of being unseen, unrecognized, unheld.

In a poem called "I Go Back to May 1937," Sharon Olds honors the necessary acknowledgment of our sorrows and how they have led us to become the person we now are. She envisions her parents as the innocent kids they were when they first met:

I see them standing at the formal gates of their colleges,
I see my father strolling out
Under the ochre sandstone arch . . .
I see my mother with a few light books at her hip . . .
They are about to graduate, about to get married . . .
I want to go up to them and say, Stop,
don't do it—she's the wrong woman,
he's the wrong man, you are going to do things
you cannot imagine you would ever do,
you are going to do bad things to children . . .
but I don't do it. I want to live. I
take them up like male and female
paper dolls and bang them together
at the hips like chips of flint as if
to strike sparks from them. I say
Do whatever you are going to do, and
I will tell about it.

An honorable spiritual practice recognizes the losses we have suffered, tells our story, and sheds our tears to free us from the past. The Sufi poet Ghalib invites the "storm clouds to weep them-

34

selves clear to the end," so that the sky can once again be spacious and clear.

Whether in grief, anger, wanting, or restlessness, we can see that much of the work with the contractions of the heart is the work of our "unfinished business." We encounter the forces and situations that have held us closed to ourselves and others. What is conflicted, ungrieved, unfinished shows itself as soon as we become attentive. It is here that we must learn how to work respectfully with the profound forces that govern human life. It is the layers of these energies that create contraction and suffering, and the freeing of them that brings awakening and release.

The Layers of the Mind

As with the body and heart, when we go into the mind, it too reveals contraction. The meditation master Ajahn Buddhadasa described the modern world as "lost in thought." Our modern minds hold layers of doubt, ambition, fear, and belief, the thousand stories and self-images, past and future, that become our defensive mental structure. We see how often the mind dismisses the present moment in order to get somewhere else, become someone else. Whether we engage in prayer, meditation, or selfless service, we will encounter the repetitive thoughts and limiting beliefs that create our small sense of self. Our thinking cup is full, and no more will go in.

In our novice years we were taught to surrender to hours of group practices, chanting, the daily cycle of communal prayer, scriptures study, devotion, and service. During these initial months I saw how often I would get lost in some fantasy or story, and not be there at all. I would imagine myself as a great saint, or proving myself to my family, or getting back at those who had slighted me, or worrying about the past, telling a story to myself or someone else about how it could be or might have been. Our mother superior chided

me that I was lost in my stories instead of being where I was,
so much so that I would miss the novitiate.

Our entanglement in thoughts and beliefs about ourselves,
those around us, and the world makes it impossible to be where
we are. It is like the Zen painter who finished a life-sized portrait
of a tiger on the wall of his dwelling. Returning home lost in
thought some days later, he was frightened upon suddenly seeing
the tiger there, having forgotten it was his own creation.

As we undertake to quiet our minds through meditation or
prayer, we see how much of our life is governed by these unconscious stories. Carlos Castaneda's shamanic guide Don Juan puts
it this way:

You talk to yourself too much. You're not unique in that.
Everyone of us does. We maintain our world with our
inner dialogue. A man or woman of knowledge is aware
that the world will change completely as soon as they stop
talking to themself.

We begin to see the themes of our inner dialogue, which can
be ambition or unworthiness, insecurity or hope, self-hatred or
self-improvement. The stories reflect our conditioning, personal
and cultural. When a group of American psychologists met with
the Dalai Lama, he asked what difficulties are most common for
Western Buddhist students. One of the most mentioned and
strongest was self-hatred. The Dalai Lama's reaction was incred-
ulous, for self-hatred is unknown in Tibetan culture. He went
around the room asking, "Have you too experienced this self-
hate?" Almost everyone said yes.

Central to the stories we tell are the fixed beliefs we have
about ourselves. It is as if we have been cast into a movie as a
depressed person or a beautiful one, as a compromiser or a clown,
an angry victim or a fighter whom no one will ever take advantage
of again. Because those thoughts and assumptions are so powerful, we live out their energies over and over. These patterns of

thought, together with the contractions of body and heart, create a limited sense of self. They are sometimes called "the body of fear." When we live from the body of fear, our life is simply one of habit and reaction.

An honorable practice unmasks these stories and releases their limiting beliefs, just as it opens the body and heart. We begin to recognize the patterns of these contractions and to learn that they are not the most fundamental reality. We learn how to step from these old skins, the small sense of self, into the reality of the present. We find ways to allow the body to ease, the heart to soften, and the old stories of the mind to fall away. This is the moment when the dragon skins are seen for what they are, a karmic spell no longer needed, and the prince and princess are revealed in their own tender beings, vulnerable and new.

With innocence and openness we return to the simplicity of direct experience. When we step out of the current of thoughts, letting go of "how it was and how it should be," of "how we should be," we enter the eternal present.

But even this shedding of our skins, the opening of the body, heart, and mind, is still only a preparation for a deeper journey. The prince and princess have seen one another. Now together they must face the life and death before them.

3

THE FIRES OF INITIATION

I recommend almost dying to everybody. It's character building.
You get a much clearer perspective of what's important and
what isn't, the preciousness and beauty of life.
ASTRONOMER CARL SAGAN,
AFTER SURVIVING A NEAR-FATAL ILLNESS

Go ahead, light your candles and burn your incense and ring your
bells and call out to God, but watch out, because God will come
and He will put you on His anvil and fire up His forge and beat you
and beat you until He turns brass into pure gold.
SANT KESHAVADAS

Now it is time to go deeper into the
forest. What we have described so far is a preparation. We have
started to release the old patterns of holding in the body. We have
consciously opened to the deep emotions that underlie and propel much of our experience. We have begun to work with the
repetitive patterns and beliefs of the mind.

Through this work, we come to find ourselves in a clearing,
standing face-to-face with the sacred ox, hearing its quiet steady
breath. The tasks depicted next in the Zen teachings require us
to tame the powerful ox and then to release both the ox and
the self so that we can come into a unified harmony with the
world. To release the full energies of life requires a radical process
of transformation, often accompanied by a demanding rite of
initiation.

In spiritual practice, initiation is no simple ceremony—it is the passage through a difficult task by which our heart is matured. In undertaking the trials and hardships of a period of initiation, we can transform our view of ourselves and the world. We can awaken our spiritual authority and inner knowing, a trust that can carry us in the face of difficulties and death. Initiation forces upon us a shift of identity in which we can transcend our small sense of self, release what is called "the body of fear," and awaken an undying wisdom, love, and fearlessness.

Initiation's transforming process is not always outwardly obvious. Some experience it as a slow spiral, a steady and repetitive remaking of inner being. The heart gradually deepens in knowing, compassion, and trust through the hundred thousand repeated practices and heartfelt sincerity of a regular spiritual discipline. The Buddha likened this process to the ocean floor which descends little by little to the depths of the sea.

The teacher Dainan Katagiri Roshi was once asked by his Zen students about the beautiful faith and warmth he radiated: "This is what we want to learn from you. How do we learn that?" The master answered, "When people see me today, they don't see the years I spent just being with my teacher!" He described how he practiced year after year, living simply, hearing the same teachings over and over again, sitting every morning no matter what, doing the rituals of the temple.

This is the slow way of initiation, putting yourself over and over into the condition of attention and respect, baking yourself in the oven repeatedly until your whole being is cooked, matured, transformed.

But more commonly, initiation entails an intense, radical, and rapid change. Such a transformation often takes the archetypal shape of a rite of passage. A rite of passage can be described as a forced journey through a rocky canyon so narrow you can't take any baggage with you—a rebirth in which you must leave your old life behind. It involves great risk, sometimes a brush with death, for only then can the seeker discover fearlessness and find that within himself or herself which is beyond death.

Sometimes initiation comes spontaneously. A great loss, crisis, or illness, tended to wisely, will cause our hearts to grow. At other times we may require a more deliberately created initiation. The longing for initiation is universal, and for modern youth it is a desperate need. When nothing is offered in the way of a spiritual initiation to prove one's entry into the world of men and women, initiation happens instead in the road or the street, in cars at high speed, with drugs, with dangerous sex, with weapons. However troubling, this behavior is rooted in a fundamental truth: a need to grow. One of the great motivations for seeking initiation, as well as one of its tools, is a growing awareness of death. One American Tibetan lama told me:

> My parents died when I was only seventeen and eighteen. The reality of death came as a huge, abrupt shock, and it took a long time to work through the grief. With my parents gone, I felt like nothing stood between me and death anymore. This realization forced me to spiritual practice. It's amazing that we don't realize the imminence of death.

Carlos Castaneda's shaman Don Juan recommends taking death as an advisor.

> Death is our eternal companion. It is always to our left, at an arm's length. It has always been watching you. It always will until the day it taps you.
> The thing to do when you're impatient is . . . to turn to your left and ask advice from your death. An immense amount of pettiness is dropped if your death makes a gesture to you, or if you catch a glimpse of it, or if you just catch the feeling that your companion is there watching you.

If we are spiritually committed, we must face our fears of death while we are alive. In Christian mystical practice, this is "reliving the mystery of crucifixion and resurrection." In Buddhist meditation it is "learning to die before death." Since death will take us anyway, why live our life in fear? Why not die to our old ways and be free to live?

Nachiketa and the Lord of Death

One ancient teaching story from India tells of a young man, Nachiketa, and the way he came to stand face-to-face with death. After the death of several friends, Nachiketa felt the brevity of life. He saw the shallowness that comes from worldly pursuits when these activities are divorced from spiritual understanding. The son of a rich merchant, he knew that the heart's happiness did not come from the amount of property we own. This explains his reaction when his father was encouraged by the Brahmin priests of the community to make a grand donation to the temple in order to insure himself a good rebirth in the afterlife. Nachiketa was appalled by the idea that virtue and merit could be purchased in a proud public display in the town center while everyone in the town looked on.

The day arrived. "I give my cattle, my gold, all of value to the priests of the temple," the father declared. "All you value? Ha!" demanded Nachiketa. "What about me, your son?" Publicly shamed and offended by these words, Nachiketa's father responded angrily, "I give you as well. I give you to Death!" Nachiketa's eyes blazed and he replied, "I accept." Then he left.

Nachiketa went to a remote spot in the deepest forest and sat, waiting for Death to show himself. For three days and three nights he sat there intent and motionless, determined to track down the white ox and look into its eyes, determined to face Death in his spiritual quest. Sitting through hunger, pain, and exhaustion, Nachiketa came at last to the land of Yama, the King of Death, also known as "the Keeper of Accounts." There he was greeted by Death's three assistants—pestilence, famine, and war—who explained that Lord Yama was away. "He is out collecting rent." "That's fine," said Nachiketa. "I will wait."

When Death returned three days later, his assistants told him of this most unusual young man who had come seeking him. Humans who hear of the Lord of Death usually run the other way, but this young man had been waiting steadily for three days. Lord Yama went to Nachiketa, they greeted one another, and then the Lord of Death apologized for keeping him waiting. "Welcome to my kingdom. I see you are a man intent on his journey. Alas, I have kept you waiting. I will make up for the three days you waited by offering you a boon. You may choose three blessings for your journey."

During the time of journeying and waiting Nachiketa had entered the liminal space between worlds where truth is revealed. Now three blessings were offered. In this luminous state of mind, he recognized what he most needed to go on. The first boon Nachiketa requested was forgiveness for himself and all he had touched. "Let my father look upon me with the same joy as the day I was born." Nachiketa knew that only by releasing his past, by reconciling with all that was incomplete in his heart, could he continue his journey.

In asking forgiveness for himself, Nachiketa was also forgiving his father, for forgiveness must always travel in both directions. This is not a simple matter of will; nor is forgiveness always easy. To forgive may require us to open to a long process of outrage, sorrow, and grief. Forgiveness does not mean we condone the injustices of the past. We may vow "Never again will I allow this to happen." In the end, rather, forgiveness is simply a letting go of past pain and hatred. Through its softening kindness, we free ourselves from blind repetition, from carrying the pain of the past into the future. To forgive means that we do not put another person out of our heart, as Nachiketa knew he could not put his father out of his heart if he was to continue on his path with his full being.

Reunion with life is the blessing granted by forgiveness, and the boon of forgiveness left Nachiketa's heart open and clear. Lord Yama looked at him directly and noted, "Your first boon was a wise one, Nachiketa. Now what will be your second? Speak!" After a moment's silent reflection, Nachiketa spoke. "I ask the blessing of inner fire."

Nachiketa knew that to succeed on his spiritual journey, he would need both ardor and courage to follow the path with his whole being. So Nachiketa asked for the strength to give himself fully to his quest: Inner fire is wholehearted energy, spiritual passion, Shakti, a full aliveness of being.

This necessary fire or fullness in initiation is not to be confused with ambition, striving, or grasping after a goal. It is not an effort to improve ourselves or to attain something special. In the boon of aliveness, Nachiketa did not ask to get to the end of an imagined journey, but to be fully where he was. It takes the energy of our entire presence to meet and tame the sacred ox. Again Lord Yama honored Nachiketa's wisdom, blessing him with inner strength.

Free from the restrictions of old conflict and filled now with the limitless energy of perseverance, Nachiketa had found much of what is necessary to pass through initiation. Finally, the Lord of Death asked Nachiketa to name his last boon. After reflecting, Nachiketa looked at Death and said, "I ask for that which is immortal." With some surprise, Death reminded this audacious young man that he had come to the last boon, and that he could choose anything. Lord Yama then conjured up visions of what Nachiketa might choose instead: a harem of beautiful maidens to travel with on his journey, a royal golden war chariot with the world's fastest steeds, a palace where Nachiketa would be king.

Nachiketa viewed all of these and more. "Why not choose among these?" Death urged again. But Nachiketa was a determined youth not easily led astray. Once we have seen the white ox, we know a flea circus for what it is. And so he questioned the visions. "Will not all of these things that you have shown me return soon enough to your own kingdom, Lord Yama?" The Lord of Death smiled at Nachiketa's understanding and answered, "Yes, it is true." "Then I ask to know that which is immortal."

At this Lord Yama said, "I will grant your third boon." He handed Nachiketa a simple and yet extraordinary gift—a mirror.

"If you wish to find the secret of immortality, Nachiketa, I cannot help you more than this. You yourself must look directly into yourself. Then you must repeatedly ask yourself the greatest of all human questions: 'Who am I?' Look beyond your body and thoughts, Nachiketa. In this way you will find what you seek."

Whether it is enacted in initiation or in meditation, we too must face Lord Yama. We must ask who it is that is born and dies. As Nachiketa gazed into the sacred mirror, he entered into the profound spiritual questioning that leads to the deathless. When everything he held was released and stripped away, a pure and timeless heart arose—Nachiketa was free.

The Lessons of Nachiketa: First, Disenchantment

Each of the steps of Nachiketa's initiation are reflected in the journeys of modern seekers. The same eternal themes arise: the need to face death, the requirement of forgiveness, the finding of energy and courage, and the seeking of truth. These tasks resonate in the heart of all who follow a path of awakening.

Like so many we have met in this book, Nachiketa's first call to initiation was a fierce disenchantment, a compelling turnaway from the superficial values of this world. Our disenchantment with our own parents, our community, even religion may actually support our journey. Joseph Campbell used to lament that organized religion all too often offers an "inoculation against the mystical," empty rituals that undermine the spiritual impulse with a secondhand version. There are many ways in which we each have lost our hearts to false gods.

It may take a shock or a blow, like the death of Nachiketa's friends or the hypocrisy of the priests who promised his father salvation for money, to return us to our heart. The value of our harshest difficulties is how honestly they cause us to question, how they intensify our courage and bring alive our deepest inner purpose, how they reawaken our soul's task on earth. The painful breaking apart of our world is often the precious opportunity our heart has needed to learn to be true to itself.

My own meditation master used to ask us about our spiritual life, "Which have been the most valuable lessons, the comfortable times, or your difficulties?" When disenchantment arises, the very suffering and struggle it causes bring us the courage to question in the face of all odds. Like Nachiketa, we are required to abandon certainty and comfort and to put our trust in the questioning itself. There comes a longing to tell the truth.

Kabir, the Indian mystic, understood this seeking. "It is the intensity of the longing that does all the work," he said.

Steadily Facing the Unknown

In many initiation stories the search for what is beyond death is described as the hero's crossing the great water, climbing the impossible mountain, confronting dragons, or facing the armies of Mara, who personifies the forces of evil. In each of these images we risk the life we have known to discover something new.

Perhaps they are so daunting because the unknown territory of initiation will open before us only to the extent that we turn our whole being courageously toward it. In willingly facing the unknown, we offer trust in a greater purpose to life. And then we must venture wherever the road leads us, in spite of the dark, in spite of the quivering of our heart.

To steadily face the unknown demands the help of the practice or ritual to which we have entrusted ourselves. For Nachiketa help came through unwavering meditation, motionless sitting for three nights and days. For others it is unceasing prayer in the midst of crisis, or a traditional ritual of initiation led by elders. The intensity of the longing and the steadiness of turning toward the unknown will bring us to Lord Yama's kingdom.

The encounter with death can take many forms. Like the remote forest Nachiketa entered, the monasteries of Thailand where I trained as a Buddhist monk were purposely situated in areas known for wild animals, dark caves, and ghosts. The training included sitting alone all night or meditating in forest charnel grounds, staying with the corpses that were being cremated until the fire went out at dawn.

In the natural course of our everyday lives, illness or childbirth can bring us face-to-face with death, changing the life that follows. Like Nachiketa's ordeal, my wife's labor for our daughter Caroline took three days and nights. We breathed together, held hands, waited. She became progressively more exhausted and surrendered hour after hour until the final intense stages of labor carried her into the world of motherhood.

In initiation we give birth to ourselves. An English-born Tibetan nun who spent twelve years on retreat in caves in the Himalayas tells of having to rely on her spiritual practice to sustain her life when a huge avalanche covered her cave and her valley, killing many. After digging an airhole, she meditated through a long winter darkness of many days and nights.

Each initiation offers a test in which we are asked to abandon the old and open to a greater vision. Sometimes an initiation occurs in private, and sometimes it asks us to enter a collective ritual of transformation, to embrace a public act of courage. During the 1970s prodemocracy movement in Thailand, the students and military police waged days of pitched battles in the streets of Bangkok, leaving hundreds of students dead or wounded. One morning after a bloody fight the day before, a Bangkok meditation master called together his monks and nuns and told them it was time to test their training. Then he led nearly a hundred robed figures with their alms bowls single file down to the conflict. They walked in the "no-man's-land" between the barricades. Guns were lowered, tensions eased as they stood there, robed figures for peace, reminding all present of another possibility. That morning the gradual process of reconciliation truly began.

Forgiveness and Reconciliation

Nachiketa's initiation also required the blessing of reconciliation and forgiveness. As long as he was enacting his journey as a fight with his father, he was inwardly diverted from his true task: to face his own fear and awaken his own heart.

Forgiveness is both a preparation and an end in spiritual life, a theme we return to many times. To forgive we must face the pain and sorrow of our betrayal and disappointment, and discover the movement of heart that opens to forgive in spite of it all. Like Nachiketa, each of us will find our hearts closed or feel ourselves hostage to the past at times during our journey.

Our process of forgiveness may include speaking out and seeking justice, but in the end it is also a compassionate letting go, for our own sake as much as for others. It is like the meeting of two former prisoners of war: When one asked, "Have you forgiven your captors?" the other replied, "No, never." The first ex-prisoner looked with kindness at his friend and said, "Well, then they still have you in prison, don't they."

The initiation of mature spiritual teachers has always required forgiveness—for others, for themselves, for life itself. Without the wise heart of forgiveness we carry the burdens of the past our whole life.

One nurse, a senior practitioner who works in labor and delivery, tells this story:

Even though they're painful, most labors go well and there is tremendous joy once the parents can hold the baby. But I noticed that when there is a tragedy, and a baby is stillborn or dies, the other nurses call me. I think it's because of what I have been through. When I was eight years old I was left in charge of my younger sister and my three-month-old baby brother for the day. That day he died a crib death. For years I felt responsible and had incredible pain about it. My mother never told me it was my fault, but she never told me it wasn't, and she never allowed any grief. I was a big girl and big girls don't cry.

When I went to nursing school I still carried that guilt. I worked at night in a cancer center, with people on respirators. Sometimes they would beg me to let them die. What was outside reflected what was inside me. It was tremendously hard. Then I went to my first meditation retreat. In the silence it all came up. So many scenes—my brother's death, the hospitals, waves of grief and sorrow from the past—and I realized that in all these years I had never forgiven my mother or myself. For days in silence I just sat with all the pain, as if I was in labor. I wept, and then came that forgiveness I had been looking for all my life. I felt a grace. My heart opened to loving myself and forgiving my mother, letting go of all that got in the way of being alive and loving.

I have been meditating now for almost twenty years. And somehow I have found the ability to be with anguish and pain, without having to control it or change it, so that now the doctors and nurses call me in. Sometimes I sit with the parents and we just hold hands and cry together in their vulnerability, holding a damaged fetus, and facing the terrible decisions they have to make. It's only forgiveness that makes this life workable.

While self-forgiveness is essential, the wounds that others have caused us are also a necessary gate for our healing. A teacher in a Hindu ashram describes a period during which he was confronted with memories of his stepfather's harshness and mistrust.

He had raised me since I was two, and for years I was either fighting him or trying to win his approval. Then one day, after a monthlong yoga retreat, I was walking out in the open fields past the ashram, and it hit me that my stepfather didn't have long to live. I realized that for all these years he had tried to love me, but because of his own harsh father he

could never let his feelings show; he was too afraid. In his
own awkward way he had raised me as his boy. And in my
own awkward way I forgave him. I went back to visit him.
So much in my life lightened up after that. Thank God for
forgiveness.

Sometimes it is not so much that we forgive harmful actions, as that we learn to acknowledge and respect the hard struggle of life itself. A story of the Second World War shows how a forgiving and tender heart can allow us to enter the world anew.

Many Japanese soldiers were stationed on islands throughout the Pacific during World War II. As the Japanese pulled back, these islands were so quickly abandoned that when the war ended, there were still hundreds of loyal soldiers on duty who had no knowledge of their defeat. Over a few years most of these men were found and brought back in by local people, but, as is common knowledge, a small number hidden in caves and forests continued to maintain their positions. They believed themselves to be good soldiers, trying to remain faithful to their country and defend the Japanese nation as best they could in the face of grave hardships.

One might wonder how these men were treated when they were finally found after ten or fifteen years. They were not considered misguided or fools. Instead, whenever one of these soldiers was located, the first contact was always made very carefully. Someone who had been a high-ranking Japanese officer during the war would take his old uniform and samurai sword out of the closet and take an old military boat to the area where the lost soldier had been sighted. The officer would walk through the jungle, calling out for the soldier until he was found. When they met, the officer, with tears in his eyes, would thank the soldier for his loyalty and courage in continuing to defend his country for so many years. Then he would ask him about his experiences, and welcome him back. Only after some time would the soldier gently be told that the war was over and his country was at peace again, so he would not have to fight anymore. When he reached home he would be given an honorable welcome, celebrating his arduous struggle and his return to and reunion with his people.

We have judged ourselves and others for so long, carrying on our battle with the past, with life itself. In forgiveness we bow to it all with mercy and respect. It is the way we begin to tame the white ox: by befriending it. With forgiveness, our hearts become clear and whole for a time. The courage of our forgiveness frees us to enter the next step in our initiation.

Inner Fire

Nachiketa's second request was for inner fire: the ardor and courage needed to persevere with his journey even in the face of death. This passion and willingness to open, to discover, to learn, is one of the central qualities of all who progress in spiritual life.

The quality of inner fire can transform any obstacle and difficulty into the very process of awakening and illumination. We each treasure the moments when we are fully alive. With spiritual passion we can awaken no matter where we are. So when one student complained to my teacher Ajahn Chah that in his very busy life he did not have time to meditate, Ajahn Chah laughed and said, "Do you have time to breathe? If you are determined, you must simply pay attention. This is our practice, wherever we are, whatever is happening: to breathe, to be fully present, to see what is true."

One Buddhist teacher recalls her early years in Zen. She describes how deeply she was inspired by the master, by the wholeness of his presence, his compassion and spontaneity. She wanted to be alive like that.

> I sat in the Zendo, but I really had no idea what to do. The one instruction I can remember is "Die on the pillow." I would sit there with considerable enthusiasm thinking, "Yes, I want to do this," but I hadn't a clue as to how to proceed. Then as I attended other retreats I gradually learned that the

way to do that was to give myself more and more fully to the practice itself. I found an organic expansion of my capacity to sit longer and sleep less until finally, at my first three-month Vipassana retreat, I found myself on fire with energy for practice and only needing three hours' sleep. As I gave myself to it, my inner strength grew.

Sometimes this inner fire is thrust upon us. One of my teachers, Dipama Barua of Calcutta, was a great yogi. After the death of her husband and two of her children, she felt compelled to begin meditation training. When she started she became quite ill in those first days at the temple, but nothing would deter her. Being too weak to walk, she crawled up the steps of the temple and sat there, so determined was she to face her fears and come to freedom.

Even those in prison can find a way to this freedom. Aware of the painful fact that we are now spending more funds on our prison system than on educating our children, many spiritual communities have begun providing teaching to the millions under lock and key. These teachings are offered under the principle that all human beings need to find inner freedom and salvation and that no one is beyond redemption. Fleet Maul, a prisoner following the Tibetan teachings of Thrangu Rinpoche, writes:

The noise and lack of privacy are the greatest obstacle to doing formal meditation practice in prison. From 7:00 A.M. to 11:00 P.M. the prison's overcrowded living areas are in an almost constant uproar. To practice during these hours I used to clean out one of the sanitation closets where the mops, brooms, and trash barrels are kept. I would set everything outside, so that I wouldn't be disturbed, take a chair, and sit for an hour or two. People thought I was a little strange, sitting in the trash closet, but they got used to my being there. When I finally got a single cell after years of hellish overcrowding, I began Tibetan practice of one hundred thousand full-length prostrations and recitations.

Now the guards come by to count heads at 5:00 A.M., so they see me doing full prostrations on the floor beside my bed.

At some point we must surrender our fears and hopes, dying to the way it was supposed to be and opening anew to the mystery. Nachiketa did not ask to get to the end of an imagined journey, but to be fully where he was. Even a prison, even a palace, can be the site of awakening.

Sometimes the surrender of initiation comes in joy and ecstasy. I visited a temple along the sacred Ganges River in Benares just as the pilgrims were completing a weeklong devotional chant to the Divine Mother. For seven days and nights they chanted without stop. When exhausted, they would drop to sleep on the floor for a few hours and then start again. Without ceasing, without food, they chanted the name of God. Over and over, circling the altar, a crowd of devotees would chant the holy name to the sound of Indian harps and tambourines. One woman told me later how on the first days the pain and hunger, family concerns, and worries would inwardly interrupt her chanting. But as she threw herself again and again into the holy name of God, gradually everything of herself dropped away, and she circled effortlessly, the spirit of the Divine filling her with ecstasy as she swayed around the candlelight.

For one rabbi and mystic, the passage through the fire came not in the temple but at the altar of a bitter American divorce. He had studied long years with Hasidic and kabbalah masters in Jerusalem and was now a schoolteacher and a spiritual leader in a devoted Jewish community.

Then my wife of fourteen years left me, condemning everything I had done, complaining that I never really cared about her, and that she had lost herself in the marriage, and her life in the bargain. She fought fiercely for custody of our three children, to gain most of our money and the house we had lived in. She got angrier and more destructive. She pub-

licly denounced me to friends and community as her demands increased. As a spiritual teacher, I found it the most agonizing period of practice in my whole spiritual life. It felt like I was dying over and over, being ripped apart, forced to go through the fire of letting go of my children, my reputation, and still keep my heart open.

Several years after this excruciating period, the rabbi says:

I could never imagine asking for this much pain, but it has given me a new humility and an honesty about myself and my spiritual life. I was forced to become simpler, more true to myself, less quick to judge others. Thankfully my relations with my children are back on track. Talk about learning compassion. It was a hard way, but I guess I needed that.

This is one of the tasks of initiation. To the extent that we give ourselves wholeheartedly to the work of the spirit, our life becomes simple and whole. The poet Rilke tells of this.

> You see, I want a lot.
> Perhaps I want everything:
> the darkness that comes with every infinite fall
> and the shivering blaze of every step up.
>
> So many live on and want nothing
> and are raised to the rank of prince
> by the slippery ease of their light judgments.
>
> But what you love to see are faces
> that do work and feel thirst. . . .
>
> You have not grown old, and it is not too late
> to dive into your increasing depths
> where life calmly gives out its own secret.
> (tr. Robert Bly)

Undying Blessings

Nachiketa's last request was for knowledge of that which is immortal, undying. Lord Yama responded, "To find that which is timeless, you must look into the heart of life itself." He then handed Nachiketa a mirror.

The mystery of identity, "Who am I?," is one of humankind's central spiritual questions. Are we this body of flesh and blood? Is consciousness merely a product of our nervous system, our thoughts, our feelings? Are we our genetic heritage and ancestors' patterns, or is our essential nature more fundamentally spiritual? Are we a creation of consciousness itself, a spark of the Divine, a reflection of the universal mind? This is the inquiry of mystics and sages.

In the forest monasteries where I practiced, a newcomer is ushered into a sacred grove to be offered ordination. Then the elders instruct each new monk in the first and most important meditation practice: an investigation of the mystery of birth and death. You are directed to meditate on the question "Who am I?" First you must examine your physical body to see that it is made up of earth, air, fire, and water, and how these form into the disparate parts of skin, hair, nails, teeth, fluid, blood, heart, liver, lungs, kidneys. In this bag of skin and bones, who are you? You are asked to investigate the question of identity, to release all that is impermanent in body and mind, and to discover a timeless awareness beyond birth and death.

The question of identity is posed in many forms. During one annual three-month insight meditation retreat, an old Korean Zen master from Nine Mountains Monastery came to speak. He told the students that whatever practice they were doing for three months was a waste of time. "The only practice that is worthwhile"—he banged on his Zen staff and pointed to himself—"is to ask, '*What is this?*' WHAT IS THIS?" he shouted.

The Indian sage Ramana Maharshi used this self-inquiry almost exclusively to awaken his disciples. When people came to see him with troubles and questions, he would look at them with what is called "the glance of mercy," a profound compassion for all the ways they were lost. Then he would direct them into the meditation of self-inquiry. Ask yourself, "Who am I? Who was born into this body?" Solve this question and all troubles will be solved. To ask this question is to look into Nachiketa's mirror. As each experience arises it is questioned: "Is this who I really am? Is this the timeless?" One experience arises after another—thoughts about oneself, images and plans, loves and fears, feelings toward or against something, changing sensations of sounds and sights of the physical world—and each is seen for what it is: transient, limited, not able to last. In turn, each is released, as "not this, not that," until finally our entire sense of self is abandoned and we rest in a deep and unutterable silence.

A Jewish mystic, the Mezritcher rabbi, taught the same truth: that we cannot change from our limited reality into another "unless we first turn into nothing, the true state, that which is before and after all things."

As we awaken we discover that we are not limited by who we think we are. All the stories we tell ourselves—the judgments, the problems, the whole identity of the small sense of self, "the body of fear"—can be released in a moment, and a timeless sense of grace and liberation can open for us.

As with facing death, the release of our old identity comes at a price. The price is paid in the letting go of all we hold and take ourselves to be, a stripping away until only the eternal remains. Through opening, initiation, difficulty, and grace, we come to know another reality. One American lama I interviewed describes her initiation in this way:

My greatest lesson came during the three-year retreat. The whole three years and three months were filled with nonstop meditations and prayers, and demanding practices, both days and nights. But then, halfway through the last year of the retreat, I received notice that my younger brother had just died, either an accident or suicide. I got the telegram and my whole being went into shock. I was so open. It had thrown my whole family into chaos, grief, and despair. They wanted me at home to help them. I had to decide whether to leave the retreat and not finish it, because if you come out you cannot return, or whether to stay. It was like standing at the edge of a huge cliff.

I asked my revered Tibetan master. He told me that in the course of a three-year retreat many people would be born and die, and that many obstacles would happen. He said I could do what I wanted but reminded me that I had vowed to stay in retreat for three years. It was a very absolute, unwavering answer. So I sat, and overwhelming waves of helplessness, grief, guilt, and fear washed over me. Every part of my conditioning, every identity I had held from my life until then was screaming to go back home. I felt the conflict in every cell of my body. I was being torn apart. But I had committed myself to practice in a realm of absolute truth, to find universal compassion for every single being. To fulfill that, I realized, I would have to let go of my personal attachment.

Then I knew I had to stay. It was like jumping off a cliff in absolute darkness. It was incredibly difficult. Yet through the practice and my teacher's spirit, I was connected to the absolute freedom of my true nature, no matter what happens. Now I simply know it is true.

And when I came out half a year later and saw my family, by then they were supportive and happy I had finished, and that I could be with them in an entirely new way. I feel now that all I went through in that retreat, and in the depth of my own conscious struggles, was ultimately helpful to them.

There is a direct parallel in the Christian tradition. To awaken to the great heart of Jesus we must "be willing to tread for a long time as a blind man in the darkness." So wrote St. John of the Cross. The contemplative masterpiece *The Cloud of Unknowing* insists that true contemplatives must "die to themselves, and lose the radical self-centered awareness of our being, for it is our own self that stands in the way of God."

One Sufi master describes how frightening his loss of identity was to him as his spiritual life opened:

As I looked at all I had held to be me, the separate individual, it began to unravel. At first there was an openness and emptiness, but with it came a rush of fear, a struggling to exist, some kind of terror. I felt that I was letting go of everything—my whole sense of self had given way. One day during this I was sitting in a window seat on an airplane, and it felt like I was falling out the window, and the terror came in big waves, irrational and very strong. I felt just like an animal falling in space. Only later when I learned to let go into it, to let myself fall, did it open up into a cloudless sky where I disappeared.

For this Sufi teacher, initiation felt like he was dying. One Hindu teacher with whom I spoke had a more literal experience of near-death. After years of yoga and meditation, mostly in the West, he returned at forty-three to spend a year in India:

After months in the ashram I went on pilgrimage to Benares, Allahabad, and Rishikesh, and then I got quite ill. I found myself in a horrible dirty hospital with very little money and no friends around, so weak I had difficulty even talking. I felt sure I would die there all alone, and in many days of high fever I did come quite close to death. I lay there shaking and afraid, and after some confused days it dawned on me that this is what my years of training were for. I closed my eyes and could feel the end of my life just a small breath away.

I could feel the whole world of birth and death circling around me. It was in my whole body—the pain, the seeking for pleasure—and as I faced the enormity of the fear, it was as if I died a little. Then there arose a pure knowing: "This is not who you are." I knew that what the yogis had taught me was true, and my resistance fell away. There is that which is deathless, and it is only found when we face death. Afterward I returned a healed and humbled man.

"I felt like I died a little" is a similar phrase used by Ijukarjuk, a renowned Eskimo shaman, to describe his initiation during a thirty-day winter fast in a tiny snow hut. By virtue of this journey, Ijukarjuk became a wise man and healer. If we are to be free, like Nachiketa, we must ask our sacred questions and follow them, even to Lord Yama and the land of death. It is there that we find undying blessings.

There is one more event in the story of Nachiketa. At its conclusion, we see the young man bowing to Lord Yama a final time, totally at peace. And then as if by magic the landscape of the Kingdom of Death changes to the spring rice fields of his native India. In this a last secret is revealed to him—death and birth are not separate. Renewal comes by dying. When we have faced death and aloneness, we are unafraid to live, and life flowers under our feet. Everywhere we go becomes holy ground.

Nachiketa knew this in his heart, and walked off toward his home, to embrace his father and start a new life. If his story were to be painted by a student of Zen, we might see walking by his side the gentle figure of a white ox, tamed.

PART TWO

The Gates
of
Awakening

THE GATES OF AWAKENING

Every spiritual tradition has stories of those who have awakened from their usual dreamlike state to a sacred way of being. Through initiation, purification, or prayer, or by a great spacious surrender to the dance of life, they come to know that which is ever-present and holy.

The founder of Japanese Zen, Dogen, explained:

The human mind has absolute freedom as its true nature. There are thousands upon thousands of students who have practiced meditation and obtained this realization. Do not doubt the possibilities because of the simplicity of the method. If you can't find the truth where you are, where else do you expect to find it?

There is a part of each of us that knows eternity as surely as we know our own name. It may be forgotten or covered over, but it is there. Like Nachiketa, we have only to ask for the truth, and we will learn that it is found in a mirror. My teacher Ajahn Chah called this center of wisdom within us "the One Who Knows."

The spiritual practitioners interviewed for this book discovered this center in themselves. But the One Who Knows is not found in practitioners alone. One famous study of American spiritual life found that the majority of those interviewed had had a mystical experience at some time in their life. However, the researchers also discovered that most of those people would not want it to happen again. Why is this?

What we have no words for, we cannot understand; it does not fit into our view of what is real. And if we stumble upon it, as the study shows, we may be taken by surprise, and frightened. On the unknown places on their maps, the ancient cartographers wrote, "Here there be dragons."

Yet, as surely as we inhabit the mystery of birth and death, as surely as the night is full of stars, as surely as we know the necessity of love, we contain the possibility of awakening. Even today, in many parts of the world, many people are recognized as enlightened or illuminated with holiness, and sages are widely revered. The sage in us can be awakened as well; the One Who Knows can be found in our own lives.

There are numerous entry points to the eternal wisdom of the heart, which can be called "the gates of awakening." Each gate is a doorway to ourselves, a doorway to the truth. Here are four of the most powerful, each described by those who have passed between their open hinges. You will recognize these passages in your own life.

4

THE HEART AS MOTHER
OF THE WORLD:
The Gate of Sorrow

Overcome any bitterness because you were not up to the magnitude of the
pain entrusted to you. Like the mother of the world you are
carrying the pain of the world in your heart.

SUFI

We enter the gates of awakening
carried by the same melodies, the same songs of joy and despair
that first called us to the spirit. The ocean of life brings us waves
of birth and death, joy and sorrow. For many, as at the beginning
of our search, it is the painful truths of life that become our sacred
gateway, that open us to the great heart of compassion. The blow
of tragedy, the devastation of our losses may have begun our return
to the spirit. Now in a deeper octave, this dimension of awakening opens our being to the shared pain of the world. To enter
through this state is called "Awakening by the Gate of Sorrow."

It is said that on the morning of the Buddha's enlightenment,
he looked out upon the vast universe with newly awakened eyes
of wisdom, and tears began to roll down his cheeks. He saw beings
in every circumstance of life striving to be happy. Yet out of misunderstanding these beings were acting in the very ways that
brought suffering to themselves and caused suffering to others.

Some say that when his tears touched the earth, they took life and became Tara, the Goddess of Compassion.

If you stand by the Wailing Wall in Jerusalem, you will see the same tears and cries for compassion, not just for the lost temple of Israel, but for the sorrows of all people who live in separation from the Divine.

Morning and evening, the heart calls out in prayer:

> Answer us, God, for we are in great distress. Please be near to our outcry, let your kindness comfort us. Before we call to you, answer us, as even the prophet Isaiah has said, "And it will be that before they call, I will answer; while they yet speak, I will hear."

Without understanding the source of suffering, human beings strive to gain happiness by possessiveness and greed, through violence and hatred. We act out of delusion and ignorance, creating pain as an inevitable result. Our grasping, our aggressive entanglement in the world brings with it unavoidable struggle and loss, yet all is done purportedly to seek safety, to find happiness.

The Buddha saw what every wise heart comes to know, that life on earth is painful as well as beautiful. Yet our confused reactions magnify this fundamental pain into an even greater suffering. As I write these words, human decisions create war in twenty-eight countries. Millions hunger, though there is abundant food available. Millions languish in sickrooms or hospitals, ill with diseases that we have medicine to cure, vaccines to prevent. This suffering is not separate from us. Buddhist teacher Sylvia Boorstein writes about attending her synagogue on the day the Mourners Prayer is said for those who have lost relatives in the Holocaust. Many members stood, reciting the prayer. "I looked at how many people were standing and thought, 'Can all these people be direct survivors?' Then I realized that we all are, and I stood up too."

There are times in spiritual life when it feels as if all the barriers we have erected to shield ourselves from the pains of the world have crumbled. Our hearts become tender and raw and we feel a natural kinship with all that lives. The cries of street children echo in our mind, images of terrorism and racism, ecological destruction, poverty, and slavery fill our consciousness. It is as if our consciousness has broken open to the struggles of humanity and the earth itself. We may feel that we are in a charnel ground, we may see the suffering of countless generations. And we recognize that there is no escape from this.

Yet only by opening our eyes and heart to the suffering of the world can we find freedom or peace. In our own way, each of us, as a Buddha-to-be, must look into this great question: What is the truth about suffering in human life and what is the cause of this suffering?

In the Fire Sermon, the Buddha addressed the genesis of the sorrows of the world.

> Everything is burning. The eye is burning and visible sights are burning. The ears and the sounds they hear are burning, the nose, the tongue, the body and mind. With what fires are they burning? With the fires of greed, of hate, of ignorance, burning with anxiety, jealousy, loss, decay and grief. Considering this suffering, a follower of the way becomes weary of the fires, weary of greed and hate that fuel the grasping at sights, sounds, smells, tastes, body or mind. Being weary, one divests oneself of this grasping and by the absence of this grasping one becomes free.

To see the truth of suffering completely is to come to freedom through the gate of suffering. We can never successfully grasp or control the changing conditions of life. We cannot possess our lover, our spouse, our homes, our work. We cannot even possess our children. Yes, we can love and care for them, but if we try to control them, we only create suffering. Pleasure and pain, praise and blame, success and failure alternate day after day. The world itself has pain and pleasure woven into it as night is woven together with day. If we resist this truth, we will inevitably suffer.

There is a story told of Ramakrishna, a Hindu sage whose visions and devotion became legendary throughout India in the last century. For days he sat by the side of the Ganges, lost in prayer, seeking a revelation of the face of the Divine Mother, the creator of life itself. Then, in an amazing moment, the surface of the water rippled, and out of the river rose a huge and beautiful goddess, shining hair dripping with the waters of the river, eyes like pools that contain all creation. She opened her legs and beings emerged from her body—children and animals, a fountain of births of all kinds. Then, in a terrible moment, she reached down and carried a newborn child to her mouth and began to eat it, blood running down her mouth and across her breasts. For she who creates is also she who destroys; she is the source, the continuation, and the ending of all life. Then the goddess slowly sank back beneath the waves, leaving Ramakrishna to contemplate her power.

When we open the heart through the gate of sorrow, we sense how pain and dissatisfaction are woven into the fabric of experience. In the midst of pleasure, we are anxious about when it will end. In the midst of possession, we worry about loss. Even the most beautiful birth and most gracious death come with pain, for entering and leaving the body is inherently a painful process. We know that throughout our day, experience changes from pleasant to neutral to unpleasant, and back again, ceaselessly. This unending change is itself a source of pain. And our habitual reactions to it can create in us a continuous sense of struggle.

One strategy for gaining liberation is to focus our attention directly upon this inherent, continuous experience of dissatisfaction and pain. We must sense it clearly, and find in its midst a freedom that releases us from any identification or grasping.

Maha Naeb of Thailand teaches her students how to understand dissatisfaction by paying precise attention to what motivates each action and movement throughout the day. She instructs them to be absolutely still and not change posture or perform any act unless they see what experience in the body and mind necessitates the change. When they awaken in the morning, they are instructed to lie there meditating quietly for a time and not move.

But after a time they notice that lying in one posture for so long causes the body to become stiff or painful, so they move in order to be more comfortable. Again, after some time they may notice the discomfort of a full bladder, so they go to the bathroom to relieve this source of pain. But the toilet seat is hard and the bathroom is cold, so to alleviate this discomfort they go out and sit comfortably in a chair. Then their belly offers up morning hunger. To alleviate the hunger pain they go to eat. But then they must clean up because leftover food will rot and smell bad. Then they go to sit quietly again for a time until the next pain or discomfort causes them to move. And it goes on.

By the careful observation of the source of each action, a constant movement to alleviate suffering is revealed. Yet those who face this truth do not find it a formula for despair, but a gateway to compassion. For within the heart is found a freedom and love even greater than the suffering. By facing the pain of the world they awaken a fearless and merciful heart, the universal birthright of humanity.

The Sufi poet Rumi celebrates the wisdom willing to immerse itself in the fires of life.

> God's presence is there in front of us,
>   a fire on the left
>   a lovely stream on the right . . .
>   Whoever walks into the fire
>   appears suddenly in the cool stream,
> Any head that goes under the water surface,
>   that head pokes out of the fire.
> Most people guard against going into the fire.
>   and end up in it . . .
>   If you are a friend of God,
>   fire is your water.
> You should wish to have a hundred thousand
>   sets of moth wings,
> so you could burn them away, one set a night.
>   (tr. Coleman Barks)

One meditation teacher describes how suffering became his gate to awakening and how he was able to open to this fire, to sit in the midst of it unmoving.

My meditation had always been very difficult. There was usually a great deal of tension and pain that I carried in my body as well as my heart. As an environmentalist I had strug-gled for years with the suffering of the world, and all these images and sorrows would come flooding past as I sat. It was as if I was in the midst of the rain forests being burned and bulldozed. I saw warfare and pollutions, all the images of what we were doing to the earth. I sat and wept, but I stuck with it even when it got intense. I did not believe in run-ning away from the world. I had to face it, go into it. Then a shift happened.

I was in the ashram, practicing with a small number of senior students. I had felt a lot of physical pain in the past few weeks, but I just sat and sat in the midst of it all, unmov-ing, and my mind became very focused and very still. My thoughts became fewer until they almost disappeared, and my consciousness dropped to the center of my heart. When any sound or sensation or thought would arise, I would feel it immediately as a subtle vibration moving through the space of my heart. That's all I felt. It's as though the stillness in my heart expanded until it was the world. All experience became like tiny vibrations, waves subtly moving through this vast, peaceful heart.

Then somehow I let go further and entered the deepest peace imaginable, without even the subtlest sound or sen-sation. It was utterly silent and empty. I didn't feel my body or mind at all, just pure consciousness. My whole identity dropped away. It was breathtaking, fantastic, beyond bliss. I knew I could never fear death after this because it is only this timeless, unborn consciousness that is real.

I felt that nothing of the world could compare with this peace. Any sight, sound, or thought, no matter how plea-

surable, was a disturbance, was painful compared to this silence. When I came back I could feel what the Buddha meant about suffering: how every birth leads to death, how the struggle of the opposites—night and day, joy and sorrow, all that arises and passes—is inherently painful.

I remember that shortly afterward walking down the road in India I saw a lamb being born. It just knocked me over, seeing the struggle of birth as the lamb came out. I realized that any identification with this life—holding on to the process of birth, aging, death—is suffering. I just stood there and wept for the suffering of this world. I could feel it with so much compassion. I knew I'd never forget it.

But it's amazing how strong desire is too, the roots of wanting pleasure and stimulation. In a few months I was back in the West looking for music and fine wine. The force of wanting and indulgence came back in the most outrageous ways, like a backlash to what I'd seen. But still I have followed my spiritual practice too, because some part of you always knows when you see the truth; somehow you can't forget.

When we honor the gate of suffering, what arises is the wondrous power of compassion. This compassion is described as the fluttering of the heart in the face of the pain of any other being. It is a tenderness for all forms of life, all that is born and dies, all creatures who live by one another's births and deaths. Sometimes it is compassion for ourselves. The need for such compassion is there in every journey, Buddhist or Hindu, Jewish or Christian. The question of human suffering is central to the journey of grace and redemption.

One nun recounts:

The month before Easter had been our usual preparation, with extra vigils and prayers. It was spring and I decided to let go and surrender myself to them as I never had before. I spent hours contemplating the mystery of Christ on the

Cross. And then Easter was over and we had gone through the joy of resurrection, and the whole community felt so opened by it all.

One evening about a week later I was in my room looking at the modern crucifix, which was all we had on our walls. Then I was overcome by sadness and pain. My body began to ache, and I lay on my bed in agony. I felt as if I was dying, it felt so real. I was taken over and began to weep for Jesus on the Cross, for His suffering and death. Then I was Mary holding her crucified child and I knew that the crucifixion wasn't over. I was all the mothers who have lost their beloved children in war, accident, or disease, who even today cannot feed their hungry children. I was the mother trapped in an earthquake in Armenia, struggling desperately, unable to save her child. I was the young men, all the soldiers in the senseless battles, I was the cows and pigs on the way to the slaughterhouse, I was the modern generals and the Roman soldiers, the welfare mothers and the slumlord, the victims and the perpetrators, all who would die, all who are in pain. I lay there, watched over by the pain of the world—so much pain. I couldn't bear it. My heart simply wept.

Then Jesus was there in my body, and we were holding it together, the suffering of the world. And I could see that to hold it in mercy was divine. It broke open my heart. It became the holy pain that opens the heart. This is God's purpose for our sorrows, to connect all our hearts. There is so much mercy. Mercy within mercy.

Sometimes this mercy is learned in the loneliness of our own cell; other times we cannot do it ourselves, we need another human being there to witness our sorrows, to touch what is closed in us.

One of the gifts a wise teacher offers is the capacity to hold up the mirror of compassion so that our hearts remember how to open. One Zen master recalls his early years of Zen:

I was trying so hard, and faced so much grief and pain in my practice. I had hit my limit—I was about to give up. Then I went to see the master, who saw the depth of my struggle, and she changed in an instant from a strict demanding roshi. It's as if she became the Goddess of Mercy. "Very good, very good." I felt like she had reached in and touched the most tender place in my heart with her compassion and her voice.

Dipama Barua, a saintly Buddhist elder and grandmother, worked in this way with students in Calcutta and in her visits here. Students would come to her with meditation questions, which she would answer patiently. Then she would offer tea and food. She would ask concerned questions about their health or family. When one student explained how upset his parents were that he was studying meditation in India, she reached under her mattress and pulled out part of her savings and said, "Go buy your mother a gift from India." When students would come with their greatest struggles or with hearts breaking to the sorrows of the world, she would encourage their practice. "You must see this too," she would say, and then bless and embrace them, stroking them all over, all the while repeating soft words of loving kindness, until they softened as if held in the grace of a great mother.

This is the way to freedom through the gate of sorrow. In it we discover enough mercy and compassion to allow the full truth of life and our own incarnation, its dance of agony and beauty, to be seen and accepted without resistance.

If we allow what Zen Master John Tarrant calls an opening to "the Tears of the Way," wisdom will be born. In his book *The Light Inside the Dark*, he quotes one senior practitioner who seemed defeated by an unexpected grief and wept day after day, until her weeping began to change.

I became flooded by memories of my father and the pain I had suffered from his absences and from being handed around to foster homes, neglected and disregarded. I had thought that I was opening up and then suddenly this, this thick, personal material seized me. I was totally caught up. I wept and wept. Everything I saw seemed a fresh occasion for tears. As I watched for several days, my mood began to change and the tears became more impersonal, causeless—the tears of being moved by life. I was seized by a tenderness, especially for unseen, neglected, and abandoned things—a particular shade of blue in the sky at dawn, the bones of mice dropped by owls. These later tears are the tears of initiation. We are taken up into largeness.

To let go in the deepest recesses of the heart, to release all struggle and wanting, leads us to that knowing which is timeless. As one teacher has said:

After I opened beyond any sense of myself, I could feel "my pain" change to "the pain," the pain of the world. I saw how the universe moves and the planet is on fire—that much pain—and yet it all could be held, and it didn't touch anything. It rested in the midst of an immense peace.

In the gate of sorrow we free ourselves from illusions and grasping, from a false separation from all life, and hold it all. We can rest in the great heart of Buddha, of Jesus, in the heart of the One Who Knows.

5

NOTHING AND EVERYTHING:
The Gate of Emptiness

You live in illusion and the appearance of things. There is a reality, but you do
not know this. When you understand this, you will see that you are nothing.
And being nothing, you are everything. That is all.
KALU RINPOCHE

From where does our life of joy and
sorrow arise? When the source of creation is personified, it is
given names like Allah, Brahma, or God. The divine source can
also be experienced outside of personification. Mystics and meditators who describe this source experience the cosmos as coming
out of a sacred emptiness, a Great Void. Jewish mystics describe
it like this:

> Out of emptiness God has made the world, it exists in the
> heart of God alone. To know our place we must again
> become as nothing, and then what is holy will move
> through us and illuminate all we do.

What does it mean to "become as nothing"? Understanding
emptiness or selflessness is disconcerting: It is hard to describe,
in the way water would be obvious, yet hard to describe for a fish.

Still, when we experience its truth, it opens us to peace and joy in remarkable ways. Angelus Silesius, a Renaissance Christian mystic, explained:

> God whose love and joy are everywhere
> can't come to visit
> unless you aren't there.
> (tr. Stephen Mitchell)

When Nachiketa was handed a mirror by the Lord of Death, he was directed to an investigation into the source of his being. In the depths of this inquiry meditators can discover the experience of emptiness. This emptiness has two sides: the emptiness of self and the emptiness of the void.

The emptiness of self shows itself first in our lack of control over our supposedly fixed "self." Anyone who turns inward to meditation or prayer immediately encounters the ever-changing thought stream of mind, and the endless ripples of moods and emotions that color each moment. These thought streams and emotions have a life of their own. In them a whole vision of our childhood or the replay of complex adult experiences appears, compels our attention, and disappears in moments. We usually take ourselves to be the sum of these thoughts, ideas, emotions, and body sensations, but there is nothing solid to them. How can we claim to be our thoughts or opinions or emotions or body when they never stay the same? Perhaps we can take a step back and look at who it is that knows this, the space of knowing in which they arise.

In meditation we can shift our attention from the sense of everything being unconsciously tied together as "my experience" to a more silent, less possessive observation. This silent observation allows us to see the first aspect of emptiness, called selflessness, or egolessness—the discovery that the usual sense of oneself as a solid separate being is only an image created in our mind. This is what Alan Watts called our best-kept secret in *The Book: On the Taboo Against Knowing Who You Are.*

When one Westerner, now a Tibetan monk for twenty years, first met his teacher Lama Yeshe in the 1960s, he was a successful filmmaker and TV producer. After they were introduced, Lama Yeshe found out this would-be student made films. "Oh, you make TV, movies? I good actor. I best actor!" Lama Yeshe laughed. "I can be anything, you see, because I am empty. I am nothing." Then he laughed again.

Emily Dickinson also pointed to our intuitive sense of this truth:

> I'm nobody! Who are you?
> Are you—Nobody—Too?

What are these mysterious descriptions of nonself about? For one meditator, the experience of emptiness of self was a signal experience in her spiritual life. She had studied with lamas and masters throughout India. When she returned from many years in Asia, she still regularly spent days meditating.

> *I was up in the mountains and awoke early, when the morning was still dark. I sat so very quietly day after day, and then the most wonderful and terrible experience came. I disappeared. All that I am was washed away. I didn't know its name at first, and you can't give it names, even Nirvana, because it's before names. And such bliss. I knew it was no longer my own heart and body, it was the world's.*

In the emptiness of self the world becomes transparent, clear, uncomplicated. We realize that our sense of separate self is untrue. Who we are in a conventional self disappears into silence, peace, and the pure experience of being, without anyone present to possess that experience. And as emptiness of self is recognized, we come to understand the second dimension of emptiness, the emptiness of all phenomena. One Buddhist text, the Samutta Nikaya, explains it this way:

Suppose a person who was not blind beheld the many bubbles on the Ganges as they floated along, and after careful examination, saw how each appeared empty, unreal, insubstantial. In exactly the same way can we carefully examine sense impressions, perceptions, feelings, and thought, all that we experience, and discover them to be empty, void, and without a self.

Emptiness of self opens us to the experience of void itself, the dynamic emptiness out of which all things are born. In the Buddhist tradition awakening to emptiness is the gateway to Nirvana, the freedom of the heart referred to as the Unborn, the Uncreated, the Unconditioned.

The realization of this gate has been heralded by mystics throughout time. It can be entered in many ways. Three of the most common are through meditation, through an encounter with another who is awake, and through immersion in a solitude so deep we become transparent.

Knowing Through Meditation

Here is one teacher's experience during an extended insight meditation retreat.

By now, after several months, I only needed three or four hours of sleep. The whole instruction was to stay absolutely present and alert, and not react to anything that happened. So many thoughts and emotions had come and passed. There were days of intense loneliness, of tears and grief, and then times of rapture. Some days I felt like I was dying, my body was falling apart. I was surrounded by a world of death and destruction. Then after, it all evened out. I felt like I was floating through hours of meditation, with waves of light and ecstasy, my body dissolved open like the sky, with no boundaries.

As I became quieter still, the experiences kept coming

faster and faster. Now it was as if I could notice every single thought, even though there was a constant stream of them. Every thought-form would create a world of ideas or memory or imagination, and then vanish as soon as it was noticed. In the deepening silence of mind I began to feel the subtle prethoughts, as if the mind were pregnant, about to release its next thought. Sounds, smells, emotions, every tiny perception was noticed and released, or rather floated free, seen like fireflies in the night. I kept up a diligence of sitting and walking, feeling often as if I were under the sea in a still and transparent world.

One afternoon I lay down to meditate in the heat of the day. My eyes closed and effortlessly there was an awareness of all the sensations of this new posture. All the perceptions floated by, arising and vanishing like bubbles in soda. I felt myself letting go into this and the perceptions came even more quickly, as if the universe was rapidly pulsing—now becoming pulses of light, like fireflies. A moment of fear came and went, then my mind opened, then somehow fell down, and all was totally silent, beyond silence. There was no me, no experience, nothing, no words to put on this. Only a knowing. The world rested in an ocean of peace out of which all appearances arise and vanish. It was stunning. I knew the essence of consciousness to be this vast peace. There was certainty that I, and everything, were just an appearance in mind. And beyond this world where everything is born, changes, and dies is this ever-present reality. Of course, everything came back, but more luminous, transparent, shining with joy.

The first moments of opening into nonself can also be simpler than this. Another teacher tells of his first understanding of emptiness:

It was during a walking meditation in the garden near the temple. I can remember the exact spot. I lifted my foot and put it down on the earth, felt all the sensations of moving and knew there was NO ONE to whom it happened, no self at all! The thought came, "It is an empty process," and this thought was as empty as the step.

For one Zen teacher an understanding of emptiness came quietly. She calls her way "gentle perseverance," explaining, "I was not one of those warrior-type Zen students."

I was sitting with the koan MU, doing zazen with the others. I was actually quite relaxed and MU was repeating itself; it had taken on its own life. Then I simply disappeared. There was sitting and breathing and sounds and MU, and it was all MU. I was nothing and I was MU, and when I went in to see the master, I smiled and laughed. It's who I was all along.

It is said that the spirit of meditation should continue as we rise from the cushion. One meditation teacher had been sitting a long retreat in India, but his realization began out in the courtyard with a sick puppy on a cloth on his lap.

People drop off unwanted dogs for the temple to care for, and at this retreat there was a new litter of puppies, several very sick. I sat for days with one whimpering puppy after another. I was completely cut open by this. Many dogs would come and go; that day, though, I saw that the underlying truth of life doesn't change although it manifests in those changing bodies. I kept meditating with the puppies and the puppy shit and then went back into the hall.

I became very still. Thoughts and intentions would arise and dissolve in an instant, but there would be no impulse to follow them. And then some deeper letting go happened, like a huge bursting of all perception into space, emptiness. Suddenly there was no self, nothing to do or solve. That was all just foolishness. I was lifted off my cushion with a smile six feet wide, and in the emptiness joy arose, a river with no edges, a dance of emptiness, a confirmation of freedom where life is no problem, "self" is no problem, even sick dogs are no problem.

Emptiness in Another's Sacred Presence

The understanding of emptiness is contagious: It appears we can catch it from another. We know that when a sad or angry person enters a room, we too often enter into sadness or anger. It shouldn't surprise us, then, that the presence of a teacher who is empty, open, awake can have a powerful effect on another person, especially if that person is ripe. In every tradition there are stories describing awakenings of students through direct encounters with their master. One teacher of meditation and raja yoga experienced a decisive opening at a lecture in California, which led to a ten-year journey of practice in India.

I was listening to Krishnamurti on a spring day at his school grounds in Ojai Valley. He sat on a single wooden chair, a slight old man with a commanding presence. There were a thousand of us resting on the grass, sheltered beneath a grove of ancient live oaks. All our focus was devoted to the speaker, who challenged everything we knew about life, about ourselves. He spoke of true attention. "Are you really listening?" he asked. "Not with the limited ideas of a thought or reflection, but in the utter silence beyond the mind?" And in that instant my mind stopped. I entered an enormous stillness. The grove seemed to expand and float, as if it were in the center of the galaxy. The words came out of the trees. I felt I was totally alive, yet dead, beyond myself. All was filled with light, and a timeless, boundless space was all that existed, ever. As the words drifted through like a dream, I knew that I had let go with Krishnamurti, as if the joy of

*awakening were contagious, and I had caught it, felt it,
entered it.*

In Zen, the phrase "turning word" is used to describe those
few words, like Krishnamurti's "silence beyond the mind," that
can turn the mind to its true nature in an instant. Such moments
of awakening are recorded in the hundreds of classic Zen stories
known as koans. An example is Zen Master Hui Neng's reply when
asked about a flag fluttering in the wind. Was it the flag that
moved or the wind? Hui Neng answered, "Neither. It is the mind
that moves."

In the presence of a skilled teacher such a question can lead a
person to turn from the particulars of a moment to a timeless perception. We remember our original nature, the boundless heart
which contains all things, yet is not limited by them. A Western
Buddhist teacher remembers a time in the mountains of India:

> *I had passionately devoted myself to meditation for several
> years. One evening the teacher called us together for chant-
> ing, prayer, and a lecture. I was seated in the front row, com-
> pletely attentive. In the middle of the talk I heard the
> teacher say, "Your face is like a mask." That was like light-
> ning in a clear blue sky: It cracked my world. In a moment
> everything I thought I knew dropped away. I had done a
> hundred acid trips before coming to Asia, but they all paled
> compared to this. This was a whole new dimension, outside
> all the senses. It completely transcended my senses and iden-
> tity, all that I thought I was. It was beyond pleasure and
> pain, ecstasy and joy. I wept for the beauty of it for a long
> time. That was twenty-six years ago. In all these years, it's
> that unborn reality that matters beyond everything. It is a
> torch that illuminates everything. That's all there is. And
> somehow it's present in this moment too.*

A variety of conditions come together in these joint awakenings. There is the openness of the student, an earnest willingness

to discover. There is often a significant preparatory period of practice or purification. The account above followed many years of strict retreats of both Vajrayana and Vipassana. There is the respect and awe surrounding a master. And there is the field of consciousness of the master—the direct presence of love, freedom, and emptiness that he or she is able to convey.

For one meditation teacher, with twenty years of practice under masters in several Buddhist lineages, "something was still missing in my life."

I had been doing a spiritual pilgrimage in Asia. In the mail came the most beautiful letter of invitation from a master I had written. He had described the moment when Buddha held up a flower to Maha Kasyapa and all of Zen was born. Somehow through this invitation my friend and I ended up in India, visiting this little-known guru, a grandfather, with a handful of students, hidden away in his little living room in a back alley.

I was struggling with the noise, the chaos of India. Days passed, and I felt, "I'm not getting it, nothing is happening." It seemed he was giving more attention to the men in the room, and I felt, "Oh, this is just an Indian male trip; he doesn't understand women." Each day people would bow to him, and I thought, "Who needs bowing? I'm not into it; I'm a feminist from America."

He taught by asking us to inquire into who we think we are, not as struggle but as letting go. "Let go of the seeker and the sought," he would say. Then one afternoon he came close and looked in my eyes and would not let me go. I felt like a cornered animal. And tremendous fear came, as if something huge was about to happen. I felt like I had been distracting myself from this thing for eons, but now I was caught and I couldn't get away. I couldn't avoid it anymore.

He said some words, but what they were didn't matter. There came tremendous light and a huge space of nothingness, and I was gone, nowhere and everywhere. And then tremendous laughter and joy and crying. Everything in my life that seemed to have led up to that moment made sense, every struggle and fear. And now it was over. I was every-thing and nothing and completely free. That was it. After that I couldn't hurl myself at his feet enough times, there was so much gratitude. I would have given him anything, but of course he wanted nothing. And now I see in my work with students, the biggest surprise is that people think there is something to get, something to do, when it's so obvi-ous that there is nothing to do—except you still do it. There's the doing that's necessary to arrive at that place of nondoing.

I had a naive idea about the ease of bringing the bounty of this freedom to others. You don't have to go to India to find it. All you need is a truly sincere intention. Wherever you are, if you really want freedom, the universe will respond. It has to. You will be shown the way.

Knowing in Solitude

The knowledge of emptiness is also born in the solitude of the heart. In the Gospel of Mark we are told:

Rising early the next morning, Jesus went off to a lonely place in the desert. There he was absorbed in prayer.

Don Jose Rios, a revered Huichol Indian shaman, visited the U. S. at the age of 106. He said:

In my eighty years of training I have suffered much. Many times have I gone to the mountains alone. But you have to do this. For it is not I who can teach you the ways of the gods. Such things are learned only by yourself, only in solitude.

In entering solitude one does not necessarily find silence. At first solitude can be noisy, filled with the conflicts of the body and the mind's ongoing commentary that Chogyam Trungpa called "subconscious gossip." Meditation practices help us to find a way to genuine stillness. In them we find that there are many levels to silence. The first is simply external silence, an absence of noise. Then there is the silence of the body, a growing physical stillness. Gradually there comes a quieting of the mind. Then we discover the silence that comes as a witness to all things, and then twenty other levels of silent absorption in prayer and meditation. Still deeper we come to the indescribable silence beyond the mind, the silence that gives birth to all things. To enter silence is a journey, a letting go into progressively more profound levels of stillness until we disappear into the vastness.

Bernadette Roberts, a respected modern Christian mystic, had been a nun for ten years, and later the mother of four children. In *The Experience of No Self,* She tells of her journey to silence, of initial bouts of fear, of finally losing herself in silence until the subtle thoughts would time and again pull her back from its embrace. But one day, sitting alone in a chapel, she began to discover where silence would lead. These experiences came as the first part of a long process, pulling her into emptiness and letting go until her life itself united into a whole. Here are her words.

> *Again there was a pervasive silence . . . but this time no movement came. I left the chapel as a feather floats in the wind. . . . Outside I had a difficult time because I was continually falling back into this great silence. But as the days went by, and I was once more able to function as usual, I noticed there was something missing and I couldn't put my finger on it. . . . I could not find an explanation in the writings of St. John of the Cross or anywhere else in the library. It was coming home that day, walking with a panorama of valleys and hills before me, that I turned my gaze inward, and what I saw stopped me in my tracks. Instead of the usual*

unlocalized center of myself, there was nothing there, it was empty; and at the moment of seeing this, there was a flood of quiet joy, and I knew, finally knew what was missing—it was my "self."

Physically I felt as if a great burden had been lifted from me; I felt so light. I looked down at my feet to be sure they were on the ground. Later I thought of St. Paul's experience—"Now, not I, but Christ lives in me"—and realized that despite my emptiness no one else had moved in to take "my" place. So I decided that Christ was the joy, the emptiness itself. He was all that was left of this human experience. For days I walked with this joy. . . . There was no "mine" anymore, only "His."

For another teacher, the opening to emptiness came as a surprise at the very beginning of his path. He spent thirty years in Buddhist training after that in order to understand and integrate where he had begun.

It was early in my spiritual life. I had gone to a few meditation classes. Now I was lying quietly, in solitude, resting after so much time thinking, wondering. My mind was in the clearest, most open state. It also felt charged, alive, yet absolutely still as well. I had not known such a balance of alertness and ease was possible. I picked up an old Buddhist text and read a few lines:

Although the One Mind is, it has no existence. In its true state, Mind is naked, immaculate, being of the Voidness, transparent, timeless, uncompounded; not realizable as a separate thing, but as the unity of all things, yet not composed of them. Arising of themselves and being naturally free like the clouds in the sky, all that appears fades away. . . . The whole of the World and Nirvana as an inseparable unity are one's own mind.

84

Everything I knew of the world shattered open. I could not say what was left, for there was nothing of myself at all. There was that which is here before the sense of self ever existed. I knew once and for all that there is no self, that any sense of self is an illusion. We are empty like a dream, a play of mind. Gradually some of the world came back, though in many ways my sense of it had changed completely. I had no idea how I was supposed to live anymore. For weeks I walked around in a kind of lightness and shock.

The gate of emptiness can reveal itself whether in solitude or in the sacred presence of another, in deep meditation or in the mountains. Attentive to this mystery, the heart can open to directly experience the emptiness which gives birth to all things.

Taoists speak of this as sacred hearing, not by means of the intellect's understanding but the "hearing of the spirit," in which all the senses are open and empty. Only then, with the emptiness of all the faculties, can the whole being listen and know what is right there before us, which can never be heard by the ear or the mind alone. This is the wisdom of those who know not and who yet, being empty, carry a heart full of light.

Isaac Newton knew this when he wrote:

To myself I am only a child playing on the beach, while vast oceans of truth lie undiscovered before me.

Through the gate of emptiness, for that child, the vast unknown is not a source of terror, but the field of his joy.

6

WHO ARE YOU REALLY, WANDERER?

Satori and the Gate of Oneness

One day I wiped out all notions from my mind. I gave up all desire.
I discarded all the words with which I thought and stayed in quietude.
I felt a little queer—as if I was being carried into something, or as if I were
touching some power unknown to me . . . and Ahhh! I entered.
I lost the boundary of my physical body. I had my skin, of course, but I felt I
was standing in the center of the cosmos. I spoke, but my words had lost
their meaning. I saw people coming toward me, but all were the same man.
All were myself! I had never known this world. I had believed that I was
created but now I must change my opinion: I was never created;
I was the cosmos; no individual existed.

MASTER S.

It is the goal of spiritual life to open to the reality that exists beyond our small sense of self. Just as we can enter this reality through our shared suffering or through vast emptiness, we can enter through the gate of oneness, and discover what can be called "Awakening as the Beloved." Through the gate of oneness we awaken to the ocean within us. We come to know in yet another way that the seas we swim in are not separate from all that lives.

This gate shows us the mystery of divine connection. Every culture has rituals and voices that call us to this truth. It is there when we hear the performance of a mass by Handel or Mozart, and when we enter an ancient cathedral with the sun shining through the stained glass. It is there dancing in ashrams in India and with the dervishes of Turkey, chanting the names of the Divine through the long night. It is there in the Native American Sun Dance. When the sacred spirit is present, we can only bow in gratitude. As one American swami describes it:

> *Blissful energy exploded up within me to the top of my head, and my heart was full of love for everyone and everything. I kept bowing and touching the ground and saying blissfully, "The earth is my witness," over and over.*

The deepest forms of meditation, rituals, prayers, and sacred art act to reopen our eyes and hearts to oneness. In the words of Symeon, an eleventh-century theologian:

> We awaken in Christ's body. . . .
> I move my hand, and wonderfully
> my hand becomes Christ. . . .
> I move my foot, and at once
> he appears like a flash of lightning. . . .
> For if we genuinely love him,
> we wake up inside Christ's body,
> whole, recognized as lovely and radiant. . . .
> We awaken as the Beloved
> in every last part of our body.
> (tr. Stephen Mitchell)

Communal rituals for awakening into oneness have been developed over many generations. A Western teacher tells of encountering one ancient ritual of connectedness while visiting Tibet for the first time:

> *Just to get to Tibet, we traveled on an old bus for fourteen hours from Katmandu, up and down rocky gorges, then up*

higher and higher into the enormous mountains. The ride become even more grueling and dangerous over the days, as we crossed the high Tibetan plateau filled with tiny flowers and brilliant rocks. The sky changed. It was huge and dark, bigger than the earth, as if the very figures of ground and heaven were reversed in these wild mountains.

After many travels we came to a mountainside temple, the famous Drepung monastery, just as pilgrims from all over Tibet arrived for a festival. For days the courtyard was filled with yak butter lamps and deep chanting and song. On the last night, at about 4:00 A.M., the whole crowd surged outside to climb precipitously onto a special hillside outside the gates to wait for daybreak. Everyone was reciting sacred prayers and mantras over and over, clutching their robes in the cold wind. The copper horns of the monastery, so huge that each was held by three men, sounded long powerful notes down the entire valley, punctuated by rhythmic cymbal clashes.

As the sky began to lighten, a giant painting of the Buddha of Compassion, nearly one acre in size, was unrolled down the great monastery wall opposite us. It reached the bottom just at dawn. The horns sounded again.

Then the first sun's rays hit the painting. The huge golden Buddha was set ablaze with light, and at the same moment the first sunlight struck my own body from behind. It was arranged so that the light seemed to come out of this glorious Buddha and I felt I was being warmed by the Buddha's own heart, as if the Buddha had come into me. I was totally transformed in that moment. I knew that the Buddha was in me.

While such a pilgrimage can inspire our awakening, traveling isn't the point. The goal is to discover this experience for ourselves, wherever we are. In *Returning to the Source*, Wilson Van Dusen explains what it is like to be a mystic in the West, as one who has experienced the Divine countless times: in a summer sunset, in the eyes of a child, in the taste of an apple.

What is it like to be a mystic in this world? In part, it is sad. Mystics can go through a long period in which they have experiences of God, but they remain unsure. Once, after a talk in a church, an old woman waited until the crowd of people cleared. She came up to me afterward. I saw that she was not long for this world. Acting very circumspectly, she recited a short dream in which an amazing gold sun came to her and asked me if it was God. I first thought of my standard reply, "We need to go into the dream, and see what is in it." But then I was struck by the emotional impact of the larger situation. This old woman is dying and it matters very much to her if she met God even once in this life. I said, "Yes, it was God," and we both broke into tears. But how sad. She had the marks of a very spiritual person, whose life was embedded in God. And yet she asks desperately if once she met Him. To me she represents most of mankind. She is already well on her way, but she does not recognize the signs.

Every tradition has its mystics and every sincere form of practice can bring the revelation of oneness. One rabbi describes how this knowledge came to him on a summer retreat:

The experience that opened my whole inner world happened in the midst of a week of prayer and retreat. It was a quiet morning and I sat down to pray. First I wrapped myself in a prayer shawl and placed the traditional prayer boxes on my forehead and my arms. ("Thou shalt bind them as a sign upon thine arms.") My eyes were closed and as I quietly prayed a huge transcendent light began to glow around me, as if it were shining throughout the world. As it shined onto me, it passed through the prayer scrolls, the prayer boxes, imprinting itself directly into my body. This luminosity

89

shone through all three prayer boxes, and in every direction it imprinted the great prayer into my cells, the essence of my being. This great prayer is "Hear, O Israel, the Lord is one," which means that in all things THERE IS ONLY GOD. In that moment I understood why the mystical tradition is so concerned that written prayers be perfect, that none of the letters be broken or damaged. Instead of saying the prayer, I was dwelling in it. It was the marvelous experience of being a prayer realized. I know that our very lives, our very bodies are a prayer.

From that point on I would read the psalms and prayers, from David to the Talmud, and it would all open up. The great sages of the past were clearly speaking from a transformed state of consciousness.

A story about a Taoist hermit in the mountains conveys the truth of our oneness with divine humor. A formal delegation from the Confucian temple below decided to visit and seek his advice. When they arrived at his hut unannounced, they were scandalized to find him completely naked. "What are you doing meditating in your hut with no pants on?" they demanded. "The whole world is my hut," he replied. "This small room is my pants. What I want to know is, what are you doing in my pants?"

This is the truth we already know intuitively. A character in one of Alice Walker's novels describes it this way:

One day when I was sitting quiet and feeling like a motherless child, which I was, it came to me: that feeling of being part of everything, not separate at all. I knew that if I cut a tree, my arm would bleed. And I laughed and cried and I run all around the house. I just knew what it was. In fact when it happen, you can't miss it.

The world is our hut. We know that the air we breathe is shared with the oaks and fir trees of the forests, that the water we drink pours down from floating clouds as rain before it comes into our cells. All that we possess and are is a gift given us by the wholeness from which we come and to which we return. Our minds and bodies are not separate. The glimpses of oneness awaken a natural compassion and sense of justice out of which we come to treat the other parts of ourselves—all that is—wisely. Awakening to oneness, we discover that we have the same last name as the mountains, the streams, and the redwood trees.

A full experience of this truth is called "satori"—the first taste of enlightenment. All of us are candidates for satori, for remembering our true name; we need only to learn to let go. For one European Zen master, the first experience of satori came at age thirty-seven. As a student, he had come to spiritual life in part to escape the pain and confusion of his family and in part to move into a bigger reality that he knew was possible. The discipline he undertook was not confined to the traditional practices of Zen. It included dreamwork, healing, and therapy, each helping him untangle and release his past sorrows and defenses. All along, he continued sitting zazen as well.

> *My first experience of satori came in the midst of Zen training, but only after nine years of both psychological healing and intensive meditation practice. Then, somehow, it was as if enough preparation and purifying had taken place—I was ripe. One night I dreamt of a sacred mountain with the shrines of ancient saints at the bottom. I knew it was visible to only a few. In the dream I was climbing the mountain while licking a big ice cream cone, and all the children of the world were streaming down from the top of the mountain. The children were joyfully racing down into the world, but I had the ice cream cone and I was giggling. For all of us there was only laughter, innocence—so different from my actual childhood. It was as if some new possibility opened inside me.*
>
> *I went into spring retreat shortly after this dream. I remember experiencing a deep, pure meditation and thinking I was beginning to find what I had quested for—but I*

knew enough to just let it go and meditate some more. Then, on the fourth day, my mind fell into chaos, and I thought, "Well, I was wrong." But instead of using my concentration as a sword to cut the confusion away, casting all out except the luminous ground, I embraced the chaos with all my heart. Then body, mind, and the world started to open. It was like a great wave opening over me. I was filled with joy and clarity. It was both empty and full, cool winter and warm spring together. I felt I could understand everything.

This went on for days, for weeks. I remember at the retreat sitting in the middle of the afternoon, when every-body is tired and stiff and struggling, and I was so happy. We would go to see the Zen master, who would ask his impossi-ble questions, and I smiled to myself, "Oh, I know the answer to this." But I just kept sitting. The energy built and built. Finally I went in to the master and he asked one of the oldest koans, punctuated with a small hand gesture. With this gesture the whole room fell away. Everything was gone—the wind, the stars, the dogs outside. We all disap-peared into the same vastness. There was nothing and every-thing. And I laughed and laughed in astonishment. I knew the mind of my teacher, I knew the age of the world. My body was transparent, the blowing of the wind was my breath, my steps were the earth moving herself. After this, life was so joyful, alive, and my oldest fears were washed away, just gone. I was finally truly alive. And even though I was smiling for weeks and months, it was an odd thing. I didn't tell anyone in the community what was happening because I knew somehow that people would feel left out. In that way I immediately became aware of all the painful lim-itations in this world, how even within the great openness, the limitations must absolutely be respected.

In awakening, our whole sense of identity shifts. We let go of our small sense of self and enter the unbounded consciousness out of which we come. What becomes known with absolute certainty is that we are not and never have been separate from the world. It is as if our heart, our knowing, expands further and further until we contain everything, until we are the world.

Another teacher describes the simplicity of this knowing:

One day during the fall intensive training period, I was eating. I had been sitting, struggling for a number of days. I was trying so hard, determined to crash through every barrier and figure it all out—who I am, what is this practice that I'm doing. I lifted my bowl and suddenly I understood completely: Everything is all right just as it is! The whole world is completely, profoundly whole. I didn't need to do anything. I didn't need to try so hard. It sounds so pedestrian when I say it now in words, but it was enormous, an astonishing revelation which instantly undercut all my questions, and released me from the hundreds of ways I had always tried to change or fix myself or the world. There was an amazing physical dimension to it as well. My whole body dropped away, the shell or container of myself vanished, the bottom of the world dropped out. I had no shape separate from the world. My whole way of being released and changed over the months that followed, so much that people began asking me what had happened.

This openness to all things can come in any circumstance, like the experience of Eugene O'Neill's Edmund on the night seas in Argentina:

I lay on the bowsprit, with the water foaming into spume under me, the masts with every sail white in the moonlight towering above me. I became drunk with the beauty and singing rhythm of it, and for a moment lost myself—actually lost my life. I was set free . . . dissolved in the sea, became white sails and flying spray, became beauty and rhythm and the high dim-starred sky. . . . I belonged within a unity and joy to life itself.

93

For a second you see, and seeing the secret, you are the secret. The Sufis call it "becoming one with the Beloved." What we have sought to know illuminates our own body and heart, as in the experience of a Dominican nun who has been in her order for forty-two years.

Even from childhood I had a very personal relationship with Jesus. As a nun I had made up this question, especially as I learned more about prayer: "Where is Jesus now?" We would pray and serve and try to make our hearts pure to receive Him. But I knew it was more than that. Jesus would come to me at night as a strong comforting spirit. He even entered my body. On many occasions a spiritual ecstasy rushed like a lover, for hours, through every part of my body. I was up for hours. I couldn't really talk about it, even though I felt radiant and profoundly fulfilled. He flooded my heart with such love. I began to see Jesus everywhere—in people who were struggling, in the poor, in the least of His creatures, in my sisters, in the rich too. I served them all with love, as "Christ in His distressing disguise." To some it might sound like heresy, but Jesus is here among us, in every human, in every stone, in our deeds, in our successes and our errors. His glory is in the apricot tree in the garden, the gift I give to my niece, in my own hands and eyes. I feel Him moving in this very body I have been given. What a beautiful kingdom to awaken to, the divine presence in the world.

When our identity expands to include everything, we find a peace with the dance of the world. The ocean of life rises and falls within us—birth and death, joy and pain, it is all ours and our heart is full and empty, large enough to embrace it all.

7

THE GATELESS GATE:
The Gate of the Eternal Present

Actually there is no real teaching at all for you to chew on or squat over. But not believing in yourself, you pick up your baggage and go around to other people's houses looking for Zen, looking for Tao, looking for mysteries, looking for awakenings, looking for Buddhas, looking for masters, looking for teachers. You think this is searching for the ultimate and you make this into your religion. But this is like running blindly. The more you run, the farther away you are. You just tire yourself, to what benefit in the end?

ZEN MASTER FOYAN

A young monk asked the Master:
"How can I ever get emancipated?"
The Master replied:
"Who has ever put you in bondage?"
ADVAITA TEACHINGS

Sometimes we meet very wise people who have never gone anywhere special, never undertaken a systematic spiritual practice, never had a mystical experience. They can appear as the generous-hearted and loving child care worker, the sage who works in the local bookstore, or the compassionate grandmother beloved by an entire community. Such people emanate wisdom, immediacy, a gracious and free heart;

they exemplify those who are unafraid to live, to love, and to let go.

When we speak about undertaking a spiritual path, such people raise a question for us. What about those who practice for many years, growing into an ever-deeper wisdom, but never have any particularly remarkable experiences of grace, satori, or awakening? This too is quite common. How does it happen?

Examining these examples helps us undo a possible confusion set up by the last chapters. Just as there is danger for a culture that ignores the process of initiation and the experiences of satori, grace, and illumination, there is also a danger in describing them in too much detail. That danger is that they will become too important in our minds, or that we will glamorize these stories and come to believe they are necessary in order to live a spiritual life. But if we hold some special experience as our goal, we may spend years seeking that goal outside of ourselves, grasping after something that is here within us all along. Or we may begin to doubt ourselves and our own experiences, and judge our heart and spiritual life as inadequate and insufficient.

When I returned to my teacher Ajahn Chah after completing a long period of intensive training in other monasteries, I told him about the insights and special experiences I had encountered. He listened kindly and then responded, "It's just something else to let go of, isn't it?"

We need to remember that where we are going is here, that any practice is simply a means to open our heart to what is in front of us. Where we already are is the path and the goal.

When I spoke to one lama about his own realization, he said he could not emphasize enough the wisdom of its ordinariness. He had done long retreats and traditional training, but that "was his job," just as a baker bakes bread. When I pressed him to recount any particular moment of illumination, he laughed and replied:

We're always trying to make something special, bigger, better than what is actually here. Any realization that has come was simply a confirmation of what is here already. The rumors and teachings are true: We are luminous beings and awakening is our nature. If you want a story, it wasn't anything, and yet I could say I was resting easily, and a monk came in. He just looked at me and said, "Aha, I see something has happened." I had been relaxing and present, and there came an eternal moment, or hours—who knows?— of perfect fulfillment and peace, but I had hardly even noticed. The monk saw it immediately, though, and it was reflected back to me in his eyes. I started to see it reflected everywhere. In that reflection I was utterly relaxed. There was nothing to do or be. Everything was totally ordinary, and at the same time it was totally clear—awakening to this moment now is all there is.

When asked about the path of practice, Buddha explained that there are four ways for spiritual life to unfold. The first way is quickly and with pleasure. In this, opening and letting go come naturally, like an easy birth, accompanied by joy and rapture. The second way is quickly but painfully. On this path we might face a powerful near-death experience, an accident, or the unbearable loss of someone we hold beloved. This path passes through a flaming gate to teach us about letting go. The third form of spiritual progress is gradual and accompanied with pleasure. In this way opening and letting go happen over a period of years, predominantly with ease and delight. The fourth and most common path is also slow and gradual, but takes place predominantly through suffering. Difficulty and struggle are a recurrent theme, and through them we gradually learn to awaken.

In this matter we do not get to choose. Our unfolding is a reflection of the patterns of our lives, which are sometimes described as "our fate" or "our karma." No matter the apparent speed, we are simply asked to give ourselves to the process. In fact, we cannot measure our progress. It is like being in a small rowboat on the ocean. We row, but there is also a larger current; we may continually head east, but cannot know how far we have gone. The question of distance and time, however, is one that arises only at the beginning. It does not matter how far we think we have gone. It is our willingness to open radically and repeatedly just now that characterizes this journey.

Perhaps to be accurate, we could add a fifth way to the four paths of spiritual unfolding described by the Buddha. That is the way that involves no effort, no speed, and no journey. Instead of passing through the gate of oneness or the gate of sorrow, we pass through the gateless gate, the realization that the whole idea of journey and striving is an illusion. Where we're going is here.

To understand this better, we need to acknowledge two complementary ways in which awakening and illumination are discovered. One is through the path of striving and effort, the other through the path of noneffort. In the path of effort you purify yourself, you struggle to release all the obstacles to being present, you focus yourself on awakening or illumination so fully that everything else falls away. Finally you are forced to release the one last grasping, the desire for enlightenment, and in this letting go, everything becomes clear. In the path of noneffort, there is no struggle. You open yourself to the reality of the present. To rest in the sense of naturalness is all that is asked. Out of this, all understanding and compassion follow.

In fact, both ways are at times part of everyone's journey. Both ways lead to letting go. As one of my teachers, Dipama, would say, "Both ways are best." Wise effort is important. Yet no matter how arduous the path, and how much effort is expended, in the end the awakening of the heart comes as an act of grace, like a spring wind that wafts away all our concerns and fears, that refreshes the heart.

To meditate and pray and listen is like throwing the doors and windows open. You can't plan for the breeze. As Suzuki Roshi puts it, "You can't make a date with enlightenment." And a similar saying goes, "Gaining enlightenment is an accident. Spiritual practice simply makes us accident-prone."

When we grasp, we miss the moment that is just now. There is a story of an eager Zen student who arrives at a temple and says,

"I want to join the community and work to attain enlightenment. How long will it take me?" "Ten years," replies the master. "Well, how about if I really work and double my efforts?" "Twenty years." "Hey, just a moment. That's not fair! Why did you double it?" "In your case," says the master, "I'm afraid it will be thirty years."

For one Sufi master, the experience of opening has taken the form of an ongoing process rather than appearing as a single, great event of transformation.

While I of course remember various insights and revelations, on the whole my spiritual life has been a process of years and years of consciousness opening. This process simply has to be respected and encouraged. If I pay attention to what is happening inside, what wants to open next, it will always intensify. And as I sense each new capacity, I also discover what is in the way, preventing my opening. So if I sense my compassion is growing, I also encounter the doubts and resistances that stop me from really living in compassion. Acknowledging this becomes the next step in the process of opening.

Even though we know the truth, we have to work through the holding and beliefs that keep us limited. For a long time you have to keep this opening process going by paying attention. But you reach a point where it goes on by itself. There's no turning back because you know what it is to rest in True Being, to trust, even though you fall back into resistance sometimes. Because you know this is who you are, your understanding can't disappear.

Rather than seeking enlightenment as a state far away, we learn to recognize that it is, as Zen teaches us, "nearer than near." The gateless gate honors this natural awakening as our birthright.

Ajahn Chah, living amid a Buddhist culture that overemphasized the long arduous journey to enlightenment, took great care to remind his monks and nuns that their own awakening was natural and just at hand. He used to say that if you hadn't tasted the stream of enlightenment in the first six months at the monastery, you had been wasting your time. He pointed out that enlightenment is our inherent state, and that we can learn to rest in our naturally silent and free heart, independent of all the changing conditions around us.

> Within itself the mind is timeless, naturally peaceful, unmoving. Rest in this natural state. If the changing sense impressions cause the mind to forget itself, to be deceived and entangled, your practice is to see this whole process and simply return to the original mind.

Ajahn Chah reminds us that our careful reflection and earnest meditation can show us this reality whenever we become still. All experiences are without self, without independent existence. They arise like the wind, and pass away, all according to certain conditions. In any quiet moment of seeing this truth, he taught, we can step out of all the conditions we call "self," to rest in the timeless knowing, the unconditioned. Thus the difficult practice we undertake is to know the changing world and not get lost in it.

In this teaching, the figure and ground of our experience are reversed. Illumination is our true state, and spiritual practice is a way to release our entanglements and live in the reality of the present. We are the goal.

A Buddhist meditation master tells how her life has been transformed. For her too there is no event, no powerful satori that she can point to. Instead it is the endless stream of awakening itself.

> Here I am, a teacher for hundreds and hundreds of students, some who have experienced powerful meditative openings. But that has not been my way. For a long time this was the hardest thing for me to accept, that "nothing happened." I'm not a person with big dramatic experiences. For thirty years now it's simply been a process of practicing without being caught by my own ideas of discouragement or success. I

*would go for months of intensive training and no spectacu-
lar experience would happen. This was especially hard for
the first ten years, but at least I never got trapped into believing I was a special spiritual person.*

*Yet somehow something did change. What most trans-
formed me were the endless hours of mindfulness, giving a
caring attention to what I was doing. I learned that the inner
dropping of burdens was not going to happen for me all in
one piece, but again and again. I simply dropped the burden of my judgments, of my fear, of distrust of myself, of
tightness of body and mind. At some point I discovered how
automatically tightness and grasping would come, and with
that realization I started letting go, opening to an appreciation of life, finding an ease. The traditional teachings
slowly dawned on me—that in reality there is neither coming nor going, that from the ground of being, nothing ever
really happens or will ever happen. Seeing this was like a
confirmation of what I already knew. I became less serious,
less concerned about myself. My kindness started to deepen.
Oddly enough, some of my friends tell me I have become
more and more like myself. They say there has been a very
big change in me, but it wasn't produced by any special
event. I guess it is just the fruit of being present over and
over. It's that simple.*

It is easy to get caught in the notion that there is a goal, a state,
a special place to reach in spiritual life. Accounts of extraordinary
experiences can create ideas of how our own lives should be, and
lead us to compare ourselves with others. In Tibet one famous yogi
had lived for years practicing ardently in a mountain hut supported by the villagers below. Then one festival day he heard that
all his supporters were going to visit him. The yogi carefully swept
his hut, polished the offering bowls on the altar, made a special
offering, and cleaned his robes. Then he sat back and waited, but
an unease came over him. Who was he trying to be? Finally he got
up, scooped up several handfuls of dirt, and threw them back onto

the altar. Those handfuls of dirt were said to be his highest spiritual offering.

When we enter the gateless gate, we come to the end of seeking. Before this in our life we may have tried many ways to find enlightenment or become something special. Finally, we enter the gate of the eternal present and discover that we are not going anywhere. Where we are is the place, the only place for the perfection of patience, peace, freedom, and compassion. Zen poet Ryokan offers this truth as the culmination of a life of seeking wisdom:

> My life may appear melancholy,
> But traveling through this world
> I have entrusted myself to Heaven.
> In my sack, three quarts of rice;
> By the hearth, a bundle of firewood.
> If someone asks what is the mark of
> enlightenment or illusion
> I cannot say—wealth and honor are nothing but dust.
> As the evening rain falls I sit in my hermitage
> And stretch out both feet in answer.
> (tr. John Stevens)

Ryokan rests in the understanding heart. No longer seeking anything from the world, he trusts the Tao. Enlightenment is his own presence, and his response to the world is compassionate and natural.

A Christian contemplative who has actively pursued a spiritual life for thirty years tells this story:

I had always been moved by the longing of mystics like St. Theresa of Avila and St. John of the Cross. When I spent a year at a convent after a failed relationship and family troubles, I read their words over and over. I had the romantic idea that I was going through the dark night of the soul. But for me it never ended, there was no big experience, no mystical illumination at the end. When I left the convent and became a social worker, I kept up my prayer life and contemplative practice, but it remained ordinary and dark for years. Now I realize that I was somewhat depressed and lonely—nothing very mystical about that.

Then ten years ago, I made a retreat with Father Bede Griffiths, a radiant old Catholic monk with an ashram in India. He had orange yogi-colored robes and white hair and deep joy beamed out of his being like daffodils shining after a long winter. We talked and he told me that I had made up a whole story of how the spiritual journey should unfold. Then he held my face in his hands and beamed such love into me and said, "Why not be your own unique self. That's all God wants from you." And I wept and I danced and laughed at all I was trying to be. And now for years my life of prayer and contemplative practice has continued in its ordinary way, but I'm not depressed and I've come to love my life. No great experience ever happened, but through loving myself, everything changed.

The Zen tradition is full of such accounts. A disciple of Zen Master Kassan first lived with the master, but finding the teachings there not to suit him, he left to go on pilgrimage. But everywhere he went, he heard praise for his own Master Kassan as the best of teachers. At last he returned. Greeting his old master, he demanded, "Why did you not reveal your profound understanding to me?" The master replied with a gentle smile, "When you boiled rice, did I not light the fire? When you handed out food, did I not hold out my bowl to receive it? When did I ever betray you?" At this the monk was enlightened.

The holy perfection we seek has been here all along. Dame Julian of Norwich described this perfection at the center of her prayers when she wrote, "And all shall be well, and all manner of thing shall be well." To recognize the perfection of "things as they are" is a radical opening of the heart, an awe of the sacred wholeness that underlies all things. It is always here, and we can awaken to it in any situation.

The question may arise, "Why hasn't some taste of enlightenment or perfection revealed itself to me?" The truth is it probably has, but we have not noticed it or recognized it. It is like the invisible air that surrounds us, that sustains our life.

Ajahn Buddhadasa, whose monastery spread across a great forest of the Malay Peninsula, invited his students to sit with him in the coolness of the trees. Then he made a point of directing his students to look for Nirvana in the simplest ways, in everyday moments. "Nirvana," he would say, "is the coolness of letting go, the inherent delight of experience when there is no grasping or resistance to life."

Anyone can see that if grasping and aversion were with us all day and night without ceasing, who could ever stand them? Under that condition, living things would either die or become insane. Instead, we survive because there are natural periods of coolness, of wholeness, and ease. In fact, they last longer than the fires of our grasping and fear. It is this that sustains us. We have periods of rest making us refreshed, alive, well. Why don't we feel thankful for this everyday Nirvana?

We already know how to let go—we do it every night when we go to sleep, and that letting go, like a good night's sleep, is delicious. Opening in this way, we can live in the reality of our wholeness. A little letting go brings us a little peace, a greater letting go brings us a greater peace. Entering the gateless gate, we begin to treasure the moments of wholeness. We begin to trust the natural rhythm of the world, just as we trust our own sleep and how our own breath breathes itself.

On a retreat, a healer and psychologist who had devoted fifteen years to spiritual practice was struggling yet again with the question of relationships. Feelings of longing and craving and blame kept coming up again and again. We talked and I suggested he spend some days directing a loving-kindness meditation toward himself. At first he resisted; like so many of us, he felt uncomfortable focusing on himself. It was awkward to offer the intention of love and kindness to himself over and over for days. But as the retreat went on, his heart softened. Forgiveness for himself and others arose. The world began to look more beautiful. And then came a realization:

It is I who must love myself. No one else can make me feel whole. Only I can provide that love. Now I know that wholeness is always accessible to me and all beings everywhere. This knowing allows me to live with a new peacefulness and kindness to myself and others. In the simplest way, it has changed my whole life.

Again, the lesson of spiritual practice is not about gaining knowledge, but about how we love. Are we able to love what is given to us, to love in the midst of all things, to love ourselves and others? Are we able to see the illumination offered by the sun every morning? If we cannot, what must we do in the body, heart, and mind to allow us to open ourselves, to let go, to rest in our natural perfection? The gate is open; what we seek is just in front of us. It is so today and every day.

Meditation teacher Larry Rosenberg went to practice with Zen Master Seung Sahn in Korea. During the journey he undertook a pilgrimage to other masters and temples, and while traveling on a remote road he came across a particularly elegant Buddhist shrine, or stupa, at the base of a mountain. Next to it was a sign, "Way to the Most Beautiful Buddha in All of Korea," and an arrow pointing to the thousand-step path up the mountain. Larry decided to climb, hiking up the steps until he reached the top. The view was breathtaking in every direction. The simple Zen stone pagoda matched the elegance of the one below. But in place of the Buddha on the altar there was nothing, only empty space and the gorgeous green-hilled vista beyond. When he went closer, at the empty altar was a plaque that read, "If you can't see the Buddha here, you had better go down and practice some more."

PART THREE

No Enlightened Retirement

8

BEYOND SATORI:
The Maps of Awakening

A priest's daughter asked him where he got his ideas for his sermons.
"From God," he replied. "Then why do I see you scratching
things out?" asked the girl.
FR. ANTHONY DE MELLO

A clearly enlightened person falls in the well. How is this so?
TRADITIONAL ZEN KOAN

Iow can we understand what lies
beyond awakening? When Socrates was in prison awaiting his exe-
cution, he heard a fellow prisoner singing a complex lyric by the
poet Stesichorus. He begged the man to teach him the poem. "But
for what reason?" questioned the other. Socrates answered, "So I
can die knowing one thing more."

Spiritual life is the same. It involves a maturing of understanding, a continual unfolding, whoever we are. This is "posten-
lightenment" wisdom. As Chinese Master Hsu Yun explained
before he died at age 120, "There are many minor satoris before
a major satori, and many major satoris on the path of genuine
awakening."

Mystics of every tradition teach that however powerful an
awakening, our ability to live in that reality will almost undoubt-
edly pass. At first it may not seem so. Satori awakens in us an
understanding and freedom so compelling that it is difficult to

acknowledge that this realization is only the first step. Still, descriptions or maps of an ongoing process of awakening appear in virtually every spiritual path.

Sometimes this unfolding is described as entering into higher levels of vision. The Christian mystic St. John of the Cross writes of ascending Mount Carmel and seeing ever more clearly from its higher slopes. Sometimes it is seen as a stabilizing of our first understanding, as the Tibetan Dzogchen masters tell us is necessary. In the last picture of the Zen ox-herding series, herder and ox are shown traveling together back to the marketplace, bestowing blessings—and still their journey is hardly over. One could say, in fact, that their adventures have just begun. Each tradition offers its own image for how life goes on once the heart awakens, but all agree the first opening is just the start.

Awakening Only Begins a Process

One of Buddhism's best-known maps of awakening comes from the Theravada tradition of the Elders of Southeast Asia. The Elders' map describes enlightenment as four progressive stages of "Noble Understanding," each of which brings a new level of freedom. The initial stage is called "Entering the Stream." Stream entry occurs when we have our first taste of the absolute freedom of enlightenment, a freedom of the heart beyond all the changing conditions of the world.

Like satori or kensho (a profound awakening) in Zen, stream entry brings a breathtaking change of understanding. In this first enlightenment a person sees through the illusion of separate self, releases identification with body and mind, and awakens to the timeless peace of Nirvana. Through it the direction of our life is forever changed, and we enter a stream that will carry us to greater freedom as inevitably as a swift-flowing current carries a leaf to the sea.

But even though we have seen the truth, the Elders say, further purification remains necessary for us to transform our character and embody this new understanding in our life. Thus begins the journey from stream entry to the second stage, "Returning Again." Through a deep process, often requiring many years, we discover and release the coarsest habits of grasping and aversion that re-create our fearful and limited sense of self. Attaining the second stage requires a continual and heartfelt attention to the suffering that comes when we cling to our desires and fears, to our ideas and ideals. As these forces of human life are understood, they lose their hold on us. Finally, in a deep realization, the strongest forces of desire, grasping, anger, and fear significantly drop away. We fulfill the second stage.

The third stage the Elders call "Non-Returning." In this we are irrevocably released from any remaining desire, grasping, anger, and fear, nevermore to return to their sway. The very few who progress to this third stage do so through a long process of abiding in profound calm and emptiness. When wisdom grows, the subtle movements of clinging in the heart are abandoned the moment they arise. At this stage we rest in freedom and the reality of the present, and the heart's deep peace is rarely disturbed.

Finally comes the fourth and most extraordinary stage, called "Great Awakening," in which the last traces of subtle clinging— even to joy, freedom, and meditation itself—fall away. Now without the slightest identification with self, we are freed from the vestiges of pride, judgment, restlessness, and separation that veil pure being. The radiance of our true nature shines unhindered throughout our life.

This map of the Elders explains how it is possible that a person who has experienced an obvious and deep enlightenment can still be caught in greed, anger, and delusion. After stream entry, a person can give genuinely inspired teachings on realization and illumination, yet still not be living them. That is why further stages of awakening are essential.

Most masters agree that after the first illumination, there can still arise periods of fear, confusion, loss of spiritual bearings, and unskillful conduct. No matter how compelling the vision, how profound the initial sense of freedom and grace, a process of maturation must follow. Over the years I have not seen a single Westerner for whom this was not true, and it seems to be true for most Asian teachers as well. If we fail to acknowledge this truth, we simply fool ourselves. When a proud mother once announced to Mullah Nasruddin, "My son has finished his studies," Nasruddin replied, "No doubt God will send him more." It is like that for us all.

Because the actual signs and means of attainment can vary, there is considerable disagreement among the Elders themselves on what constitutes stream entry. In one lineage it arises from the deepest meditation, which dissolves the solidity of the body and all identification with it. In another lineage it is freedom from identification with the mind. Other monasteries teach that stream entry has nothing to do with deep meditation, saying it comes naturally in the first months of practice when we let go of all attachment. According to certain teachers, a single encounter with the master, or a moment's pointing to the ever-present selfless perfection, can awaken stream entry. Some say stream entry comes after a long struggle with a koan in Zen. And even within individual monasteries, masters may dispute among themselves whether a student has actually attained these realizations.

Maybe it is best to honor many ways as true. Stream entry occurs whenever we truly let go of the small sense of self and open fully to freedom and trust. Perhaps it is like what Louis Armstrong said: "I can't tell you about jazz—you know it when you hear it."

In following the path beyond stream entry students have found it even more difficult to get precise, unambiguous instructions. A senior Buddhist teacher who was known as one of the strongest Western practitioners told me:

After years of retreat practice I went to Burma. The teacher called forth our fullest effort and I experienced many stages of insight leading to an amazing realization of the dharma— what seemed like stream entry, which the Sayadaw appeared to confirm. It was an awe-inspiring period, and the effects of that level of awareness lasted for a long time. So I thought it would be straightforward to go to the next stage of enlightenment. I threw myself into the practice the following year, but only seemed to repeat what I had touched already, with nothing new happening. I became frustrated, and as I pushed further I sensed how deep the next level of attachments really is.

I tried to get direct answers from several masters about what I needed to do to attain the second stage, but all the answers were surprisingly vague and unclear. Eventually my Sayadaw did say his own next stage of practice was a purification that took many years. What I know at this point is to keep following the direction of the dharma, but I'm not clear that we can know exactly how far we've come or how far we have yet to go.

Humility and the Dark Night

Christian contemplative maps describe the higher spiritual paths as a process of growing humility and purification. St. John of the Cross teaches us that after certain initial experiences of grace there will come long painful periods in which we lose our sense of connection with the Divine, and that such dark nights are necessary stages of the sacred journey.

First, according to St. John, comes the "Dark Night of the Senses," in which the things of the world lose their taste. This is a period of profound loss, when all that has given comfort in the past loses its meaning. After the most splendid illumination, we enter a dry and barren place, without a clear understanding of the heart's road. St. John of the Cross describes this as a time of patient purification of character from pride, greed, and wrath. In it we deepen our realization of the sorrows in the world caused by our separation from the Divine.

After the Dark Night of the Senses comes the "Dark Night of the Spirit," in which yet greater purification and surrender is required. This is a purgatory of grief and confusion, such as we see in the trials of Job. Out of this time of stripping away arises a vehement love and longing for only the Divine.

A great reward awaits those who honor the soul's dark nights: St. John sings of an unutterable sweetness, the swoon of grace which flows into a soul that has deeply surrendered to this "splendid darkness." In this long journey, it is humble perseverance that matters. St. John says, "The love of the heart is the candle flame that carries us through the road of darkness."

The dark night came to one meditation teacher after years of inner contemplation and an opening to the Divine.

After many years in both Catholic and Buddhist communities, it was on a long solitary retreat that the indescribable happened. The closest I can come is to use St. Augustine's words—I saw that God was closer to me than I was to myself. God was like a vast ocean and everything I was used to experiencing as myself was a thin membrane, floating on the surface, insubstantial and then gone. . . .

When the bliss and divine openness that came with this realization subsided some months later, I fell into profound heaviness and dread. It was the beginning of a period of hell. After a huge emotional outpouring, everything became stuck in a deadness, without feeling, without meaning. I had moved from the Buddhist center back to Ohio to be near my daughter, taking a meaningless cleaning job. My body developed hives and asthma. The endless inner pain and loss made me feel desperate, close to suicide or psychosis, though outside it all looked normal. Prayers and meditation had become impossible.

After months of this suffering I finally got so overwhelmed I threw myself down on the bathroom floor and cried out to God for mercy, because I couldn't go on. In an instant the whole tortured state of being drained out of me, like water out of a bathtub. For two hours I sat there on the floor in bliss, joy, and peace. I saw that all the difficulty was

God's work and I remembered my trust in God and that these sorrows are part of the path. After two hours' rest I was able to acknowledge that I could take it, and that if it was part of God's work, I wanted it. The very moment I saw that, unbelievably it all came right back—rising up from below as if the bathtub were filling again. Everything was exactly as before, exactly as painful and terrible, but that tiny period of God's mercy made all the difference. I knew I could take it, that I wanted to live through whatever God had given me no matter what. A huge gratitude arose for the grace and tenderness God showed to me then, like the tenderest of mothers, following just out of sight, longing to help us and catch us if we fall. It was there in the worst of my pain that I learned I had no choice but to live in God's grace.

Just as St. John speaks in terms of a dark night, St. Theresa of Avila uses the image of an "interior castle" to describe how the sense of mystery and humility must grow, "as the soul moves toward God's seat in the center of the castle." She maps the years of the soul's journey through seven stages, or inner dwellings. Each brings a gradual purification from the dangers of fear, wealth, and honor, a release from the "consolations of the world." Like St. John of the Cross, she tells how experienced contemplatives must pass through stages of aloneness, grief, and deception, sustained only by the continuing ardor of love and prayer. "The important thing is not to think much, but to love much." She tells how, through a long journey of steadfast love and grace, we finally enter a spiritual rebirth in which the soul becomes a caterpillar in the cocoon of the Divine, dying to its old ways and breaking forth with wings.

Yet even after we awaken and break forth with wings, the clouds only become more subtle. The anonymous fourteenth-century mystic who wrote *The Cloud of Unknowing* reminds us that although "through contemplation a person is purified of sorrow . . . we never arrive at perfect security in this life."

The Path Is Not Linear but Circular and Continuous

These systematic depictions of spiritual stages can make it seem as if the path is simple, linear, and progressive, as if spiritual life were a step-by-step development of oneself over time. In one way, the maps are correct, and we do gradually purify, open, release, and stabilize over the years of spiritual practice. But whatever happens does not happen in a straight line. Whether in the monasteries of Burma and Tibet or in the accounts of Christian, Jewish, and Sufi mystics, we almost never see anyone whose path is simply linear.

The unfolding of the human heart is artful and mysterious. We might wish the path to enlightenment were orderly and predictable, but the ways of the heart are a landscape discoverable only in the journey. We cannot capture freedom and place it in time. For the mature spirit, freedom is the journey itself. It is like a labyrinth, a circle, a flower's petal-by-petal opening, or a deepening spiral, a dance around the still point, the center of all things. There are always changing cycles—ups and downs, openings and closings, awakenings to love and freedom, often followed by new and subtle entanglements. In the course of this great spiral, we return to where we started again and again, but each time with a fuller, more open heart.

Jewish mystics say that the most exalted mystical states circle back to the simplicity of each day's prayers. In the kabbalah, the most sublime meditations of timeless awareness, called "binah" and "cochma," must be connected back to a life of daily generosity and devotion. The highest states of the Divine inevitably return us to our family and our prayers, to the lighting of the weekly sabbath candles and the holy practices of service and forgiveness. "As above, so below" is the mystic's formula.

For St. Theresa too there is a cycle. The interior life of ardor and selflessness does not find its end in union with the Divine. She insists that we return from that holy source again and again, to bring its radiance into the world, for "from this we are given a new life." The demand of "the splendid favors of awakening granted us is that they be embodied," so that we might live a holy life in this world. The fruit of the inner journey "is in our good works"; the mysteries open "only that we may return and have the strength to serve." Like the Zen ox herder, we circle back to enter the marketplace with bliss-bestowing hands. We return to bring the blessings of an awakened heart to everyone we meet.

More Poetry Than Mapmaking

The heart awakens as a lotus opens: Its natural beauty and scent both fill itself and perfume the garden around it. But the nature of flowers is to open in the daylight and close at night. How can we map and describe such a process? Yes, there are the stages of shoot, bud, and blossom. But this description omits more than it tells. It misses the nurturance of roots in the mud, the drinking of sunlight, the pollination of the bees, and the lotus sisters and parents that surround this flower and fill the world with more beauty. It misses the growth that takes place at night and the invisible buds below the surface of the water that don't yet remember the world of sunlight.

Because the unfolding of this mystic spiral is so richly organic, many traditions turn to poems to express its spirit. Poetry has a mysterious power in its ability to hold meanings almost impossible to speak directly. Zen writings offer almost no literal descriptions of stages of enlightenment, only metaphors and images, such as a finger pointing to the moon or the famous ox-herding story we have been following. The image of a white crane standing in snow or a black crow at midnight can convey the mind of awakening more keenly than hundreds of pages of abstract explanation, if the listener's ears are open.

The Buddha became enlightened on seeing the morning star. The Elders say his first words were a poem.

Builder of this house of sorrow
you shall build your rafters no more. . . .

In Zen, a different image appears, also poetic in its inclusion of connection.

With this star, I
and everything awaken.

Kabir, the Indian mystic, sings the marvels of awakening within the clay of this very body.

Inside this clay jug there are canyons and pine
mountains, and the maker of canyons and pine
mountains!
All seven oceans are inside, and hundreds and millions
of stars.
The acid that tests gold is there, and the one who
judges jewels.
And the music from the strings no one touches, and
the source of all water.

If you want the truth, I will tell you the truth:
Friend, listen, the Holy One who I love is inside.
(tr: Robert Bly)

The poemlike language of koans is used in Zen to foster enlightenment. One repeats a profound poem or koan over and over, inquiring into it until the mind opens in a radically new way. Then dozens of other koans follow to invite the student to embody more deeply the freedom which he or she has found, or to illuminate the directions in which understanding can go astray. Taken together, they create a poetic map of the life of practice. These koans and stories lead the student to the integration of the world of enlightenment with this one: "Bring me a pearl from the bottom of the sea without getting wet," a Zen master may demand, or "Show me the sound of one hand clapping" or "What is the straight within the bent?"

The student who encounters these stories, questions, and poems cannot meet them with a conceptual mind alone—any easy response is firmly rejected. These koans' answers come only as we deepen our ability to live in the reality of the present, to open and close like the lotus, to enter the dark forest and dance in the market. They do not point to an ideal state, but to the flexibility of the Tao, the naturalness of the lotus. They teach a letting go of fear and self-consciousness, of worldly and spiritual clinging, until we are free to be ourselves.

The ultimate end of the koans might be seen in the following story, a bit of modern Zen humor regarding a disciple who sent his master faithful accounts of his spiritual progress. In the first month, the student wrote, "I feel an expansion of consciousness and experience oneness with the universe." The master glanced at the note and threw it away. The following month, this is what the student had to say: "I finally discovered that the Divine is present in all things." The master seemed disappointed.

In his third letter the disciple enthusiastically explained, "The mystery of the One and the many has been revealed to my wondering gaze." The master yawned. The next letter said, "No one is born, no one lives, and no one dies, for the self is not." The master threw up his hands in despair.

After that a month passed by, then two, then five, then a whole year. The master thought it was time to remind his disciple of his duty to keep him informed of his spiritual progress. The disciple wrote back, "I am simply living my life. And as for spiritual practice, who cares?" When the master read that he cried, "Thank God. He's got it at last."

The story reflects the Zen teaching of the perfection of things as they are. The white crane in the snow is a white crane standing in snow, the black crow at midnight is truly itself.

Ideals Are Not Realities

What, then, are we to make of maps that do not include poetry and humor, that seem literally to prescribe a steady, linear, upward ascent? The risk is that we may try to climb their stages only to become lost in a cloud of unreachable ideals. It may be useful to examine how such a map can function in our actual life of practice, taking Tibetan Buddhism's Ten Bhumis as our example.

Described as the ten stages of awakening to Buddha Nature, the Bhumis are called in sequence: Stage One, "Joyous"; Stage Two, "Immaculate"; Stage Three, "Luminous"; Stage Four, "Radiant"; and so forth. The "Joyous" level begins after stream entry; though lofty and pure, it does include some ordinary human practices, such as vows of great generosity and the wish to bring awakening to all sentient beings. The practitioner who has attained the second Bhumi, however, must be able to see clairvoyantly into the past and future, to enter a hundred forms of deep meditation, to make the body multiply and appear in many places and forms at once, to cause a hundred Buddhas and bodhisattvas to appear around them wherever they go. And the third through tenth stages speak of powers even more miraculous and remarkable than this.

When I asked an old lama from Tibet about whether these ten stages are in fact a part of the practice, he said, "Of course they really exist." But when I inquired who in his tradition had attained them, he replied wistfully, "In these difficult times I cannot name a single lama who has mastered even the second stage."

Of course, there is an archetypal truth to these stages beyond what this exchange may acknowledge. In moments of grace or illumination, we are indeed surrounded by Buddhas—we see the Buddha Nature in every being we meet. And we make our body multifold whenever we experience how every being is interconnected with our own body, how the web of life, of rain forest, redwood, mushroom, and mitochondria is who we are. In other words, even these ostensibly literal maps may be better read as if they were a kind of poem, rich in possible meanings.

Zen Abbot Norman Fischer explains the difference between ideals and reality this way:

> Ideals are reflections of our deeply religious nature. But, as we know, ideals can be poison if we take them in large quantities or if we take them incorrectly; in other words, if we take them not as ideals, but as concrete realities. Ideals should inspire us to surpass ourselves, which we need to aspire to do if we are to be truly human, and which we can never actually do, exactly because we are truly human. Ideals are tools for inspiration, not realities in themselves. The fact that we have so often missed this point accounts for the sorry history of religion in human civilization. . . . If rightly understood, ideals make us light-hearted and give a sense of direction.

Two Visions of Awakening

When we compare a linear ascending path with a spiral unfolding, we find two quite different conceptions of spiritual fulfillment. The linear path holds up an idealistic vision of the perfected human, a Buddha or a saint or sage. In this vision, all greed, anger, fear, judgment, delusion, personal ego, and desire are uprooted forever, completely eliminated. What is left is an absolutely unwavering, radiant, pure human being who never experiences any difficulties, an illuminated sage who follows only the Tao or God's will and never his or her own. If this is the ideal we hold, we also have to acknowledge that such beings are exceedingly rare or may not exist at this time on this earth.

The more circular vision of enlightenment presents freedom as a shift of identity. In this vision, too, we awaken to our true nature, and rest in a timeless freedom of spirit. We know that our true reality is beyond body and mind. And yet because we also live within this limited body and mind, the ordinary patterns of life may continue. In the prophets of Judaism, Christianity, and Islam, and among indigenous elders worldwide, awakened beings are more complex figures who combine sanctity and flawed humanity. The difference, though, is that the old difficulties are ungrasped, held in an easy and harmless manner. As the sage Nisargadatta says:

> Pain and difficulty may arise, even impatience and irritation, but these have nothing to do with me. I was not born and will never die. . . . Though this body and mind are limited according to conditions, my life is an eternal unfolding in the timeless.

Whether we hold to a perfect ideal or to freedom within our humanity, awakening is a mystery with which each tradition and student has to grapple. The resolution of this mystery will finally be answered in the heart. It is here that the opposites can be held, understood, reconciled. Only the heart can contain both our perfection and our humanity.

Leaving maps and expectations behind, in the end we must turn our hearts in the direction of love and awareness, come what may. In living from this awakened heart we all become bodhisattvas, all servants of the Divine. We replace any claims of levels of enlightenment with a vow to awaken each moment, together with all beings. This is the path of patience, compassion, wisdom, and generosity, the path of our willingness to live in the reality of the present. Only here can we find freedom and rest in a timeless perfection.

As Suzuki Roshi put it: "Strictly speaking, there are no enlightened people, there is only enlightened activity." If there is a self who claims enlightenment, that is not it. Instead, he went on, "What we are speaking about is moment-to-moment enlightenment, one enlightenment after another."

9

NO ENLIGHTENED
RETIREMENT

If there be anywhere on earth a lover of God who is always kept safe, I
know nothing of it, for it was not shown to me. But this was shown:
that in falling and rising again we are always kept in that
same precious love.
JULIAN OF NORWICH

You cannot stay on the summit forever. You have to come down again. . . .
One climbs and one sees; one descends and one sees no longer, but one
has seen. There is an art of conducting oneself . . .
by the memory of what one saw higher up. When one no longer
sees, one can at least still know.
RENÉ DAUMAL

On the night of the Buddha's
enlightenment, after vowing to awaken, he was attacked by the
armies of Mara, the god of illusion and evil. Seated under the
Bodhi Tree, he was able to meditate unmoved by Mara's strongest
temptations of greed and pleasure. Then with a heart of compassion he overcame the anger and aggression unleashed by Mara,
and Mara left, defeated. After this the Enlightened One rose to
teach throughout India for forty-five years.

In the stories of the Buddha's later life, however, we learn that
Mara's disappearance was only temporary. Many times afterward

Mara returned to fight or tempt or undermine the Buddha. It is said the Buddha recognized Mara each time he appeared and so was not caught by temptation, fear, or doubt. "Is that you again, Mara?" the Buddha would ask, and being recognized, Mara would slip away, only to try again another time.

In other texts the Buddha and Mara actually become friendly. In one version the Blessed One is seated in a cave when Mara reappears. The disciples outside become frightened and try to get rid of Mara, calling him an enemy of their teacher. "Did the Buddha say he had enemies?" counters Mara. Seeing the untruth of their words, they reluctantly summon the Buddha, who responds immediately with interest.

"Oh, my old friend has come," says the Buddha, as he warmly greets Mara, inviting him in for tea. "How have you been?" As they sit together, Mara complains about how difficult it is to be an evil one all the time. The Buddha listens to Mara's stories sympathetically and then asks, "Do you think it is easy to be a Buddha? Do you know what they do to my teachings, what they do in the name of the Buddha at some of my temples? There are difficulties being in either role, a Buddha or a Mara. No one is exempt." In one scripture the story ends when Mara becomes awakened as a Buddha himself.

Inevitable Transitions

No matter what version we read, Mara does not go away. There is no state of enlightened retirement, no experience of awakening that places us outside the truth of change. Everything breathes and turns in its cycles. The moon, the stock market, our hearts, the wheeling galaxies all expand and contract with the rhythm of life. All spiritual life exists in an alternation of gain and loss, pleasure and pain. For each of us, even the Buddha, it is only by letting go into this truth that we awaken to that which is timeless, the reality of freedom.

For almost everyone who practices, cycles of awakening and

openness are followed by periods of fear and contraction. Times of profound peace and newfound love are often overtaken by periods of loss, by closing up, fear, or the discovery of betrayal, only to be followed again by equanimity or joy. In mysterious ways the heart reveals itself to be like a flower that opens and closes. This is our nature.

The only surprising thing is how unexpected this truth can be. It is as if deep down we all hope that some experience, some great realization, enough years of dedicated practice might finally lift us beyond the touch of life, beyond the mundane struggles of the world. We cling to some hope that in spiritual life we can rise above the wounds of our human pain, never to have to suffer them again. We expect some experience to last. But permanence is not true freedom, not the sure heart's release.

Every wise voyager learns that we cannot hold on to the last port of call, no matter how beautiful. To do so would be like holding our breath, creating a prison from our past. As one Zen master puts it:

> *Enlightenment is only the beginning, is only a step of the journey. You can't cling to that as a new identity or you're in immediate trouble. You have to get back down into the messy business of life, to engage with life for years afterward. Only then can you integrate what you have learned. Only then can you learn perfect trust.*

Like the monk in the ox-herding pictures, most of us have to reenter the marketplace to fulfill our realization. As we come down from the mountain, we may be shocked to find how easily our old habits wait for us, like comfortable and familiar clothes. Even if our transformation is great and we feel peaceful and unshakable, some part of our return will inevitably test us. We may become confused about what to do with our life, about how to live in our family or society. We may worry how our spiritual life can fit into our ordinary way of being, our ordinary work. We may want to run away, to go back to the simplicity of the retreat or the temple. But something important has pulled us back to the world, and the difficult transition is a part of it.

One lama remembers:

When I came back it was as if my twelve years of experiences in India and Tibet were a dream. The memory and value of those transcendental experiences was in some way a dream challenged by the culture shock of returning to my family and to work in the West. Old patterns came back surprisingly quickly. I got irritable, confused. I wasn't taking care of my body, I worried about money, about relationship. At the worst point I feared that I was losing what I had learned. Then I realized I couldn't live in some enlightened memory. What became clear is that spiritual practice is only what you're doing now. Anything else is a fantasy.

All spiritual life is preparation for transition, from one state to another, from one circumstance to another. The ability to make wise transitions is the ability to keep a beginner's mind. Change is not the enemy. Like Mara, it returns to ask the heart to be present and trust at deeper and deeper levels.

The integration of spiritual experience is a process of many years. After a three-month silent insight meditation, retreat participants are cautioned to expect twelve months of transition states, of joys and disappointments and newfound wisdom, as they learn to take into their lives all they have seen. The rule of thumb for those who have been in a monastery or traveled to Asia is that five, ten, fifteen years away usually means five or ten years of transition just to reestablish one's life in a whole and grounded way.

One insight meditation teacher tells of five-year cycles. Her first five years of intensive practice opened her to a vast inner world and profound, liberating understandings.

It's as if my heart absolutely needed that stability and nourishment before I could begin to touch the grief of my past. But then when it finally came up, the next five years was the

*opposite. The well of pain and agony was equal to the ecstasy
of the years before. I guess I had to have both.*

In a similar spirit, a Christian contemplative abbess found an
enormous grace on first entering her monastery, but then a cycle
of difficult practice arrived.

*The life of our community was simple and sane, and I threw
myself into it with all my love and energy. I did this with all
the skill of a very strongly formed and defended personality.
Deep prayer and meditation experiences sustained me for a
long time. After some years I felt I could trust the community, so I rested for a breather. Around this time one of the
older sisters died. I had been close to her, and it triggered a
succession of memories: the death of my twin brother at our
birth, the near-death of my mother, the distance, hatred, and
loss of my father. I realized how split off my life had been
because of my sorrow. I saw that even in the monastic community I had lived on the surface, had been running from
the grief and emptiness. I finally stopped. That realization
started years of healing work to find the place where the
grief, the monastery, the pain of my own life, and the pain
of the world could be held in the same sacred heart.*

Crash and Burn

These ordinary cycles of opening and closing are necessary
medicine for our heart's integration. In some cases, though, there
are not just cycles, there is a crash. As far as we ascend, so far can
we fall. This too needs to be included in our maps of spiritual life,
honored as one more natural part of the great cycle.

The Zen koan that introduced Chapter 8 is asked of students
who have experienced a first awakening: "A clearly enlightened
person falls in the well. How is this so?" One Zen master reminds
his students, "After any powerful spiritual experience there is an

inevitable descent, a struggle to embody what we have seen." The well we fall into can be created by clinging to our experience and spiritual ideals or by holding inflated ideas about our teachers, our path, or our self. The well can be the unfinished business of our psychological and emotional life—an unwillingness to acknowledge our own shadow, to include the human needs, the pain, and the darkness that we carry, to see that we always have one foot in the dark. As bright as it is, the universe also needs us to open to its other side.

A teacher of the Sufi Order was twenty-three years old when she joined a tradition filled with praises of God and songs of prayer. She sold her belongings and lived in a prayer-filled ecstatic Sufi community for over ten years. It was a glorious and heart-opening period of her life. Then she decided to marry and was drawn back into the world.

> *I had been taught how to be open and loving. I had amazing experiences of ecstasy and joy; our prayer life was filled with that. I didn't know what to do when I left the community and jealousy, fear, and loneliness came that I had to deal with on my own, without the support of my teacher or Sufi friends. I didn't have experience dealing with my pain and needs. My Sufi partner was worse. He couldn't bear to face the anger, the frustration, the demands of an individual householder's life. Then he left me. I was alone in this little house. As high as I had been able to go, the fall was deeper. His departure opened a tidal wave of despair in me that came from my sister's drowning and my mother's subsequent abandonment of the family—everything that I had run to the Sufis to heal. Oh God, it was hard. There was no light at the end of the tunnel. In the middle of it was just darkness. It didn't matter if it was in the middle of the night, if it was summer or winter. This went on for a year. All I could do was seek out people who could hold me, who could just listen to my tears and rage until finally I could be with*

myself. Although it was painful, a lot of healing and inte-
gration happened in those years. I just wish I had had more
perspective at the time, or better spiritual guidance.

Even recognized teachers are not beyond the experience of
finding themselves shattered. One American, a seeker for twenty
years, finally realized the fullness of freedom with a guru in India.
He was ecstatic for a year, "resting in perfection, drenched in
silence and love." After his wife became pregnant they returned
to the U.S. and in a short time the spiritual joy he had found drew
friends and seekers. Within two years he had daily meditation
groups, a center, hundreds of students. His path seemed to be
unfolding perfectly and he thought he had gone beyond the troubles of the world, until a crisis came.

I had always worried about my students, how unstable their
wisdom seemed. After the first profound realizations of
emptiness and freedom, the painful tendency of many
people was to become caught again in separation. But then
it happened to me! I received a crash course in confusion,
panic, and depression. It started when I became very sick
with leftover parasites from India. Then all the money I had
saved for years and invested in two thriving businesses was
lost through bankruptcy and betrayal. All of a sudden the
"guru" was sick and poor. I became terribly frightened. My
family life became a place of conflict. We had to leave our
home, to struggle with money, to worry about ordinary
things. I had difficulty with my mother. And all the while I
thought I shouldn't be feeling these things—I'd been to the
peaks, after all. I thought I knew the whole game.
  Finally I had to stop teaching. I lost all control. I
reached a childlike stage where I wasn't trying to understand
things; I was just broken down completely, living moment
to moment, and in some way that's when my spiritual life
really became genuine for the first time.

Celebrity is no protection from this kind of crash; in fact it may bring it about. Bhagawan Das, a six-foot-four blond-topknotted yogi, spent seven years in India walking barefoot, meditating in caves, chanting in ecstasy the names of God. He introduced Ram Dass to his guru, Neem Karoli Baba, a story Ram Dass tells in his 1960s classic *Be Here Now*. Bhagawan Das later traveled throughout the West with Ram Dass, teaching and singing for great spiritual gatherings.

I came back to America and found myself onstage before thousands of people, I named babies and blessed people, and people fell at my feet. I felt like a king with my patrons and movie stars, but I was still a kid, a guru at twenty-five, sitting on a tiger skin in a Manhattan town house.

If you play with the Divine Mother, she will play with you, because she's everything. . . . She's all the desire, the anger, the lust; she is everything. If you want name and fame, you can have it—Mother will give it to you. But what I had attained in practice came through the grace of being with saints. You hold that space through the blessings of the saints. And when I began indulging myself, I stopped my real practice, and I lost everything.

Spiritual life is not a once-and-for-all game; it's an ongoing process. After three years of "spiritual life" that was really a party, I got sick of it and wanted to be home with my children. I rejoined the world and sold used cars in Santa Cruz, I became a businessman, and I gradually lost my sense of divine completely.

Twenty years later a friend took me to see a visiting saint. I fell into a deep meditation for three hours. Then my guru's voice came and I wanted to sing God's name. So that's what I have been doing. But this time I'm being more cautious, watching who I spend time with. You need to be careful if you think you've attained something, because you can still lose it. You have to keep your spiritual commitments and keep your practice going. Now I'm just trying to be a real human being, and if others can learn from my experiences, then it all happened for a reason.

Honoring the Fall

When the Christian mystic Julian of Norwich says she knows of no lover of God who is kept safe from falling, she is voicing the understanding that to descend is also God's will. Whether we understand this or not, Mara does return. The fall, the descent, and its subsequent humility can be seen as another form of blessing.

Whatever success we have is usually one-sided. Then our less developed aspects, or "our shadow," as Jung calls it, come into the light. These are more raw, less controlled aspects of ourselves. There are certain truths we can learn only by descent, truths that bring wholeness and humility in surrender. In times of our heart's greatest vulnerability, we come close to the selfless mystery of life. We all need periods of fecund time, fallow time, of being drawn closer to the humus of the earth. It is as though something in us slows down, calls us back. And out of that time a deepened knowledge and beauty can emerge.

We can learn this from the myth of Orpheus. Because he is a son of the Muses, Orpheus is able to create the most beautiful human music ever heard. But then shortly after his wedding, his beloved wife, Eurydice, dies, and a grieving Orpheus follows her spirit all the way to the underworld. With his lyre, confronting the Lord of Death, he sings of undying love, as the poet Rilke describes:

A woman so loved that from one lyre came more lament than from all lamenting women, that a whole world of lament arose, in which all nature reappeared: Forest and valley . . . field and stream and animal in sorrow. . . . So greatly was she loved.

(Tr. Stephen Mitchell)

So moving is Orpheus's song that Hades allows Eurydice to return to the land of light, but on one condition: that Orpheus promise not to turn back or look behind him to see her on the long journey home. Led by Hermes, the god who mediates between two worlds, she silently follows behind Orpheus on the slow trek back to the world of light.

Again Rilke:

> He said to himself, they had to be behind him . . .
> but their steps
> were ominously soft. If only he could
> turn around, just once. . . .

It is the way of the heart, our human nature, to turn around— as Orpheus eventually does, though it loses Eurydice to him forever. We cannot live only in the world of the light. The heart knows that to open it must touch all of the truth, all of what we are, even when that risks the loss of what we love. Finally Orpheus's music must include the eternal strains of loss and grief, to sing fully our deepest understanding.

Traditionally it is said that if we don't honor our unfinished tasks, our karma will remind us, our unresolved conflicts will rearise; we will be forced to turn toward what we have not faced in ourselves. Put simply, the circumstances of human life will insist on getting our attention. Our falling needs to be honored along with our rising. Sometimes simply recognizing this is all that is necessary. As one Zen teacher describes it:

> *After months of joy from the retreat in which my Zen master acknowledged an authentic awakening in me, I became depressed. Later I went to another retreat, just to have an experience with Toni Packer. In one of the evening talks she mentioned that after people have big openings they often get quite depressed. The moment I heard this, my depression began to lift. It's as if I needed permission to accept what was so, and then the cycle could again begin to move.*

The fall is an invitation to both inward and outward transformation. Sometimes a spiritual fall does not resolve quickly; it can take years to move into the next phase. One Catholic monk and teacher who left his abbey after a dozen years to reenter the world of work and relationship describes what happened this way:

> *Our days in the abbey were a harmonious rhythm of prayer and silence, of sacred community and solitude. When I left, it was because of what was unlived in me. With all the beauty and ecstasy in the cloistered life, I had tried to fully include my passion, my physical being, my humanity, and while it worked for some, in the end it didn't feel possible for me. When I left, the initial euphoria was quickly overtaken by a dark night. I had learned how to be still, how to listen, how to trust in prayer; in that way my spirit was mature. But many parts of my life were immature.*
>
> *I couldn't go back, I couldn't go forward, and so I decided to serve others. I got work in a soup kitchen. I found a lover; we tried to live together. I had to rely on the strength of the spirit to get me through the doubts and suicidal depression. Those were the hardest three years of my life. Now I can see that they were essential to discovering my true spiritual vocation, a life of service. It was through them that I learned to trust what my life would bring. I am grateful now for all that I went through. It brought me closer to God.*

Letting Go

In the inevitable rising and falling, the cycles of expansion and contraction that come as you give birth to yourself, there may be moments to push, to strive toward a spiritual goal. But more frequently the task is one of letting go, of finding a gracious heart that honors the changes of life.

Suzuki Roshi once summed up all of Buddhist teaching in three simple words: "Not always so." Conditions always change.

We come down from the summit. Mara returns. Honoring the truth of transience allows our experience of darkness and falling to be part of the greater whole.

One Western lama came out of seven years of silent retreat to travel and teach for seven more.

The biggest surprise for me was how much I still needed to learn to trust. For years I thought spiritual life was about some special state of perfection or enlightenment. It is really about releasing attachment. Life doesn't depend only on what you do. The big illusions we strive for, whether in the world or our spiritual life, turn out to be false. When you learn to let go, you find a tremendous faith in the ground of all things, that which is true before and after all our plans. Everything arises and passes—this is the true perfection. I found I could trust this.

In all practices and traditions of freedom, we find the heart's task to be quite simple. Life offers us just what it offers, and our task is to bow to it, to meet it with understanding and compassion. There are no laurels to acquire. Charismatic teachers and spiritual attainments can become traps of striving in which we lose sight of our own Buddha Nature here and now. Ajahn Sumedho, the first American abbot of a Theravada Buddhist monastery, cautions us against trying so hard to get something special.

For minds obsessed by compulsive thinking and grasping, you simplify your meditation practices to just two words— "let go"—rather than try to develop *this* practice, and then develop *that*, achieve *this*, and go into *that*. The grasping mind wants to read the suttas, to study the Abhidamma, and to learn Pali and Sanskrit, then the Madhyamika and the Prajna Paramita, get ordinations in the Hinayana, Mahayana, Vajrayana, write books and become a renowned authority on Buddhism.

Instead of becoming the world's expert on Buddhism and being invited to great international conferences, why not just "let go, let go, let go"? For years I did nothing but this in my practice. Every time I tried to understand or figure things out, I'd say "let go, let go, let go" until the desire would fade out. So I'm making it very simple for you, to save you from getting caught in an incredible amount of suffering. There's nothing more sorrowful than having to attend international Buddhist conferences. Some of you might have the desire to become the Buddha of the age, Maitreya, radiating love throughout the world. Instead, just be an earthworm who knows only two words—"let go, let go, let go." You see, ours is called the Lesser Vehicle, the Hinayana, so we only have these poverty-stricken practices.

Letting go is the essence of this story about Tibet's favorite yogi and saint, Milarepa. Long after his enlightenment, Milarepa went to collect firewood outside the cave where he had been blissfully practicing. When he returned he found in the cave seven metal demons with enormous bodies and eyes the size of cups. Some were grinding barley and making fire, others were performing magical tricks. As soon as Mila saw them he became frightened. He meditated on the Buddha, uttered a subjugating mantra, but was unable to pacify them. He thought, "These might be the local deities of this place. Although I have been here for months and years, I have not praised them or given them any torma." So he sang a song of praise.

You nonhuman demons assembled here are obstacles.
Drink this nectar of friendliness and compassion and be gone.

The first three demons who were performing magic went away. Realizing that the remaining demons were magical obstacles, he sang this song of confidence.

It is wonderful that you demons came today.
You must come again tomorrow.
From time to time we should converse.

With this, three more demons vanished like a rainbow. The remaining demon performed an imposing dance, and Mila thought, "This one is vicious and powerful." So he sang another song, the pinnacle of realization.

A demon like you does not intimidate me.
If a demon like you could intimidate me,
The arising of the mind of compassion would be of little meaning.

Demon, if you were to stay longer, that would be fine with me.
If you have friends, bring them along.
We will talk out our differences.

Lord Vajradhara, Buddha,
Grant your blessings so that this lowly one may have complete compassion.

Then with friendliness and compassion, and without concern for his body, Milarepa placed himself in the mouth of the demon—but the demon could not eat him and so vanished.

Tibetan practices teach us that we benefit by honoring and feeding the demons. When the demons arrive we must recognize that they are part of the dance of life itself. When they threaten, it is only our illusions that are in danger. The deeper our bow to the awesome changing powers of life, the wiser we will be, and when we embrace them, they turn into a rainbow. Every color shines in the awakened heart.

As Julian of Norwich tells us, "In falling and rising again we are held in that same precious love." Only to the extent that we let go into change can we live in harmony with those around us and with our own true nature. No matter what the situation, awakening requires trust: trust in the greater cycles of life, trust that something new will eventually be born, trust that whatever is, is perfect. Wise letting go is not a detached removal from life. It is the heart's embrace of life itself, a willing opening to the full reality of the present.

This is the wisdom of the Tao:

> Rushing into action, you fail.
> Trying to grasp things, you lose them.
> Therefore the master takes action by letting things
> take their course.
> She remains as calm at the end as at the beginning.
> (tr. Stephen Mitchell)

The Secret Embrace

Though it sounds simple, letting go is also an advanced practice. It is demanded in the greatest trials of our lives and in our final moments. It is here that the heart learns the secret: that to let go is also to embrace what is true.

For one Buddhist teacher who had trained for years in a monastery, a painful divorce and the death of one of her children catapulted her into profound grief and a reexamination of all her years of practice.

> *I became overwhelmed. I would weep for days on end, not knowing how I could live, what to do. It was a teaching that no amount of meditation could help me through. I really had to face the suffering of the world and the suffering of my own mind. In those years I finally learned the necessity of letting go, of opening to the truth no matter what.*

When the fall occurs we must give ourselves to it. The freedom of the heart was revealed to the Buddha only when he could touch the suffering of Mara with compassion. This is a secret taught in martial arts such as aikido: to enter into the energy of our opponent, to embrace his or her aggression and move together with it. In this embrace we reconcile and make peace with all things. We and our opponent are both protected.

A playful statement by Emerson makes the point well: "When a dog is chasing after you, whistle for him." It is a truth of the heart that what we resist makes us frightened, hard, inflexible, and what we embrace becomes transformed.

When we honor Mara by name and invite him in for tea, the fear and confusion and conflict of descent become our allies. The vulnerability and humility of our heart become our safeguard. In letting go trust is born; in releasing struggle true strength is revealed; in a compassionate heart our love for sentient beings is fulfilled. We cannot stay on the summit, but we can find peace and oneness with all things. In meeting all the changes of the seasons with this secret embrace, wherever we are becomes holy ground, the seat of enlightenment.

10

THE DIRTY LAUNDRY

People commonly feel that because I am considered a living Buddha I
must experience only serenity, perpetual happiness, and have no
worries. Unfortunately this is not so. As a high lama and
incarnation of enlightenment I know better.
KANJU KHUTUSH TULKU RINPOCHE

When confronted by a human being who impresses us as truly great,
should we not be moved rather than chilled by the knowledge that he
might have attained his greatness only through his frailties?
LOU ANDREAS-SALOMÉ,
BIOGRAPHER OF FREUD

In her recently published book, *Lives
in the Shadow,* Radha Rajagopal Sloss gives an intimate account
of growing up with Krishnamurti. She portrays the gifts of courage
and awakening he brought to tens of thousands of students worldwide, and writes of the many years Krishnamurti was a loving second father to her. But she also tells of her shock when she learned
the details of his twenty-year affair with her mother, which took
place while her father was Krishnamurti's business manager and
one of his closest friends. Beyond that, she tells of Krishnamurti's
compulsive but secret need for still other women in his life, and
of hidden abortions, duplicitous cover-ups, growing attachment
to luxury, and an arrogance and rigidity that led to prolonged
legal battles with his own staff. These tales have also been told by
others who knew him well. Yet when he was asked about his part

in this by Radha, Krishnamurti angrily remonstrated, "I have no ego."

What do we make of such a story, and of the many others like it? Is each spiritual scandal a unique failure, or are there certain dynamics, almost archetypal, we might discern, which might help us navigate more consciously this aspect of the spiritual path?

How to Respond Wisely:
Learning Discriminating Wisdom

Before beginning any inventory of our own and others' failings, it is important to examine our eyes and heart, to be sure that we enter this terrain with an open and careful spirit, rather than in a spirit of anger, comparison, or self-justification. What is needed at such a moment is the spirit of discriminating wisdom.

In the Kalama sutra the Buddha instructed each practitioner to look honestly at what is wise and healthy and what is unwise and unhealthy, independent of any text or teaching or authority. This "fearless moral inventory," as it is called in Alcoholics Anonymous, is a fruitful and necessary practice for students and teachers alike.

Discriminating wisdom means seeing clearly. Just as we have to recognize when our literal laundry is dirty and needs to be washed, the first step in attending to any problem is an honest appraisal of what is so. In collective spiritual difficulties, we have to be courageous enough to question our beliefs, our community, our teacher, ourselves. We have to end our isolation by seeing and telling the difficult truth to ourselves and to one another, but always in the spirit of compassion, and in the knowledge of interconnection. This step alone is enormously healing, if at first frightening. We have to learn that we can trust the truth and that the truth will lead to freedom.

Discriminating wisdom, however fearless, must also be based in compassion. It sees not only the problems, but the causes and misguided intentions that preceded them. Because it sees without harsh judgment, it can separate and distinguish what is skillful from what is deluded. More than this, discriminating wisdom recognizes that every tradition and every teacher has strengths and weaknesses. Thus it is able to take the good and leave the rest.

There is a modesty and kindness in discriminating wisdom: It does not expect perfection but is willing to see two sides, to learn from every situation, to acknowledge difficulties and understand their causes. Let us look then in this openhearted way at some of the major areas of teacher-community difficulties along the spiritual journey.

Four Major Areas in Which Difficulties Arise

One common area of danger in spiritual communities is the misuse of power. This is most likely to occur when a teacher or master wields all the power in a given community. When the master's wishes are paramount, when students wait on his or her every word, when questioning is discouraged and feedback absent, the teacher can all too easily begin to control students' lives, claiming that it is for their benefit. Gradually an unconscious intoxication with power can replace wisdom, and love becomes a reward, dispensed only as the teacher decrees. Sectarianism and rivalry inevitably grow when power is misused. There are those who are "saved," and those who are lost or punished. There are cliques, in-groups, secrets, and power struggles. At its most painful, the misuse of power creates paranoia, cults, and other horrors.

A second problem area for teachers and communities can be the misuse of money. The grace found in spiritual life evokes great generosity, and as a community becomes successful, money flows in: for God, for the temple, for the holy work of the leader. Because most religious traditions are steeped in simplicity, their teachers are not trained to deal with money. Without a continuing rededication to the core of practice, it is all too easy in our materialistic society for spiritual leaders to become overwhelmed by money, to clutch after security, or to fall from need into greed in the name of the spirit. In the worst cases, abuses of money can lead to secret bank accounts, high living, and fraudulent use of donations, even while other community members are asked to live austerely and work without compensation.

A third common area of harm is misuse of sexuality. The abuse of sexual energy is unfortunately prevalent in our times, and this can easily become a problem in a spiritual community when a teacher is unconscious in this area. The teacher's needs, combined with the ambivalence toward and denial of sexuality that are found in most spiritual teachings, can lead to secret affairs, sex in exchange for access to the teacher, students serving the teacher by sex "in the name of tantra," and other forms of sexual exploitation. Such relationships bring unnecessary suffering. At the extreme, sexual misconduct has led to secret harems, abuse of children, even the transmission of HIV by a teacher who told his students that his special powers would serve as protection.

A fourth problem area is the misuse of alcohol and drugs. Modern culture is full of addictions, and these carry over into spiritual communities. Certain spiritual traditions celebrate drunkenness as a metaphor for spiritual transformation. Taken literally, this can be used as an excuse for open or secret addictions. Alcoholic or addicted teachers have led to the downfall of whole communities and major suffering in the lives of students who became caught in the culture of addiction.

Why Difficulties Happen

How do the problems we have described happen to communities of well-intentioned people? Clearly something has gone terribly wrong. One way to gain a broader perspective on how things go awry is to turn to the world of myth.

Greek mythology is rich in tales of rising and falling and what happens when we forget our true place. One of the most instructive is the story of Icarus, whose father Daedalus was considered the most clever of all artists and craftsmen. Originally from Athens, Daedalus traveled to Crete to design the amazing labyrinth where King Minos held captive the deadly Minotaur. But when Daedalus fell out of favor with King Minos, he and Icarus were imprisoned, first in the labyrinth itself, and then in a stone tower along the beach. Soon Daedalus conceived a way to escape. Father and son saved the crumbs from their food to entice seagulls into the tower, and then patiently collected their feathers, while also hoarding the wax drippings from their candles. Daedalus made a set of wings from the feathers, held together by thread and wax, and taught himself to fly. He then made a second set of wings for Icarus.

At last they were ready to set out on their journey to freedom. As he tied the wings to his son's body, Daedalus warned him to fly modestly and not soar too high, lest the sun melt the wax. When the two finally sped from the island, fishermen and shepherds looking upward mistook them for gods.

As Crete disappeared behind him, Icarus rejoiced in the lift of his great sweeping wings. He began soaring, abandoning himself to the freedom of flight. Higher and higher, closer to the sun he went, feeling as if he could touch the heavens. But soon the heat melted the wax, and the feathers fell from his wings. Crying out for help, Icarus fell like a leaf into the sea and drowned, leaving a few feathers on the water. With grief and despair in his heart, Daedalus returned to his homeland, hung his wings in a temple of Apollo, and never again attempted flight.

So, too, we may find ourselves, like Daedalus, imprisoned in a labyrinthine life of our own making. Through a long and patient practice we may acquire the means by which we might escape. The part of us that knows its limitations can navigate the dangers of liberation's flight. But if we forget we are human, if a part of us thinks it can soar upward without any limits, then flight itself will abandon us, and we will inevitably be plunged into the dark sea.

Intoxication and Identification with the Gods

Flight, as we see in the myth of Icarus, is the domain of the gods, not humans. During practice, our consciousness may indeed identify with the gods, with an archetype: the ideal possibility. This can be valuable, but only as long as we understand what it entails. An archetypal identification means trying to be a perfected being, a Buddha, a Christ, a master who is totally pure. The world of the gods is enticing—when we taste the fruits of freedom, the experiences can sweep us away. Yet problems arise if we believe we can stay there, never returning to the realities of time, of earth, of our human life. In psychology, this dynamic is called "inflation."

In most cases where the role of teacher is abused, the teachers are not purposely dishonest. Surrounded by crowds of disciples who want to think of them as perfect, they have come to believe their own press releases, to identify with the authority of being a "master." A collective intoxication grows, created equally by teacher and student, each out of good intentions. But within this climate of unreal expectations it is easy for the teacher to get disconnected and out of touch, to feel, like Icarus before his fall, that he or she can fly forever.

Isolation and Denial

When a community sets itself apart from the world, or tends toward cultlike enclosure, there is no possibility for real feedback. Similarly, when teachers are highly elevated and viewed as perfect they can become isolated and cut off from honest equals, partners, and spiritual friends. Community members in this situation can lose sight of what is actually occurring. Teachers surrounded by adoring students rather than peers can fall prey to loneliness and unacknowledged needs for genuine intimacy, or worse, to blind self-assurance, arrogance, and intolerance. Isolation coupled with inflation becomes fertile ground for delusion, thought control, and transformation from practice community to cult.

Cultural forces often contribute as well to these problems. Our patriarchal cultures have conditioned us to look up to authorities, to distrust our own bodies and feelings, to follow the ones who "know better." We have not been encouraged or empowered to think for ourselves. The longing to be rescued, to find someone who knows the truth in this confusing world, is the basis for many communities of mindless followers.

Idealization and isolation lead to a culture of shared denial. Idealization blinds us to the evidence of our own eyes, and isolation means no one else will point out the facts. At times the level of denial in spiritual communities is shocking, especially to someone who looks in from the outside with open eyes. There is denial about the leader, denial about the cultlike qualities of the teachings, denial about how much community members have lost themselves in the spiritual system and forgotten their own innate wisdom.

I have heard the story of the charismatic master of an ancient lineage who told a nationwide string of married women they were each his secret love and had them oil and shave their bodies and wait for his visits and his "higher teachings." I have been told of a world-famous rabbi who mixed his intoxicating songs of prayer with the sorry intoxication of alcoholism and fondled every woman and young girl he could.

Whether it is the arrogant and tyrannical guru who bullies and controls his students' lives "to destroy their egotism," the organized cover-ups of pedophile priests in the church, or the Burmese teacher I knew who was finally beaten by his younger monks after years of abusive and scandalous behavior, the painful results of denial and isolation can last for years.

Most traditions warn against misuse of the teacher role. Yet, many followers in the community cannot imagine or believe these warnings apply to them. They are like Icarus, ignoring the words of his father amid the headiness of flight. Our human capacity for self-deception is almost as vast as our capacity for awakening. Because questioning the teachers puts us in touch with our own shadow and pain, students deny that abuses exist and carry on as before, in spite of the obvious painful truth. Even when students are explicitly told about problems with their teachers, when there are national exposés of cult control or of abuses of power, money, or sexuality within a spiritual movement, students cannot believe it. Meanwhile deluded teachers justify what they are doing with elaborate explanations: "I was using the money, the power, for everyone's benefit." "It isn't sex, it's tantric teachings." "I'm bringing benefit to so many people, I need a little support and comfort." The allure of flying is difficult to resist.

Confusing Charisma with Wisdom

Another source of spiritual misunderstanding is our confusion of charisma with true wisdom. Certain spiritual leaders possess the ability to evoke extraordinary states. Amplified by our hopes, feelings of bliss and transcendence arise easily around these charismatic ministers, priests, Zen masters, mystics, rabbis, and gurus. It is easy to mistake such spiritual powers as definite signs of wisdom or enlightenment or divine love. We forget that power and charisma are just power and charisma, that these energies can just as easily serve demagogues, politicians, and entertainers.

It is possible for someone to be charismatic but not wise. Conversely, wisdom is not necessarily flashy or powerful—it can manifest in a humble and simple heart, and in the most ordinary-seeming of lives. In communities where special spiritual power is highly valued, students should take special care: When secret teachings or ancient lineages are evoked, when one group is chosen to be saved or awakened above all others in the world, spiritual communities are ripe for becoming cults. This does not always happen, of course, but it is a particular risk within the blinding arena of charisma. Wise traditions include safeguards against such misuse, often by the creation of a network of elders, respected teachers able to watch over one another's spiritual condition and behavior.

The Temptations of Worldly Power

From crusades to jihads, from corrupt holy men and tyrannical bishops to the sale of indulgences—the history of abuse of power by organized Western religions is well known. Somehow, though, we may have imagined that Eastern religions and meditative traditions were immune to this form of corruption. But Korea, Japan, Sri Lanka, China, Tibet, and Burma all have religious histories that include periodic grave abuses of power. In *The Zen of War,* Brian Victoria describes in painful detail the ways that many charismatic Japanese Zen masters such as Sawaki Kodo Roshi and Harada Daiun Roshi abused and twisted Zen teachings during World War II to foster war and killing. In the name of Buddhism, Zen teachers over many centuries have encouraged practitioners to join in the military killing of non-Japanese as a "beneficial war of compassion." Military killing has been described as an expression of enlightenment, and major temples have provided soldiers, money for weapons, and blessings for cannons and military campaigns. There are even cases of monasteries warring against one another, vying for increased power.

In a similar fashion, wars between sects, monks, and monasteries are a part of Tibetan history. Tsipon Shuguba, former Tibetan minister of finance and author of *In the Presence of My Enemies,* describes the power struggles and fighting during the decades before the Communist Chinese took over Tibet. Great monasteries like Sera, high lamas like Reting Rinpoche (the Dalai Lama's regent), and hundreds of monks were involved in battles using horses, guns, and cannons in which many monk-soldiers died. Sectarianism and battles for power have continued to occur in the Tibetan community in exile, all in the name of "correct" religious practice.

Many established religious hierarchies have come to possess

vast properties, art treasures, international visibility, and moral influence. The task is to find ways to hold these without becoming caught up in their glittering appeal. A wise spiritual leader will have a simple spirit and a free heart whether he or she is wearing brocade and speaking with kings or wearing rags and living in desert solitude. Genuine love for all beings recognizes political power as shabby and useless, compared with the wealth of living in the midst of the truth.

Not Including Our Full Humanity

The denial of ordinary human longings is a form of idealization so prevalent in spiritual traditions worldwide that it requires looking at in its own right. Certain spiritual traditions, both Eastern and Western, teach that it is best not to have any personal needs or desires. This ideal of otherworldly perfection does not recognize the value in ordinary relationships and needs, and denies that spiritual beings might benefit by having any life outside their narrow religious roles. This ideal expects teachers, abbots, and masters to be above the world, to maintain a saintly simplicity and ascetic purity.

While choosing simplicity is of great value, the practices of an ascetic life must be distinguished from denial. Asceticism on its own is the conscious choice of a path of simplicity. Simplicity of diet, dress, and action can be a deliberate way to learn inner renunciation and free oneself from the external pulls of the world. Celibacy too can be chosen as an expression of renunciation and simplicity.

By stepping outside the sphere of sexual and paired relationships, the nun, priest, or monk enters a way of life that can be devoted entirely to prayer, service, and the community. In such a context, the deliberate path of celibacy and asceticism can be both valid and valuable. One sign of a healthy purity is this: The person taking this role has not simply suppressed his or her needs or denied that they exist. Instead, Eros, human intimacy, and the full range of emotions are acknowledged and included in a rich spiritual life.

The problem comes when denial of our humanity is built into our spiritual view. For students this means cutting themselves off in a puritanical or fearful way from their own experience. For teachers, too, the prolonged expectations of selfless or sinless purity can translate into repression or ignorance of their own shadow.

For spiritual leaders caught up in such false idealization, human needs, sexuality, grief, and vulnerability often simply go unacknowledged. These idealistic spiritual systems offer little instruction or real help in how to work with these realities. Yet, no matter how pure and exalted the state, our ignored humanity will return, and whatever unmet needs we have will reappear. Icarus's body has human weight; Mara graciously comes back to pay us a regular visit.

If the needs of body and humanity are not acknowledged, they can be demonized and projected onto others, fueling paranoia, witch-hunts, inquisitions. The community will live in fear of many aspects of life. One Catholic abbess widely regarded for her wisdom and holiness founded a contemplative community several decades ago. She knew that her nuns and postulants needed to attend to the energies of their bodies and emotions. Yet she was punished for this. The church authorities abruptly closed down the abbey after hearing rumors of "other practices" such as meditation, breath work, and personal therapy being used to complement the daily rounds of prayer and sacred silence. She said, "I cannot believe how our community was treated for including breath and body in what is sacred." And yet Thomas Merton undertook Buddhist meditation with permission of his spiritual director. Spiritual "authorities," like any others, vary widely in their understanding and vision.

A more humble approach to our full human nature can be seen in the life of Zen teacher Dainan Katagiri Roshi, who lived with his family in Minneapolis at the center of a large Zen community. When he was diagnosed with terminal cancer, many students came to help, but they also were frightened and confused at the thought that their teacher was subject to ordinary human frailty. One day he called the students to his bedside. "I see you are watching me closely. You want to see how a Zen master dies. I'll show you." He kicked his legs and flailed his arms with alarm, crying out, "I don't want to die, I don't want to die!" Then he stopped and looked up at them. "I don't know how I will die. Maybe I will die in fear or in pain. Remember, there is no right way." Here is a teacher who did not separate himself from the life of others, who knew that the moment brings what it brings.

If a teacher and community live in open acknowledgment of human needs and emotions, they will find a certain ease in these matters. Certainly problems will arise, but they will be recognized as common problems, something everyone must encounter sooner or later. But if the spirit of community is one of judgmentalism and fear, secrecy and hypocrisy will creep in, and far more damage will occur when the facade of being above-the-human cracks. This is true whether the community is one in which celibacy is the rule or one in which spiritual practice occurs amid ordinary family life—no one, monk or layperson, is immune to the storms emotions and relationships can bring. These storms are part of the rich field of our practice.

Cross-Cultural Confusion

Asian-based traditions in the West face another difficulty: cross-cultural confusion. Teachers coming from an environment where dress is modest and the sexes are strictly separated can lose their sense of what is appropriate when suddenly immersed in American culture. Conversely, Western students can be confused as well. The story of the Venerable Kalu Rinpoche, a wise and respected old lama from Tibet, serves as a warning. He was an excellent teacher in many ways, yet he created a situation of long-standing suffering for his devoted young disciple and translator

June Campbell when he made her his sexual partner. Her book *Traveler in Space* tells of a twenty-year struggle to come to terms with her confusion and pain, and with what she saw as general denigration of the feminine in Tibetan Buddhism.

One Western teacher and devotee of Tibetan Buddhism tried to reach a cross-cultural understanding of teacher/student relations, but in the end remained grounded in her own wisdom.

Because I have a background of abuse in my childhood, and have fought for women's rights, I couldn't understand it. How could this old lama, a realized master of the supreme Vajrayana practices of Maha Mudra, choose a thirteen- or fourteen-year-old nun from the monastery to become his sexual consort every year? What did the lama's wife think? I know that India and Tibet are a different world. It was explained that taking a young consort was a "long life practice" to give strength to the lama. Powerful men have always believed this, and both religious and political figures in Asia have done so.

Then it was explained to me that in a society like Tibet—still feudal—it was an honor to her family. They were probably poor and now they'd become part of the court around the lama and they'd all be better cared for. But still I have to wonder, how about the young girls? What about them?

I talked to a number of Western women who had slept with their lamas. Some liked it—they felt special. Some felt used and it turned them away from practice. Some said they mothered the lama. But no one described it as a teaching; there was nothing tantric about it. The sex was for the lama, not them.

Sexuality is a complex terrain in our times. We cannot clearly judge an ancient culture by contemporary Western standards. Nor can teachers from other cultures expect to come to the West and have students serve them sexually or otherwise. In the long run, we will have to bring consciousness to this area or it will continue to produce more harm and pain.

Turning Difficulties into Healing

In the Arthurian legends, the young knight Parsifal joins the Knights of the Round Table to seek the Holy Grail. His mentor, Gournamond, tells him that to remain honorable, he must follow two rules: First, he should neither seduce nor be seduced. And second, if he reaches the Castle of the Holy Grail, he must ask, "Whom does the Grail serve?" As he travels, he sees all around him signs of suffering and disarray. But when Parsifal finally makes his way to the Grail Castle, he is utterly intoxicated by the court. He meets the wounded Fisher King and is offered a magical banquet that includes everything he could desire. He forgets his purpose and does not ask the essential question. The next morning the whole castle and kingdom disappear and Parsifal must wander and suffer for many years until by hard-won maturity he returns a second time. This time he remembers. "Whom does the Grail serve?" he asks. The Fisher King answers, "The Holy Grail serves the Grail King." (The Grail King is God.) As soon as the Fisher King is reminded of this holy truth, he is healed, and in being healed, all that has rotted in the fields, all disharmony in his nation, all the sufferings of the kingdom are restored to peace and well-being.

The resolution of the journey to enlightenment comes when we recognize that both our suffering and our awakening are in the service of a higher good. Unless we serve the Divine, our unfulfilled needs can become entangled with our quest, and our spiritual experiences can work only to create a more expanded form of ego. A teacher who is overidentified with spiritual energy may subtly believe that, as the one who carries the teachings, it is he or she who must be served. We should be wary when there is a court around a teacher that focuses more on the person than on the wisdom of the lineage. When the Fisher King forgets whom he serves, the bounty of the kingdom fails, and all suffer from the king's spiritual sickness.

A Humble Recognition of the Truth

A wise heart knows that whatever spiritual energy we discover is not ours, it is only entrusted to us. The bodhisattva vows and the Prayer of St. Francis advise us to dedicate whatever blessing we receive to the benefit of others. A wise heart also acknowledges that on some days we are more connected to the blessings of awakening than on others.

Several years ago I was in Indonesia visiting a number of shamans and healers. My translator told me that his uncle had been a famous healer, but after many years had stopped completely. When I asked about this, he explained:

> *My uncle was a rice farmer who learned to heal by meditating and going into a trance. From the first day he started healing people, the energy of the gods would come to help him see the illness in his patients; they would show him which herbs to use and where to touch. For twenty years the gods came, but then one day the gods stopped appearing. So my uncle told people he could no longer heal and went back to being a farmer.*

There is an amazing integrity to this. It is hard to imagine a therapist, or doctor, or spiritual teacher having a bad day and admitting, "The gods aren't available to me right now." Yet we all know this happens.

Integrity and Ethical Foundations

Every wise religion recognizes that a foundation of human virtue, honesty, and integrity is necessary in spiritual life. Whether it is the Buddhist precepts, the Hindu Yamas and Niyamas, or the Muslim or Judeo-Christian commandments, the care we take with our conduct underlies all spiritual development. It is not just that it is difficult to meditate or pray after a day of killing, lying, and stealing; it is that there is no freedom to be found, no grace-filled life possible when we are so caught in our anger and desires that we lie, kill, steal, or deceive.

While virtue and compassion naturally grow out of awareness, the spelling out of ethical guidelines is still essential for the health of any community. These guidelines must apply to the teacher as well as the students, for if masters put themselves above virtue, then, like the Fisher King, they are destined to create suffering. Even the Zen and tantric traditions, which were created to free students from the rigidity of spiritual rules, regularly acknowledge the foundation of virtuous behavior. Otherwise the path they teach would be a sham.

Spiritual traditions brought to the West from other cultures may have unwritten rules and guidelines for teacher conduct. The limits on teachers' and students' behavior are usually safeguarded by the broader community, on whose support the practitioners depend. But coming to the West, to a culture with so much emphasis on money, sex, power, drinking, and drugs, it may seem that these old rules do not matter. Foreign teachers can mistake popular culture as an invitation to excess, and America as a country without a need for rules.

To avoid harm, as the Buddha advised his monks, spiritual communities have to spell out clear ethical guidelines for all members, including the leaders. Many are doing so. Where they have not, students have the responsibility to ask for an explicit statement of principles. Creating a spiritual community without clear ethics is a recipe for betrayal. The values of compassion and love that underlie all great traditions rest on our commitment to virtue.

Betrayal as a Fierce Initiation

We entered this investigation in the spirit of discriminating wisdom. The goal of reflecting on past failures is to seek understanding that contributes to healing and redemption rather than blame. The fact is, no matter how many warnings there are, betrayal will still happen—it is a surprisingly common theme in the journey. Half of those with whom I spoke about their spiritual life described some form of significant betrayal. Betrayal is a fiery gate to pass through, a painful destroyer of illusion and innocence. It functions as an uninvited initiation into the complex truth of humanity, of the shadows cast by the light. The grief and the lessons of spiritual betrayal can last for years.

One woman's lesson in betrayal came in her yoga ashram after she lost a baby by miscarriage. Heartbroken, she asked her guru if the ashram's strenuous physical regimen in the summer heat might have contributed to the loss of her child. Angry at hearing his yoga teachings questioned, the master had her stand up in the midst of hundreds of students and announced, "She spread her legs for her husband and now she wants to implicate yoga in the loss of her child. Maybe she is simply not fit to be a mother." In that moment, years of unquestioned faith shattered. She left the ashram. A long process of grief and anger, reflection and inner work led her to understand that the biggest betrayal was that she had given away her own authority.

In 1993, at the first large meeting of American Buddhist teachers, attended by 120 Buddhist leaders, several teachers asked for a forum to speak safely about misuse of power and betrayal. Because these experiences had been a taboo topic for so long, there was a remarkable amount of pain and many tears were spilled. In some cases, the struggle for healing and forgiveness had been going on for years—and in other cases more healing was necessary. Eventually it is not the betrayal by teachers that shocks or awakens us most—it is the growing recognition of the ways we have betrayed ourselves. We pretended we did not see the shadow even when it was in full view. Through our needs and idealism we abandoned our heart's wisdom, our own true nature.

From truth telling and grieving to letting go and forgiving, we will need the support of our spiritual friends and the strength of our practice. We will need to find our own authority and our own greatness of heart. "Be a lamp unto yourself, make of yourself a light" were the last words of the Buddha. No teacher or outside authority can give us the truth or take it away. In the end we will find that our heart holds the simple wisdom and unshakable compassion that we have sought all along.

Betrayal itself becomes our teacher. We must bow to betrayal, because it brings us back to the truth. It demands that we learn discriminating wisdom, that we speak honestly, that we examine our ideals and our faults, that we wrestle with forgiveness. Few tasks are as rich in their teaching.

When yogi Amrit Desai's Kripalu Yoga community fell apart in 1994, an enormous sense of betrayal swept his disciples. A public disclosure of the master's secret affairs and manipulation of power and money over twenty years disillusioned many. Yet because he was also a creative and wise teacher, students were able to use the very practices he had taught them—of inquiry, balance, and compassion—to deal with their loss. After months of difficult meetings and councils, the master was asked to leave and the students were left to work with their confusion and despair. Over the years since, the community has rebuilt itself, dedicated to the principles of yoga and healthy spirituality that the crisis of betrayal taught them. And the master too claims he has learned important lessons from this process.

Zen Master Dogen said that a Zen master's life is one continuous mistake—that is, an opportunity to learn, one mistake after another. In betrayal and the misuse of power we encounter the failures that come with the territory of being human. As a consequence, whether we leave a troubled community or we stay, we will be required to truly learn the practice of wisdom and compassion.

As we air the dirty laundry, let us not be too hasty to judge.

The impersonal forces of idealism and inflation, the depths of illusion and fear, the subtleties of self-deception and ambition are a part of our human nature. The Greek plays, the Indian Vedas, the African tribal myths, the Zen koans wrestle with these forces, which have shaped our human lot since ancient times. To believe in a spiritual life with no shadow, where Mara never visits, is to imagine a sky where the sun always stays at noon.

In India there is a saying that even a ninety-year-old saint is not safe. We are vulnerable as long as we are alive. The great Zen Master Hui Neng reminds us how quickly the mind can change:

> As far as Buddha Nature is concerned, there is no difference between a sinner and a sage. . . . One enlightened thought and one is a Buddha, one foolish thought and one is again an ordinary person.

The effort to understand the dirty laundry of spiritual practice can best be seen as an invitation to truth. Just as awakening can succumb to delusion, so understanding and redemption can rearise in a moment, no matter how lost we have become. In a moment of truth we can reconcile what is broken, we can begin to heal our betrayals. In a moment of truth we can acknowledge how we have been lost and we can make amends. Out of our errors and frailty come some of our most profound lessons. In a heartfelt conversation, in a quiet moment when we take stock, even on our deathbed, freedom awaits. In acknowledging the suffering and betrayals of ourselves and others, we can truly awaken to the great heart of compassion.

PART FOUR

Awakening
in the
Laundry

11

THE MANDALA OF AWAKENING:
What Am I Leaving Out?

And having entered the Stream of Dharma the practitioner regularly
examines his or her own heart and sees: This is the freedom thus won
and these are the fetters, the entanglements still to be released in me.
BUDDHA

An old Trappist monk, Father
Theophane, tells a story about a Magic Monastery where the true
gifts of spiritual life can be found:

> I knew there were many interesting sights, but I didn't
> want any more of the little answers, I wanted the big
> answer. So I asked the guestmaster to show me directly to
> the House of God.
>
> I sat myself down, quite willing to wait for the big
> answer. I remained silent all day, far into the night. I
> looked Him in the eye. I guess He was looking me in the
> eye. Late, late at night I seemed to hear a voice: "What are
> you leaving out?" I looked around. I heard it again. "What
> are you leaving out?" Was it my imagination? Soon it was
> all around me, whispering, roaring, "What are you leaving
> out? What are you leaving out?"

Was I cracking up? I managed to get to my feet and head for the door. I wanted the comfort of a human face or a human voice. Nearby was the corridor where some of the monks live. I knocked on one cell.

"What do you want?" came a sleepy voice.

"What am I leaving out?"

"Me," he answered.

I went to the next door.

"What do you want?"

"What am I leaving out?"

"Me."

A third cell, a fourth, all the same.

I thought, "They're all stuck on themselves." I left the building in disgust. Just then the sun was coming up. I had never spoken to the sun before, but I heard myself pleading, "What am I leaving out?"

The sun too answered, "Me." That finished me.

I threw myself on the ground. And the earth said, "Me too."

Father Theophane's tale points to the challenge of spiritual maturity: If we hope to open our heart to all of the world, we must leave nothing out. Freedom and awakening are only found exactly where we are. If we wish to love God we must also learn to love each of His creations—including ourselves, in all our complexity and imperfection. This all-encompassing spirit creates a mandala or circle of awakening where we open to the reality of the present, we include every dimension of life.

The Mandala of the Whole

A "mandala" is an image, often complex, which represents the great circle of existence, sacred wholeness, a complete world. The aim of a mature spiritual life is to discover and embody this sacred whole in our life.

There are two central principles for awakening to this whole-ness. First, each major area of our experience on earth must be included in our spiritual life before freedom can blossom fully. No significant dimension can be excluded from awareness. The Buddhist Elders speak of cultivating four foundations of sacred awareness: the body, the feelings, the mind, and the governing principles of life. Then their teachings extend the same sacred attention to family, community, livelihood, and relations to the world at large. It is only through attention to each of these that we fulfill our awakening. These areas will be discussed more fully in the chapters that follow.

The second principle for awakening to wholeness is that con-sciousness in one area does not necessarily transfer to other parts of our lives. We know that Olympic-level athletes, however highly tuned and aware physically, may be quite emotionally immature or mentally undeveloped. Conversely, certain brilliant intellectu-als may suffer from ignorance and disregard of their bodies or their emotions. Other people, quite conscious of their feelings and expert in human relationships, may be utterly unconscious of the thought constructs and beliefs that limit them.

It is no different in spiritual life. Meditation masters skilled in navigating expansive states of consciousness may be confused in the realm of emotions or relationships. Devoted nuns or monks with a close relationship to God may have troubled or even destructive relationships with their families—or with their own bodies. Yogis and gurus who have amazing physical dexterity and breath and thought control may have unexamined beliefs and opinions that cause those around them to suffer. Most mature monks and nuns, meditation masters, and spiritual adepts even-tually discover whole areas of life about which they were uncon-scious. For many teachers, their spiritual training itself may have taught them to neglect or to deny their basic human needs. Yet until these dimensions are included in their practice, they may suffer unnecessarily with everything from poor health to emo-tional problems. Any area that is still unconscious brings with it suffering, conflict, and limitation. As Gandhi says, "One cannot do right in one department of life while still occupied in doing wrong in any other department. Life is an indivisible whole."

When we look at the spiritually unattended areas of our life, we often find in them underlying judgment or fear. We may believe that the body, or relationships, or future planning, or money, or sexuality, or family, or community, or politics is "unspiritual," dangerous, ugly, a trap. This fear puts up walls, isolates our heart from living, divides the world so that part of it is seen as not holy. Our experiences of realization remain compartmentalized and unfulfilled, like bonsai trees, beautiful but stunted.

The truth is that these interior boundaries must be dissolved. As Father Theophane's story shows, it is in a deep and honest listening to whatever has been feared or left out that our freedom will be found. And if we don't choose to look, that which is unattended will come find us; the lost parts of ourselves will present themselves, knocking ever louder if we don't listen to their cries. We end up hearing their voices in divorce or depression, in illness or some strange failure. If we do listen to and welcome all parts of the self, we will find they enrich our garden as compost, as nourishment for life itself.

There is an underlying unity to all things, and a wise heart knows this as it knows the in-and-out of the breath. They are all part of a sacred whole in which we exist, and in the deepest way they are completely trustworthy. We need not fear the energies of this world or any other. We need fear only our confusion about them. Zen Master Rinzai describes a truly wise being as one who can "enter fire without being burned, go into water without being drowned, and play about in the three deepest hells as if in a fairground; one who enters the world of ghosts and animals without being harmed by them." None of the realms of existence lie outside of our practice.

Meditation Master Vimala Thakar says, "As a lover of life, how can I stay out of any area of life?" So in the spirit of Gandhi her community works in the poorest villages of Gujarat in India to dig wells, foster irrigation, and plant new crops. And in the spirit of her friend and teacher Krishnamurti she teaches contemplative retreats worldwide. Her meditation and prayers do not separate spiritual practice from politics, compassion from justice, or self-knowledge from livelihood; all are included as a whole.

A Mature Spiritual Language

When we first enter the spiritual path, we often speak of the overcoming of obstacles, necessary striving, the purification of defilements, and the ardor of seeking God. But this language, though it may once have served us, can become excessively one-sided, setting one thing against another: worldliness against freedom, self-will against God's grace, sin against redemption. It is a language built upon exclusion.

With the awakening of wisdom, the heart gradually expands to hold the full paradox of life. As Walt Whitman writes, "I am large, I contain multitudes." In the mature heart there arises a deeper perfection that is not opposed to the things of this world, but holds them all in compassion. Our spiritual life becomes more about mercy and loving kindness than about struggles over self, or battles with ego or sin. Our heroics become a fearless love for the whole of creation, leaving nothing out. We can be present for what Zorba the Greek called "the whole catastrophe."

In Buddhist psychology this maturing is described through the image of a poisonous tree, which represents the suffering of the world. When we discover that a tree in our midst is poisonous, our first impulse is to try to cut it down—to remove it, so it no longer can be harmful. At this initial stage of practice our language is one of conflict: fear of poison and impurity, and the effort to root out and destroy that which is dangerous.

But as our compassion deepens, we recognize that the tree too is a part of the web of life. Instead of destroying it, we respect even this tree, though we also put a fence around it, warning others of the poison so they will not be harmed. Now our language changes to one of compassion and respect, rather than fear. Our difficulties, inner and outer, are now met with mercy. This is the second stage of practice.

Finally, as our wisdom deepens, we understand that our very problems and poisons are our best teachers. It is said that the wisest beings will come looking for this poisonous tree to use its fruit as medicine to transform the sufferings of the world. The energies of passion and desire, anger and confusion become transformed into the ardor, strength, and clarity that bring awakening. We understand that it is through facing the very sufferings of the world that the deepest freedom and compassion arise. What we once named poison is now recognized as an ally in our practice.

This growing freedom of heart brings the courage to question, to clarify and refine for ourselves the teachings we have swallowed whole. We shift from believing in ideals to discovering the wisdom that emerges from our own experience. We gain a direct understanding of what nourishes and sustains freedom. Now we can finally see and know for ourselves.

With maturity we are released from our initial one-sided language. We move beyond the simplicity of good and bad, right and wrong. The world is no longer a battle between black and white, pure and impure; it is no longer a poisonous tree to be cut down or removed. Our vision of the sacred includes complexity, paradox, irony, and humor. The heart becomes clear, able to understand the world rather than struggle with it, able to harvest the fruit of the poison tree rather than cut it down.

With our growing clarity, the language of nonattachment and renunciation is understood in a new way. "Attachment is the cause of suffering," says the classical Buddhist teaching. "It is easier for a camel to go through the eye of the needle than for a rich man to enter the Kingdom of God," Jesus declared. Indeed, attachment and greed are causes of suffering. But a mature teaching is more complete, recognizing that there is unhealthy attachment and healthy attachment. A mother must demonstrate her deep and natural attachment to her child or the child will be damaged and suffer. An employer can have a healthy attachment to the well-being of her workers.

As we learn to distinguish what is painful attachment from what is not, we become clearer about the meaning of commitment. Wise commitment, whether to an exclusive relationship, to virtue, to prayer and meditation, or to God and a sacred path, becomes an expression of our inner freedom rather than a limitation. Renunciation brings freedom not primarily because we give up things (although we may indeed do so), but because we give up grasping and possessiveness, we relinquish fear, anger, and delusion in the heart.

In the same way, nonattachment and discriminating wisdom are reconciled as a whole. Discriminating wisdom can set boundaries, say yes and no, stand up for justice and act for compassion. It becomes an unselfish and fearless expression of wise nonattachment. With discriminating wisdom we act without grasping or aggression, we seek to tell the truth and benefit all beings.

As we grow on the spiritual path, desire and passion, too, are understood in a new way. As William Blake wrote, "Those who enter the gates of heaven are not beings who have no passions or who have curbed the passions, but those who have cultivated an understanding of them." Instead of condemning all desire, we engage it with wisdom and sensitivity. We see the world as a play of desire, and the difference between unskillful and skillful desires becomes apparent. Some desires cause suffering, but others, such as the natural needs for familial love, food, and shelter, are healthy. The desire to learn, to understand, to serve God, can help carry us to awakening. We come to respect passion and ardor as human energies which can be associated with compulsion and grasping, but can also be directed toward commitment and integrity of being.

These energies are no longer deadly sins to be feared; they are transformed into the medicine for awakening. We are able to be in the world but not caught by it, using the energies of life to teach and awaken wherever we go. Even Socrates, who lived a very frugal and simple life, loved to go to the market. When his students asked about this, he replied, "I love to go and see all the things I am happy without." The luxuries of Athens were not his enemies, and his wisdom could walk with undisturbed pleasure in their midst.

A mature heart helps us to work even with the forces of anger and hatred. We learn to distinguish anger from the deeper suffering of hatred. We understand both as powerful energies. So when Shantideva, the Buddhist sage, warns us, "A thousand eons of wholesome deeds will be destroyed by one moment of anger," we do not cling to the absoluteness of this statement. Sometimes even anger has value. The Dalai Lama, a passionate advocate of nonviolence, admits that although anger is dangerous, "There can also be positive anger moderated by compassion and a sense of responsibility that can act as a force to bring about swift and helpful action." If we hate and fear our anger, we will end up continuing the battle. Our test is to understand and transform these energies into clarity and strength.

The Middle Path

This wider vocabulary of understanding shows how the heart becomes more flexible and sensitive. The dogmatic and rigid qualities of religious fervor give way to the middle path, with a wise presence that is neither indulgent nor fearful.

My teacher Ajahn Chah demonstrated this flexibility when he was most inconsistent, contradicting things he had previously said, reversing teachings he had earlier emphasized. When this was pointed out to him by a frustrated student (me), Ajahn Chah laughed. "It's like this," he said. "There is a road I know well, but it can be foggy or dark. When I see someone traveling this road about to fall in a ditch or get lost in a sidetrack on the right-hand side, I call out, 'Go to the left.' Similarly, if I see someone about to fall in a ditch or get lost in a sidetrack on the left-hand side, I call out, 'Go to the right.' That's all I do when I teach. Wherever you get caught, I say, 'Let go of that too.' "

The middle path embraces opposites. It rests between them, acknowledging both truths, caught by neither side. In this way we can see from one perspective that human life is suffering, with its inevitable string of losses culminating in sickness, aging, and death. Yet from another perspective it is also grace—filled with gifts and blessings, expressing a divine beauty. Our very suffering can be seen as the grace that brings us to compassion, surrender, and humility.

Awakening dissolves the labels we have put on our experience. Every notion of who we are—defiled beings or Buddhas, sinners or children of God—unravels in the wise heart. Yes, a mature heart knows the dimension of egotism and sin. But it also holds our humanity in a larger reality, one of original blessing and basic goodness. It rests in our divine nature, our Buddha Nature.

With this understanding we can better approach spiritual teachings that instruct us to destroy our self-cherishing attitude, and balance them with the need to encourage self-love, as in the Samutta Nikaya where the Buddha says, "You can search the ten-fold universe and not find a single being more worthy of loving kindness than yourself." Sometimes we need to let go of self. And sometimes it is our self-hatred and unworthiness that is the problem, and our healing and freedom of heart will only come through love of the self we have rejected.

The wise heart brings compassion to imperfection itself. A study of "wounded healers" was done at Stanford University comparing those psychologists who worked in a detached way, not revealing anything about themselves, with those who shared some of their own difficulties and woundedness. The wounded healers fostered the greatest healing in their patients.

The wise heart is at peace with the way things are. No longer struggling against the world or lost in it, we rest. The holy qualities of understanding, humility, and a patient caring are our gifts. Our body, speech, and mind become like the Tao, "content with the changing of the seasons." We become the love we have sought. And in this love we are also returned to ourselves.

Zen teacher Edward Espe Brown is the author of many Zen-inspired cookbooks, beginning with *The Tassajara Bread Book*. Through describing his kitchen practice, he writes of the truths of the heart.

When I first started cooking at Tassajara, I had a problem. I couldn't get my biscuits to come out the way they were supposed to. I'd follow a recipe and try variations, but nothing worked. These biscuits just didn't measure up.

Growing up I had made two kinds of biscuits. One was from Bisquick and the other from Pillsbury. For the Bisquick you added milk in the mix and then blobbed the dough in spoonfuls onto the pan—you didn't even need to roll them out. The biscuits from Pillsbury came in kind of a cardboard can. You rapped the can on the corner of the counter and it popped open. Then you twisted the can open more, put the premade biscuits on a pan, and baked them. I really liked those Pillsbury biscuits. Isn't that what biscuits should taste like? Mine weren't coming out right.

It's wonderful and amazing the ideas we get about what biscuits should taste like, or what a life should look like. Compared to what? Canned biscuits from Pillsbury? *Leave It to Beaver*? People who ate my biscuits would extoll their virtues, eating one after another, but to me these perfectly good biscuits just weren't right.

Finally one day came a shifting-into-place, an awakening. "Not right" compared to what? Oh, my word, I'd been trying to make canned Pillsbury biscuits! Then came an exquisite moment of actually tasting my biscuits without comparing them to some previously hidden standard. They were wheaty, flaky, buttery, sunny, earthy, real. They were incomparably alive—in fact, much more satisfying than any memory.

These occasions can be so stunning, so liberating,

these moments when you realize your life is just fine as it is, thank you. Only the insidious comparison to a beautifully prepared, beautifully packaged product made it seem insufficient. Trying to produce a biscuit—a life—with no dirty bowls, no messy feelings, no depression, no anger, was so frustrating. Then savoring, actually tasting the present moment of experience—how much more complex and multifaceted. How unfathomable.

As Zen students we spent years trying to make it look right, trying to cover the faults, conceal the messes. We knew what the Bisquick Zen student looked like: calm, buoyant, cheerful, energetic, deep, profound. Our motto, as one of my friends said, was, "looking good." We've all done it, trying to look good as a husband, a wife or parent. Trying to attain perfection. Trying to make Pillsbury biscuits.

Well, to heck with it, I say. Wake up and smell the coffee. How about some good old home cooking, the biscuits of today.

When we accept our place in the mandala of the whole, we come back to just where we are. And in this is found joy, ease, simplicity, and courage, and what T. S. Eliot calls the freedom "to care and not to care." The following chapters illustrate the flowering of this wholeness, of coming home to ourselves.

12

THIS VERY BODY, THE BUDDHA

Within this fathomlong body is found all of the teachings, is found
suffering, the cause of suffering, and the end of suffering.

BUDDHA

It's also helpful to realize that this very body that we have, that's sitting
right here right now . . . with its aches and its pleasures . . . is exactly
what we need to be fully human, fully awake, fully alive.

PEMA CHÖDRÖN

Before enlightenment we have to
live with our body. After enlightenment we still have to live with
our body. Zen Master Dainan Katagiri says, "The important point
of spiritual practice is not to try to escape your life, but to face
it—exactly and completely." He speaks both to those who are
beginning on the path and to those who have realized some measure of awakening. No matter where we are on the journey of
awakening, the body must be included.

Yet it is also true that both Eastern and Western religious traditions have dishonored this truth. There are aspects of every tradition that stress denial and aversion to the physical self, that fear
the body and have disdain for its impulses. In one Burmese
monastery where I practiced, certain masters forbade yoga,
stretching, and exercise, telling their students to throw themselves
into months of intensive meditation and "to abandon all concern
for the body." Many students accepted this admonition—how

could they distrust their teacher's words? Years later they found themselves struggling to reclaim their bodies and health in order finally to live wisely.

In Hinduism, Islam, Judaism, and Christianity, it is equally common to meet teachers who encourage puritanical detachment, who fear or despise the body. One older Ursuline nun describes the view of the body in her community:

I was taught to be ashamed of my female body from the start. In years of training in the church, I was forced to ignore every aspect of my body, and instead they held up to me all these saints who sacrificed their sinful bodies and died as martyrs. It was an uptight spirituality that deeply reinforced my own inner shame.

A traditional story attempts to awaken students to our loss of connection. In ancient China there lived a widower with two loving daughters. When his eldest daughter died, he was left with only the youngest, Sen-jo. Because she was beautiful, many sought her hand, and when she came of age, Sen-jo's father selected a good and prosperous husband for her from among her suitors. But alas, Sen-jo had long before fallen in love with Ochu. They had known each other since playing in childhood; when Sen-jo's father had laughingly told them they were well matched and should get married when they grew up, they took him to heart. Imagining they were engaged, they came to love each other deeply.

When Sen-jo heard that she was promised to another, she was so distressed she almost fainted. So greatly grieved was Ochu that he felt he could only withstand the pain of his broken heart by secretly running away. That evening at midnight he untied his small boat from the village dock and began to paddle downstream. He saw a figure rush out of the bushes, then run alongside the river. It was Sen-jo. They embraced and wept and Sen-jo climbed into the boat and joined him and they drifted to a remote village downstream.

They married and lived there for five years, starting a farm and raising two children. But in her heart Sen-jo was worried for her father and felt ungrateful to have fled. Her unresolved past haunted her, tingeing her happiness with grief. When she told Ochu, he admitted he too was longing for his home. They immediately decided to return and beg her family's forgiveness. Hiring a larger boat, they took the children upstream and docked in the village at dusk.

When Ochu went to Sen-jo's father's home to beg for pardon, he was received with bitter astonishment. Her father would not believe his daughter was in the boat. "From the day you left, my daughter has lain here in bed, too sick to speak." Ochu was taken aback. "She is in the boat, Father, with two fine grandchildren," he pleaded. "Come to the dock and see for yourself." But the father sent his servant to look, and when the excited servant returned to say, "Yes, it's true," the bewildered man went back to the sickbed of his silent daughter and told her the story.

Immediately the ill Sen-jo became filled with energy and rose from the bed without a word. She walked out of the house and down the road, followed by her father. As soon as she met the other Sen-jo and her children, the two embraced and instantly became one. Later the reunited Sen-jo said that all along, in both lives, she had had the feeling she was living in a dream.

What can we learn from this story, with its sorrowful tale of a divided life? Sen-jo had to cut off a great part of herself in order to live at all, and each half suffered in its own way. But there is also hope, for Sen-jo's determination to return invites our return as well. Like Sen-jo, many of us discover we live partially in a dreamworld, cut off from whole pieces of our life, our body, our past. It was not always this way. When we are born there is an original wholeness, a oneness with our mother and our own body. Then over the years of growing to be an individual in society, we lose this wholeness. As we repeatedly encounter the lack of respect and nurturance that is typical of many modern families, the judgments and fears of those close to us, the inevitable frustrations, loss, and cultural fragmentation that trying to meet society's expectations brings, we begin to separate from our own sacred body and our deepest feelings. This often takes place invisibly and unconsciously, in the dark, just like Sen-jo's running to follow Ochu's boat at midnight. Though we can sense our disconnection, we do not know exactly what is wrong.

James Joyce captured this dilemma when he wrote of one character, "Mr. Duffy lived a short distance from his body." Joan Tollifson, a Zen teacher, writes about how difficult it can be to simply acknowledge the truth of our body. She was born with the lower part of one arm missing. She describes a childhood in which children gasped in horror. "Some people told me how amazingly well I tie my shoes, and even more deadly, some people pretended not to notice, and nobody would say a word." If she was in an elevator with children and they asked her what happened to her, their parents would instantly silence them: "Shhh. Don't talk about it."

Then Joan discovered meditation, and for years she would sit with one hand making half of a circular mudra, trying to be a proper Zen student. But in some way she still had not actually looked at herself. "I remember the first time I really looked at my arm. I was twenty-five years old." It took that long to develop the courage to see what actually was. "And yet when you do so," she writes, "the horror is not in your body, but in your head."

Although it may be painful to look closely at our arms and legs, our belly and breasts, our face and our skin, our genitals and our hair, the cost of not looking is greater. Not looking brings a loss of feeling and connection with ourselves and this earth, with our very human life. It engenders a loss of our innate and instinctive wisdom. Even after years of spiritual practice we can still be like Sen-jo before her return, our contentment and happiness weighed down by abandoned and unfaced parts of ourselves.

One Buddhist abbot describes what happened after he survived surgery and radiation for cancer.

When I finally returned to my community and looked at it with a new perspective, I saw old students who had been there a long time and were just coasting, I saw others who were not practicing but were simply dependent and needed a place to live. I had taken bodhisattva vows which I thought at the time meant to unconditionally try to take care of everyone. As a bodhisattva I wanted everyone to stay; but my body, which had faced the truth of life and death, wouldn't let me. I kicked half the students out. In the end I was forced to listen to the wisdom of my body.

A loss of connection to embodied life is not just our individual predicament; this loss is embedded in the speed and pervasive disconnection of modern consumer society. The poet Adrienne Rich voices the sorrow hidden beneath our busy lives:

The problem, unstated until now, is how to live in a damaged body in a world where pain is meant to be gagged uncured, ungrieved over. The problem is to connect, without hysteria, the pain of anyone's body with the pain of the world's body.

One Western Tibetan lama speaks about how he encountered this.

I've seen a lot of pathological detachment in myself and others. Long years of retreat put me in touch with a lot of things, but I also went along with the old Buddhist culture where things get ignored, pushed away. I don't know how many meditation teachers, lamas, Vipassana teachers I have met who were having trouble with their health. You could say sickness is natural, is part of Buddha's First Noble Truth of suffering. But most of these teachers hadn't taken care of their bodies for years. And me? I used to pride myself on how calm and detached I was, never upset or letting myself feel anger, beyond all stress, flatlining my brain. But what about my body? Which organs have I been stuffing it all into, to the detriment of my health? Now, twenty-five years later, I'm starting to respect my body, my need for rest, for exercise, to find the physical wisdom I lost for so long.

Alice Miller, whose life's work is focused on reclaiming our authentic being, writes passionately about the body as the key.

The truth about our childhood is stored up in our body, and although we can repress it, we can never alter it. Our intellect can be deceived, our feelings manipulated, and conceptions confused, and our body tricked with medication. But someday our body will present its bill, for it is as incorruptible as a child, who, still whole in spirit, will accept no compromises or excuses, and it will not stop tormenting us until we stop evading the truth.

If we are to become whole, we must reclaim the body—holding even its pain and limitation as our own. This was true for a senior Buddhist practitioner whose parents were Holocaust survivors, and who said, "I was born into trauma, and I've discovered I have been holding my breath for my whole life." It was true for the yoga teacher who pushed her body to be perfect, until "I realized I was terrified of aging, of losing my looks, of my own weakness and vulnerability. My yoga was a way of trying to control my life."

One rabbi had traveled far on her journey before she fully realized the need for integration of her body.

Women have such fear around the body. I guess men do too. In my spiritual life I've worked with deep wounds in this area. In its wisest teachings Judaism holds sexuality and the body as sacred, and recognizes that to abuse it is to abuse what is divine. Now after many years of being a rabbi and of healing, I've started learning yoga and movement and Jewish dances. I realize that the energy of the body is the energy of God. We have to value it. Everything comes through it.

Embodied Enlightenment

Enlightenment must be lived here and now through this very body or else it is not genuine. In this body and mind we find the cause of suffering and the end of suffering. For awakening to be an opening into freedom in this very life, the body must be its ground.

Embodied enlightenment is not about special psycho-physical accomplishments, mastering the yogas of inner fire, fulfilling sexual tantras, or developing a rainbow body. Yes, certain Tibetan lamas can sit naked in the snow at 18,000 feet and generate sufficient heat to melt the snow in a twenty-foot circle around their bodies. And Catholic saints have demonstrated stigmata and miraculous healing powers. "But these powers are not the true miracle," said the Buddha. "Awakening to the truth is the miracle." Embodied enlightenment is about living wisely in your particular body, as it is, on this day, in this amazing life.

Western Buddhist meditation master and nun Pema Chödrön calls this understanding "The Wisdom of No Escape."

It is helpful to realize that being here, sitting in meditation, doing simple everyday things like working, walking outside, talking with people, eating, using the toilet, is actually all that we need to be fully awake, fully alive, fully human. It's also helpful to realize that this body that we have, this very body that's sitting here right now in this room, this very body that perhaps aches, and this mind that we have at this very moment, are exactly what we need to be fully human, fully awake, and fully alive. Furthermore, the emotions that we have right now, the negativity and the positivity, are what we actually need. It is just as if we looked around to find out what would be the greatest wealth that we could possibly possess in order to lead a decent, good, completely fulfilling, energetic, inspired life, and found it all right here.

Enlightenment flowers not as an ideal, but in the miraculous reality of our human form, with its pleasures and pains. No master can escape this truth, nor does enlightenment make the vulnerability of our body go away. The Buddha had illnesses and backaches. Sages like Ramana Maharshi, Karmapa, and Suzuki Roshi died of cancer in spite of their holy understanding. Their example shows we must find awakening in sickness and in health, in pleasure and in pain, in this human body as it is.

How do we touch this body of life, the joys and sorrows of it? An embodied awakening neither denies nor reviles the body, nor does it grasp and mindlessly indulge in pleasures. In embodied awakening we become present for the life that is given us, respectful of what the Tibetans call "this precious human form." Tsong Khapa, the Tibetan master, taught: "This human body is more precious than the rarest gem. Cherish your body; it is yours for this one time only . . . a thing of beauty that passes away." Such a respectful presence allows the life of our body to be blessed. Galway Kinnell described this blessing in "St. Francis and the Sow."

> The bud
> stands for all things,
> even for those things that don't flower,
> for everything flowers, from within, of self-blessing;
> though sometimes it is necessary
> to reteach a thing its loveliness,
> to put a hand on the brow
> of the flower
> and retell it in words and in touch
> it is lovely
> until it flowers again from within, of self-blessing;
> as Saint Francis
> put his hand on the creased forehead
> of the sow, and told her in words and in touch
> blessings of earth on the sow, and the sow
> began remembering all down her thick length,

from the earthen snout all the way
through the fodder and slops to the spiritual curl of her tail . . .
the long, perfect loveliness of sow.

One elder, a Catholic father and teacher, speaks of the gratitude and blessedness he has learned in the body.

I came from a poor white family where we drank and lived hard; the men treated the body like a truck that you used and ignored. In the church it got worse. I hated to deal with my body. I lived on coffee and then on scotch. Gradually as I looked at the simple people who came to talk to me, and saw how many tortured bodies there were, as well as tortured souls, my faith and love got past all the junk about sin and the body in church. It doesn't have to be so hard. I realize that Christ taught I had to love my enemy. I took a vow of nonviolence, and this included my body. My practice became, "Do not torment myself, do not escalate the pain." I began to teach it to others. It turned into a practice of gratitude. I get up in the morning and the care of my body is where I start. It's poignant how simple it is.

We must include the sacredness of the body if we are to be wise. One spiritual teacher describes a time, long after her first experience of awakening, when she had a serious bout with cancer.

A large abdominal tumor was removed, and with it all that I had clung to as certainties in my life. I quit work and I stopped the spiritual teaching. I turned to anything I thought might help me change what had led to that cancer, from acupuncture to depth therapy. I became humble before the body. That was fifteen years ago, and I can now say that it was the biggest turning point and awakening of all. I had used my body to practice. Now I had to inhabit it, respect it, love it with all the feminine force and nurturing and understanding I had withdrawn into my spiritual life. Keeping my heart in my body became my practice, and it has become glorious. Even the first awakenings into perfection and grace did not come close to showing me the joy of living in the body, in the senses, in each moment. I love my life in a new way. This has become the place of freedom.

No Part Left Out

As we have seen, one of the most important challenges to living an embodied enlightenment is in the area of sexuality. Religious traditions often warn us about the dangers of entanglement with the senses, and it is true that we can become overly attached and identified with this body and its pleasures. Our culture has exploited this to an extreme. But in spiritual circles the opposite danger of aversion, fear, and unconsciousness is perhaps even more common. There is, as the Buddha suggests, a middle path to be found in each of our lives. One yoga teacher paused in the midst of teaching a difficult stretch to caution her students, "You strivers here, relax. And you sensualists, straighten up."

Jung writes of the necessary balance between our animal body and its connection through Eros to the highest forms of spirit.

The erotic instinct is something questionable and will always be so whatever laws may have to say on the matter. It belongs, on the one hand, to the original animal nature of man, which will exist as long as man has an animal body. On the other hand, it is connected with the highest forms of the spirit. But it blooms only when spirit and instinct are in true harmony. If one or the other aspect is missing, then an injury occurs, there is a one-sided lack of balance which easily slips into the pathological. Too much of the animal disfigures the civilized human being, too much culture makes for a sick animal.

The most rigid forms of spirituality simply condemn sexuality. More wisely it is the misuse of sexuality that is described as a cause of suffering. The Ten Commandments teach us to refrain from adultery. The Buddhist precepts call on us not to bring suffering by inappropriate sexuality. But the fear of causing harm can easily turn into a fear of the body and of sexuality in general. By contrast, one Sufi master told me that in his tradition it was taught that "masters become sexier as they become more highly awakened." He did not mean simply sexual, but more full-bodied, awake, and alive. Jack Engler, a Buddhist teacher and Harvard psychologist, once spoke about his training as a novice under the renowned Trappist monk Thomas Merton. "Thomas Merton," he reported, "was the sexiest man I ever met."

In the early 1980s, in an attempt to understand and honor sexuality as a conscious part of the spiritual path, I interviewed fifty-three Zen masters, lamas, swamis, and/or their senior students about their sexuality. Here is part of the article I then wrote for the *Yoga Journal*.

> Like any group of people in our culture, their practices varied. There were heterosexuals, bisexuals, homosexuals, exhibitionists, monogamists, and polygamists. There were teachers who were celibate and happy, and those who were celibate and miserable; there were those who were married and monogamous, and those who had many clandestine affairs; there were teachers who were promiscuous and open about it; there were those who made conscious and committed sexual relationships an aspect of their spirituality; and there were many more teachers who were no more enlightened or conscious about their sexuality than everyone else around them.

> While we know that wise sexuality can bring intimacy, connection, and surrender, wise and holy celibacy can do the same. Both choices can be an expression of love and awareness. An embodied enlightenment brings consciousness and respect to our

body without our becoming lost in the extremes of indulgence or self-denial. In Hindu and Buddhist tantra, sexuality is valued as a route to awakening; in Jewish and Sufi traditions it is celebrated as divine. Embodied sensuality and Eros are honored and transformed. In the same spirit, celibacy can be honored and transformed in the holiness of the heart. The vital life of the body can be known through both paths.

This precious human body is a holy treasure-house for action and awakening. Holy the heart, holy the ears, holy the limbs and breasts, holy the feet and hands, holy the heart and skin, holy the hair and genitals, the liver, the lungs, the blood, the tiniest cells and the breath of life.

The writer Eduardo Galeano put it his way:

> The church says: The body is a sin.
> Science says: The body is a machine.
> Advertising says: The body is a business.
> The Body says: I am a fiesta.

When the precious human body is properly tended, its benevolence spills over to all of life. The impulse to tend, to care for, to heal, to embody love and freedom grows in us. The worlds that have been separated in us come together to make a whole.

At one of his last teachings before retiring at age eighty, Robert Aitken Roshi talked to a gathering of a hundred Buddhist teachers about his half century of Zen practice, starting in prison in Japan during World War II. At the end he was asked if he would offer a koan and be willing to give us the answer. He told us this tale: In 1951, when he was practicing in New York under Master Nyogen Sensaki, Master Sensaki held up an elegant bowl painted with a spiral from the rim to the center. He asked, "Does this spiral go from the outside in or from the inside out?" This was the koan, and we quietly contemplated its solution. Then came the moment to offer an answer. Aitken Roshi stood up from his cushion, trembling slightly, and extended his arms outward like a great frail bird, making the shape of a bowl with his whole outstretched body. First he turned one way, as if spiraling in. Then he turned the other way, as if spiraling out. He became the bowl with his whole body, with his whole being, inside and out. This was his answer.

The Wisdom of Incarnation

In May of 1998, at the Spirit Rock Meditation Center, we hosted a large benefit for the medical care of Ram Dass, who had suffered a major stroke the year before. After almost a year of rehabilitation Ram Dass was able to talk, though haltingly, and he still groped for words. At the end of the day his wheelchair was placed on the stage so he could speak. Noting to much laughter that he had been warned it was tacky to come to one's own benefit—and that's why he came—Ram Dass addressed his predicament and the question of identity.

> *For years I practiced as a karma yogi, the path of service. I wrote books about learning to serve, about how to help others. Now it is reversed. I need people to help me get up and put me to bed. Others feed me and wash my bottom. And I can tell you it's harder to be the one who is helped than the helper!*
>
> *But this is just another stage. It feels like I died and have been reborn over and over. In the sixties I was a professor at Harvard, and when that ended I went out with Tim Leary spreading psychedelics. Then in the seventies I died from that and returned from India as Baba Ram Dass, the guru. Then in the eighties my life was all about service—cofounding the Seva Foundation, building hospitals, and working with refugees and prisoners. Over all these years I played cello, golf, drove my MG. Since this stroke the car is in the driveway, the cello and golf clubs in the closet. Now if I think I'm the guy who can't play cello or drive or work in India, I would feel terribly sorry for myself. But I'm not him.*

*During the stroke I died again, and now I have a new life
in a disabled body. This is where I am. You've got to be here
now. You've got to take the curriculum.*

This is the wisdom of incarnation. In it, we willingly step into
life, neither frightened by it nor lost in it, but awake and free in
whatever the moment presents. Kabir, the Indian mystic poet,
writes:

Jump into experience while you are alive. . . . What you
call "salvation" belongs to the time before death.

To enter life requires a radical understanding that holiness,
God, or Nirvana are not found apart from experience, but are its
essence. What we seek is what we are. The Heart Sutra teaches
this truth in the phrase "form is no different than emptiness,"
while Symeon, the Christian mystic, speaks of "awakening in
Christ's body as Christ awakens in ours."

The key to this open and free heart came to the Buddha after
years of fighting against his body. He wandered through India for
six years fasting and undertaking extreme and arduous ascetic
practices in a battle to overpower all bodily desires and fears.
Finally, he found himself exhausted, close to death, lying on the
earth. Spontaneously a memory arose from when he was a boy
seated under a rose apple tree in his father's garden. He remembered how there had come to him on that spring morning, all
unbidden, a wondrous sense of wholeness and stillness, his heart
at rest and at home in the midst of all things. Amazed, he realized
that his whole spiritual quest for liberation had been misguided,
a fruitless fight against his body and the world.

With this vision he discovered the middle path, an inner unity
that neither struggles against the world nor becomes lost and
entangled in it. He opened his heart to the suffering and beauty
in life as it is, and rested in peace. And at that moment a young
woman came by and, seeing the emaciated sage, gave him a bowl
of the rice milk she was carrying. The Buddha drank gratefully,

now refreshed in body as in spirit. Then he returned to his meditation with a renewed understanding of his path.

A modern-day version of this story took place in Dr. Jon Kabat-Zinn's first clinic, in the basement of the University of Massachusetts Medical Center. When he started his mindfulness-based Stress Reduction Program, he invited the doctors at the medical center to send him the patients they could no longer help, after the best of modern surgery and medicine had failed. He did this because, as he later told me, "We can offer the strongest medicine of all—the truth." So cancer patients and pain patients, patients with degenerative diseases of bone and joint, and those with back problems who had tried everything in their struggles with their body—all were sent to him. Dr. Kabat-Zinn taught them a deep mindfulness, how to simply be present with what was true in their bodies rather than to treat their illness as an enemy to be beaten down. With this attention and acceptance, remarkable results ensued. Some were healed of their stress, pain, and diseases. Others, though still not completely well, learned new, compassionate ways of being with their bodies that transformed their lives. Now his program has spread to hundreds of hospitals nationwide.

Embodied Courage

The fruits of embodiment, fullness, wisdom, and compassion do not come without a price. When my teacher Ajahn Chah was sixty-three he entered a hospital for a combination of water on the brain, diabetes, stroke, and heart problems. He was hospitalized for nine months, in grave pain and often unable to speak. When he was released the following year, some of his capacities returned, and he was able to resume teaching in a limited fashion. I went to visit him at a temple near Bangkok and saw how much weaker and older he looked after this ordeal. I bowed respectfully. At some point in our conversation I was reminded of how often over the years he had exhorted us to reflect on the inevitability of old age, sickness, and death, and noted out loud how they were now visibly happening to him. Ajahn Chah fixed me with a piercing gaze and said, "Don't say that so lightly!"

Spiritual dedication gives us no immunity from the joys and sorrows of life's body. Every spiritual master faces the difficulties of fatigue, sickness, and death, just as we do. What dedicated practice gives us are the tools to awaken compassion and awareness in this human realm, ways for the heart to hold it all.

Every part of life is a fertile field for practice. Rachel Naomi Remen, a physician and healer, speaks of sickness as a gateway, an invitation to deepen our soul's connection with life. She says the goal of illness is to bring us back to what is important to us, to wake us up. The point of spiritual practice is not to wait for illness or death to awaken us, but to draw on the life and health we have now to bring peace to our body, heart, and mind.

And if we do not have the courage to enter our body fully, then life itself may simply insist. As Marcel Proust reminds us:

Illness is the most heeded of doctors. To goodness and wisdom we make only promises; pain we obey.

One rabbi who worked ceaselessly for many years as a teacher and scholar found himself overworked and became seriously ill. Over the year of his recovery he prayed for the blessing of a new life, and vowed to dedicate his prayers to the holiness in the body.

At first it was not easy. I had ignored my body for so long. But I realized the body is an essential way of being in contact with God. This is what we are given. I began to pray each morning that I might experience the God-given senses of each moment. I had a regimen of physical exercise and movement, but that was not what made the difference—it was the intention each morning to be alive, present, with the energy of the universe through my body. That was my prayer, and over the months my body changed; through this intention my life changed and became more beautiful and blessed.

A full appreciation of the particulars of our incarnation brings blessings. One Zen master explains:

My Zen teaching has deepened to encourage people to really plunge into the world, into life. I want them to enter life, to embody their practice, tend it with their hearts. To attend to life, to this body, is to love it and bless it. Particularly we need to find a way to bless our wounds and the darkness we find ourselves in. It takes patience to bless our woundedness, because we haven't been taught a respect for it. But if you do bless your body, you notice that you find what is right for you. You have the kind of pains that are right for you, as well as the kind of joys that are yours, the experiences that you have honestly earned.

When we listen to our bodies, our bodily wisdom grows. We can feel the body's urge to move and honor its cycles of rest, we can meditate and dance, we can respect its need for solitude, we can allow its lively senses, and we can know its pleasures and limitations. Instead of fearing our body, its losses and strange vulnerability, we honor it. When the mandala of awakening includes rather than excludes the body, our gifts can flower and our heart remains free.

Rabbi Nachman of Bratzlav tried to get his disciples to understand that:

If you never want to see the face of hell, when you come home from work every night, dance with your kitchen towel, and if you're worried about waking up your family, take off your shoes.

Embodied courage chooses not to wait until the specter of sickness and death demands attention. Instead, let us willingly enter this bodily existence, let us sacrifice false ideals for the reality of the present. It is all we have. One Zen story concerns a fervent disciple asking his master for the truth of enlightenment. The master, pointing to two nearby groves of bamboo, asks, "See that bamboo on the left, how tall it is? And see that bamboo on the right, how short it is? That is their nature." The disciple was enlightened. Accepting the truth is the gate to awakening. At this moment, what is our nature? Can we accept this too?

Embodiment and the Laundry

Hakuin Zenji wrote in his ancient Song of Zazen, "All beings by nature are Buddha, as ice by nature is water. How sad that people ignore the near and search for truth afar like someone in the midst of water crying out for thirst. . . . Truly, is anything missing now? Nirvana is right here, before our eyes; this very place is the pure Lotus Land; this very body, the Buddha."

For Hakuin the gateway to living in Nirvana is embodied awareness. Holiness of being comes by entering the moment fully, with our wholehearted attention. All the outer forms of religion— the temples, the teachers, the practices—simply call us to the eternal present, invite us to bend down the heart to touch each moment.

A Chinese fable tells of a young man observing a sage at the village well. The old man was lowering a wooden bucket on a rope and pulling the water up slowly, hand over hand. The youth disappeared and returned with a pulley. He approached the old man and showed him how the device worked. "See, you put your rope around the wheel and draw up the water by cranking the handle." The old man resisted. "If I use a device like this, my mind will think itself clever. With a cunning mind I will no longer put my heart into what I am doing. Soon my wrists alone will do the work. If my heart and whole body are not in my work, my work will become joyless. When my work is joyless, how do you think the water will taste?"

The water reflects our spirit. In Zen it is said that the whole moon and sky are reflected in a drop of dew on the grass. Each small thing, each moment is a contribution to and a reflection of the whole. Tucking a child in bed, paying the bills, listening to a business associate, paying the attendant at the gas station, writing a letter or typing a memo, meeting over a meal, planning a job, watering the garden—each becomes the embodiment of the awakened heart. It is amazing that we can forget this truth.

A young girl aged six asked her mama to tell her what she did at the university where she went every day. "I am in the art department. I teach people how to draw and paint," replied her mother. Astonished, the girl inquired, "You mean they forget?"

When we forget, awakening calls us back to bless the simple activity of each moment. One Western lama recalls using prayerful physical work to stay awake and grounded after returning from a three-year Tibetan retreat:

> *It was the hardest thing to keep my spiritual life alive in the stream of so many daily activities, and the enormous, unnecessary complexity of Western life. The first five years were the most difficult, keeping my heart simple inside while being with people who have no sensibility other than getting and hurrying. Initially it felt unstable, almost crazy. I was afraid I would forget what I learned, so I relied on the physical work to stabilize my practice and mind. I did a huge amount of cleaning. I specialized in washing, mopping, laundry. Nobody around me wanted to clean anyway. Everybody was happy to have someone else doing it.*
>
> *I used to quietly sing a mantra of compassion with each dish that I washed, each floor I cleaned. And I included the prayer that as I clean, may the eyes and hearts of all beings around me be clean and purified, made innocent and clear. Time would stop as if I was part of the earth cleansing itself in spring. It was a beautiful way to work. The simple physical tasks are the entry to learn to be with this world in a sacred manner.*

Hindus and Sufis teach that each act can be done for the Beloved. Embodying mindfulness, we fold the laundry as if folding the robes of Jesus or Buddha, we serve a meal not for ourselves or our family, but for the Holy One. When the body is included in the mandala of practice, every small act is held in the heart as well as the hands. One Dominican sister calls this "Incarnation Theology."

At the age of sixty I have gone back to the simple things I learned when I was young. If I'm grading papers, I pray for each student as I read. Or if I find myself worrying about a patient, I'll say the rosary. Adoration, thanksgiving, supplication. I try to enjoy everything, even the hard things, even serving in the face of injustice. This is what is given now. That's the truth. My life has become one of interconnectedness, the small epiphanies of each moment well lived. I don't trust the big ones where my ego gets all puffed up. It's either here and now or we've missed it.

There are so many simple practices to return us to our body, to our heart, to this moment: a prayer before entering each door, a reflection before we eat, a pause to breathe mindfully before answering the phone. A prayer or verse can be created even for watching television, says Zen Master Thich Nhat Hanh: "Watching the evening news, I know it is my story. Breathing in calmly, I hold us all in compassion." Remembering the breath, we return all things to their seat in the body.

When one Zen student told his master, "All that's left to finish up are some of the details," the master exclaimed, "But details are all there are." Embodied presence reminds us to be with each thing in turn. Gandhi called this "Blessed Monotony," and likened the round of each day to the sun and moon in their regular orbs, the silent cycles of the stars and the seasons. Zen teaches it is like baking bread in the oven: You do it over and over and you eat each loaf's particular flavor. Claude Monet lived in Giverny for thirty-five years, painting the same water lilies year after year in each new day's light. To look with the freshness of eyes that see today's light anew—this is the beginner's mind.

This simple intimacy of actual, physical service was at the center of Mother Teresa's work as well.

> I never look at the masses as my responsibility; I look at the individual. I can only love one person at a time—just one, one, one. So you begin. I began—I picked up one person. Maybe if I didn't pick up that one person, I wouldn't have picked up forty-two thousand. The whole work is only a drop in the ocean. But if I didn't put the drop in, the ocean would be one drop less. The same thing goes for you, the same thing in your family, the same thing in your church, your community. Just begin—one, one, one.

Mystics, teachers, and adepts tell us that we must awaken to the sacred in the ordinary. As Thomas Merton puts it, "Life is this simple: We are living in a world that is absolutely transparent and the Divine is shining through it all the time. This is not just a nice story or a fable. It is true."

In one Middle Eastern story, a man falsely identified as a criminal was put in prison. His friend visited and left him a prayer rug. The prisoner went angrily back to his cell. He had hoped for a hacksaw or a knife and all he'd gotten was this rug. But since he had it, he figured he might as well use it. So he started bowing on the rug to pray. Each day he became more familiar with the pattern woven into the rug, and he started to see an interesting image there. It was a diagram of the lock that allowed him to open the cell and escape.

Freedom of the heart is found not by looking up—it is right here, woven in colors beneath our feet.

13

AWAKENED EMOTIONS AND ORDINARY PERFECTION

Monks, you must be aware of pleasant feelings, neutral feelings, and
unpleasant feelings; you must establish mindfulness of the
feelings in the feelings.

SATIPATTHANA SUTRA

When a student asked, "You teach us to just sit when we sit, just eat
when we eat; could a Zen master be just angry in the same way?"
Suzuki Roshi replied, "You mean to just get angry like a thunderstorm
and be done when it passes? *Ahh*, I wish I could do that."

SHUNRYU SUZUKI ROSHI

I'm very brave generally, only today I happen to have a headache.

TWEEDLEDUM

How are we to understand emotional life after awakening has begun? Some traditions portray the awakened heart as totally unmovable. In the Anguttara Nikaya the Buddha tells us, "Just as a solid rock remains unmoved by the wind, even so, neither sense impressions nor contacts of any kind, pleasant or unpleasant, desired or undesired, can cause the heart of one who has truly awakened to waver." I was taught this in many ways. Once as I was weeping in meditation, our visiting meditation master, Dipama Barua, said that such grieving was unnecessary for a yogi. "Meditation teachers don't cry," she told me. Yet, my first meditation master, Ajahn Chah, had said exactly the opposite: "Tears are part of meditation. If you have not wept deeply, you have not begun to meditate."

In some situations the Buddha decries grief as unnecessary clinging. Yet at other times the Buddhist texts tell us he will evoke grief in his listeners, "to awaken the tears and softness of their hearts," so that "fully open and attentive they can know the depths of the teachings."

Different lineages regard the emotions in different ways. In some traditions the unconscious patterns of greed, hatred, delusion, and fear are said to disappear completely; others teach that they remain but are transformed into experiences of wisdom and compassion. But every wise tradition offers the possibility of a deep freedom of spirit. This unquenchable spirit must be discovered amidst the power of life's emotions and storms, its love unshakable.

Vulnerability and the Tender Heart

Several years ago some friends arranged for the Gyuto Tantric Choir, the Tibetan monks famous for their deep multivocal chanting, to perform in San Quentin Prison; then the San Quentin Gospel Choir would sing in response. But as the day approached it became clear to the organizers that there would be a cultural gap to overcome.

The members of the San Quentin Gospel Choir were all African-Americans, many of them big men who worked out with weights. In their years in prison they had been born again, touched by the spirit of Jesus, and their songs were testimonials to their depths of suffering and to the light of the gospel that had been awakened in them. The organizers feared that the Tibetan monks would appear to be merely foreigners and heathens to these newly awakened Christians. When the "heathen monks" arrived, the contrast was even more apparent. Dwarfed by the African-Americans was a group of small Asian men wearing maroon skirts. The question was how to bridge this gap.

A key sponsor of the event found the solution in an inspired introduction. "Almost all of these Tibetan men who have joined us today have spent years in harsh prisons. The Communist Chinese Army not only imprisoned them for expressing their beliefs, but tortured them as well. Somehow they were released or able to escape from prison. Then, to find freedom, they walked across the Himalayas, the highest mountains on earth. Some tied rags on their feet because they had no good shoes. But even now they are in exile. They are forced to live far from their home, apart from their families and community, and they do not know if they will ever be able to return. What has kept them going through all of their struggle have been their songs and prayers. This is what they will sing for you today."

In an instant the gospel choir and the Tibetan monks looked at one another with eyes that shared the vulnerable depths of human sorrow, and they found understanding. Each group sang to the other from the heart, and when their music was finished, they came together to hug and embrace like long-lost brothers.

The songs these men sang expressed the emotions of their hearts. Their struggles and capacity to endure, their hopes and aspirations for freedom and redemption were carried by their voices. Feelings are what connect us to life and to one another. To be able to feel is one of the extraordinary gifts of humanity. To neither suppress our feelings nor be caught by them, but to understand them—that is the art.

Working with the Emotions After Awakening

The Buddha taught we must become aware and accepting of the entire range of feelings—of pleasant, neutral, and unpleasant feelings as each arises. He went on, "By becoming aware of the entire range of the emotions" and "experiencing the feelings in the feelings" we can find peace in their midst and become free. But the process does not stop after an experience of realization. One Buddhist teacher recalls her study with her Zen master.

> *I was working on koans, and there were times I would go for interview and couldn't even speak about my koan. I'd have to talk about my emotions, because they were so central to my practice. Sometimes it was joy, but more often it would be the difficult feelings and struggles with my parents or in my relationship. He would listen and weep with me about it. He would say, "Yes, I know how hard it is. It's like that sometimes in my family too." I thought he wasn't supposed to say that. His openness to feeling my life would open my heart. He was so human in his willingness to be right there.*

I first met Buddhist teacher and psychiatrist Robert Hall in 1974. One of the chief protégés of Fritz Perls, he cofounded the Gestalt Institute in San Francisco in the 1960s. Then he began the Lomi School, one of the first trainings to combine spiritual work with that of the body and emotions. I was a new psychologist, and I remember telling him that I was learning to diagnose the difficulties of those who came to me reasonably well, to recognize their problems and sort through their clinical history, but what I was still shaky about was how to best help them change. "Oh, I don't do that," said Robert. "You don't?" I asked incredulously. "No," he went on, "I help them be with what is true. The healing comes from that."

Without the ability to be present to our own feelings, we continue to blame our troubles on others, individually and collectively. As James Baldwin put it, "I imagine one of the reasons people cling to their hates so stubbornly is because they sense once hate is gone, they will be forced to deal with their own pain." Only when we are permeable to what is true in us will our practice go forward.

To encourage an awareness of inner emotional richness during retreats, I sometimes recite from a list of five hundred feelings. These include: affectionate, ambitious, ambivalent, amused, antagonistic, antsy, apathetic, appreciative, argumentative, blissful, brokenhearted, calm, cheerful, claustrophobic, compassionate, concentrated, concerned, curious, delighted, depressed, disheartened, driven, ebullient, fearful, frightened, hateful, honored, humble, hysterical, glad, gluttonous, grateful, grave, greedy, jealous, jovial, joyful, pissed-off, pleased, prudish, sad, silly, sleepy, sober, spacious, sympathetic—and so on.

In the awakened heart we find a capacity to touch all parts of this amazing feeling-life with tenderness. As we begin to accept the rhythms and range of feelings, we bow to "the ten thousand joys and the ten thousand sorrows" of the Tao. Accepting inner and outer circumstances as they arise, the men and women of Tao did not "fight their way through life. They took life as it came, gladly. . . . They did not try by their own contriving to help the Tao along."

The Mind and the Heart

The "Jewel in the Lotus" is the translation of the universal compassion mantra "Om Mani Padme Hum." While it has many meanings, one explanation of its symbolism is that compassion arises when the jewel of the mind rests in the lotus of the heart. The awakened mind has a diamondlike clarity. When this clear insight rests in the heart's tender compassion, both dimensions of liberation are fulfilled.

In Buddhist psychology, mind and heart are often described by one word—"citta." This heart-mind has many dimensions. It contains and includes all our thoughts, our feelings and emotions, responses, intuition, temperament, and consciousness itself. When we speak of mind in the West, we usually refer only to the rational thought process. Observing this aspect of mind, we see an endless stream of thoughts, ideas, and stories. While this discriminating mind has a practical value, it can also separate us from the world; our ideas easily create "us" and "them," good and bad, past and future. Our thoughts also like to create imaginary problems. As Mark Twain put it, "My life has been filled with terrible misfortunes . . . most of which never happened." Or, in the words of one of my teachers, Sri Nisargadatta, "The mind creates the abyss, the heart crosses it."

Along with thoughts and impulses, Buddhist psychology also describes feelings as a natural aspect of heart-mind. Initially we notice that pleasant, neutral, or unpleasant feelings arise with each experience. If we notice them mindfully, without clinging to the pleasant or condemning the unpleasant, we can discover how these basic feelings give rise to a full range of emotions. Some people believe that emotions are dangerous. But the emotions themselves are rarely a problem; it is our lack of awareness of them or the stories that we believe about them that create our suffering. Without awareness, painful feelings can fester into addiction or hatred or degenerate into numbness; eventually we can lose touch not only with what is felt but also with our heart's essential wisdom. As the twentieth-century Christian mystic Simone Weil noted, "The danger is not that the soul should doubt whether there is any bread, but that, by a lie, it should persuade itself that it is not hungry."

The first woman I became involved with after I disrobed from being a monk was a college friend who was newly teaching at Harvard. Inside I still felt like a monk who had no preferences for or against anything, taking whatever was put in the begging bowl. When she would ask what I wanted for dinner or what movie I would like to see, I answered, "Whatever you like, dear; for me it doesn't matter." When she would ask how I felt about going out in the country or staying home, I said it was all okay with me. It drove her crazy. This wasn't just a wise spiritual detachment; she observed that I was afraid of engagement and out of touch with feeling, and reminded me that I had been that way before the monastery too. It was true. I didn't know what I felt. So she got me a small notebook with the suggestion that I write down ten things each day that I liked or disliked, until I could start to know my own feelings. Recovering my feelings was a long and life-changing process.

Feelings and Temperament

Awakening to the emotions means to feel them—nothing less, nothing more. It does not require changing our feelings—feelings change all the time on their own. Nor does it mean changing our temperament. If we are intuitive or philosophical, sanguine or melancholic, that will likely remain the same. Our range may expand, but our temperament and personality will likely continue. One Buddhist teacher said that he had expected awakening to bring a "personal transformation," only to be surprised that it was actually an "impersonal transformation." The transformation is the opening of the heart and not a personality change.

This teacher went on:

In many ways the spiritual transformation of the past decades is different than I had imagined. I'm still the same quirky person, with much the same style and ways of being. So that on the outside I'm not that amazingly transformed, enlightened person I first hoped to become. But there's a big transformation inside. Years of working with my feelings and family patterns and temper have softened the way I hold them all. In the struggle to know and deeply accept my life, it has been transformed, and my love has grown larger. If my life was like a crowded garage where I kept bumping into the furniture and judging myself, now it's like I've moved into an airplane hangar with the doors left open. I've got the old stuff there, yet it doesn't limit me like before. I'm the same, yet now I'm free to move about, even to fly.

As we have seen earlier, it is a mistake to think we can evade our karma, the history of who we are. I saw this very clearly twenty years ago when I first taught a large retreat in Switzerland.

Participants came from all over Europe. In private interviews with students I tried to open to each individual without prejudice, regardless of his or her culture or country. So I was shocked by the end of the retreat to discover that the interviews with nearly every German student who came to me were about struggle and anger and self-judgment, while most of the French students were plagued by existential questions of doubt and motivation. For the Italian students, the interviews and meditations were filled with emotion; they came in passionately gesticulating about how painful and beautiful and difficult and wonderful the process had been—every single one of them. Every individual was singular, but each was also conditioned by a greater cultural whole.

Emotional awakening, then, is not about becoming a different person. We may naturally be an introvert or an extrovert, a joyful person or an impatient one. Dzongsar Khyentsie Rinpoche goes so far as to say, "Sometimes a master can be a great teacher but not necessarily a great person. Perhaps he or she is short-tempered, not easy to get along with, or makes many demands." When Ram Dass was asked after his years of spiritual discipline whether he had transformed his personality, he laughed and answered no. Instead he said he had become "a connoisseur of my neuroses."

Like our gender, hair color, and height, personality and temperament are given to us for this life. They may be damaged in our childhood and redeemed with inner work, but they are part of our nature. In Buddhist psychology personality types remain after awakening, but are ennobled by a wise and compassionate heart. There are desire temperaments, aversion temperaments, deluded temperaments. Yet each may become refined through awakening to express a love of beauty, clarity, and spaciousness. Nor is humor excluded. So when Joshu Sasaki Roshi, now the senior Rinzai Zen master in the West, was asked why he came here to teach, he replied, "I did not come to America to teach. I came to America to have a good time. I want Americans to learn how to truly laugh."

There are many ways we have been taught to fear our emotions, and many misconceptions that trap us in this fear. The trauma, judgment, fear, and shame we encounter in childhood can be terribly constricting. Sometimes we imagine that spiritual quietude is the best answer—don't feel too much, don't get excited or angry or you'll rock the boat to enlightenment. Spiritual practice gets mixed up with ideas of passivity and self-effacement, a cessation of passionate aliveness.

Even sincere practitioners can mistake a false outer decorum for the peaceful demeanor of inner freedom. We may secretly believe that if we truly allow ourselves to experience our feelings and desires, our self-indulgence will run rampant, or our aggression and indolence will overwhelm us. In thinking this, we confuse our true nature with the feelings of a deficient and small sense of self. For while emotions are indeed powerful forces, it is not fear and repression that will release us from their grip—awareness is the answer.

We fear the destructive power of our emotions when we haven't seen them for what they really are. We confuse allowing ourselves to be aware of them with the necessity to act them out. But to include our full selves in our journey we need to understand how we have been entangled by and identified with our emotions. We need to see the identity of "the body of fear," to see how the hurt and frustration of childhood, the forces of anger, greed, pride, sexual longing, and need have been conditioned in us. Experiencing the full range of these feelings as they come and go in our consciousness, we can begin to ask of each the question, "Is this who I am?" If we can hold our feelings in a spacious and fearless heart, the lonely, broken, spiteful, confused feelings arise in a new way, transformed by our acceptance.

Weeping Buddha, Wrathful Buddha

We armor and defend the heart not only against the world, but against ourselves. Some of us fear sadness, others fear joy; some fear weakness, others fear strength. There is a cartoon showing two generals striding down the halls of the Pentagon. One is whispering to the other, "Last night I had a real nightmare. I dreamed the meek inherited the earth."

Unlike the Pentagon, the awakened heart is undefended. It allows the full sorrow and beauty of life. Lama Chogyam Trungpa said: "It is this open and tender heart that has the capacity to transform the world."

When a society has lost its ability to feel its grief, to mourn the dead of its battles, the wasted lives of youth in its ghettos, the loss of pristine forests and noble values, the racist warehousing of men in its vast prisons, it closes some part of its heart to hope. If we cannot grieve, we cannot take the lessons of the past and use them to open our hearts to new love.

In Japan, Jizo bodhisattva is one of the manifestations of this open heart. Like St. Christopher, Jizo is the protector of travelers and children. He is a saint of grief and renewal. Zen teacher Yvonne Rand has adapted a Jizo ceremony offered for the parents of "water babies"—children who were stillborn or aborted—even if their losses occurred in the distant past. In the ceremony parents offer prayers and sew tiny robes for these lost children, placing the robes ceremonially on the childlike figure of Jizo in the temple garden. An astonishing amount of unacknowledged tears and grief pour out of the parents who attend, many of whom had no idea how much was held in their hearts.

In the same way the Vietnam Veterans Memorial has become a public altar for the grief and loss of that war. It is one of the few places in America where one can see grown men weep in public. A thousand offerings are made there daily, and the notes, prayers, and poems are collected and held by the Smithsonian. They have been published in several books. In one, the following notes appear, a testimony to the connection between acknowledgment and the beginning of healing:

> Your name is on a black wall in D.C. A lot of people walk by all day. You can tell which are vets. . . . We just stand and look and weep, not caring who sees us cry.

How angry I was to find you here, though I knew you would be. I wished so long that I could have saved you. I would give my life if I somehow knew it would bring you back.

I've carried the anguish of your death for so long, but I can stop looking for you now. I think I can start living (again). . . .

Asian Buddhist temples are filled with figures of peaceful Buddhas, but also there are weeping Buddhas and wrathful bodhisattvas, figures with flaming swords, each expressing the power of emotions after awakening. Even masters like Thich Nhat Hanh and the Dalai Lama admit occasional bouts of anger. When the 1991 U.S. bombing of Iraq evoked in him the horrors of Vietnam, at first Thich Nhat Hanh felt so angry he canceled his American teaching schedule. He writes that it took him several days to breathe and calm his heart and transform the anger into grief and the power of fierce compassion so he could come to America and speak passionately to the root of the problem.

The Dalai Lama has written, "In situations of great injustice I can get angry for a time, but then I think 'What is the use,' and gradually this anger turns into compassion." His teachings acknowledge that great strength is needed to act in this world, but the wrathful Buddhas wield the sword not of hatred but of a powerful compassion.

Both collectively and individually, there are times to use this sword skillfully. I saw a Korean Zen master use his strength of compassion with a senior student who had fallen in love with a new female student in the community. Less than a year later this woman abruptly left the senior student for another man. For several months the Zen master was sympathetic to his senior student's grief and ministered to his sorrow. Then the master took a nine-month teaching trip to Europe and Korea. Upon his return, he spent time checking in with each of the community members.

When his senior student let him know he was still mourning his loss, the Zen master reached into his bag and pulled out an exquisitely carved set of prayer beads as a gift. He carefully placed them in the delighted student's two hands, which he held with one of his own. Then in an instant the master raised his other hand and fiercely smacked the student across the face, shouting as he did so, "Put her down."

Then the master bowed and walked away. All of us standing there were in shock. But we all soon noticed that the senior student was dramatically changed by this blow. He let go and moved on with his life.

With a strength of heart we can respond to the full range of human emotions, unafraid of feelings, neither identified with nor embattled by them. When we accept the feelings as impermanent and impersonal forces, we can be free to honor them without being shut down or frightened or caught by them. Wilhelm Reich once pointed out to a patient who was trying hard not to feel, "You have a mask." The woman replied, "But Dr. Reich, you have a mask too." He answered, "Yes, that is true, but the mask hasn't *me!*"

Morrie Schwartz, who taught social psychology at Brandeis, was the subject of the best-selling book *Tuesdays with Morrie,* his final teachings to his friend Mitch Albom before death. In the midst of the agony of Lou Gehrig's disease, he told his last student:

> "What I'm doing now," he continued, his eyes still closed, "is detaching myself from the experience."
>
> Detaching yourself?
>
> "Yes, detaching myself.... You know what the Buddhists say? 'Don't cling to things, because everything is impermanent.'"
>
> But wait, I said. Aren't you always talking about experiencing life? All the good emotions, all the bad ones? How can you do that if you're detached?
>
> "Detachment doesn't mean you don't let the experience penetrate you. On the contrary, you let it penetrate you fully. That's how you are able to leave it."
>
> I'm lost.

"Take any emotion—love for a woman, or grief for a loved one, or what I'm going through, fear and pain from a deadly illness. If you hold back on the emotions—if you don't allow yourself to go all the way through them—you can never get to be detached, you're too busy being afraid. You're afraid of the pain, you're afraid of the grief. You're afraid of the vulnerability that loving entails.

"But by throwing yourself into these emotions, by allowing yourself to dive in, all the way, over your head even, you experience them fully and completely. You know what pain is. You know what love is. You know what grief is. And only then can you say, 'Alright, I have experienced that emotion. I recognize that emotion. Now I'm free to detach from that emotion for a moment'. . . .

"I know you think this is just about dying, but it's like I keep telling you. When you learn how to die, you learn how to live."

Ordinary Perfection

In mature spirituality we have to find perfection in nonperfection. The Zen founder Seng-Tsan teaches that enlightenment dawns only when we are "without anxiety about nonperfection." We meet the world with our heart as it is, unafraid of its beauty and its blemishes. We find trust in the body, the emotions, in life itself as it unfolds. Our struggle to become someone different, to grasp after an imagined happiness drops away. As the Tibetan sage Gendun Rinpoche puts it:

Only our own searching for happiness prevents us from seeing it. It is like a vivid rainbow which you pursue without ever catching it, or a dog chasing its own tail. Although peace and happiness do not exist as an actual thing or place, they are always available, and accompany you every instant.

205

Waiting to grasp the ungraspable, you exhaust yourself in vain. As soon as you open and relax this tight fist of grasping, infinite space is there—open, inviting, and comfortable.

Make use of this spaciousness, this freedom and natural ease. Don't search any further. Don't get into the tangled jungle looking for the great enlightened elephant who is already resting quietly at home in front of your own hearth.

Robert Fulghum, the author of *All I Really Need to Know I Learned in Kindergarten,* describes coming to the end of a difficult practice period in the 1960s at a famous Rinzai temple in Kyoto. He had a last interview with the abbot, Zen Master Kohara Roshi. Instead of focusing only on the meditation or koan practice, the master emphasized that there was nothing to become. Then he spoke about his own life, about the stress involved in running such a large old temple, about the poor quality of the young priests, about his difficulties in fund-raising and "dealing with my wife and children, who are not"—he smiled—"as 'holy' as I am." He went on, "Sometimes I would like to get a little place in Hawaii and just play golf." He smiled again.

"It was this way before I was 'enlightened,' you know. And now it is the same after enlightenment." After a suitable pause for Fulghum to digest this wisdom, the master bade him to go home, where, according to the author, he had been "a thirsty man looking for a drink and all the while standing knee-deep in a flowing stream."

Without the understanding of ordinary perfection, spirituality can put us at odds with our life. The images we have been taught about perfection can be destructive to us. It is like the Eskimo hunter who asked the missionary, "If I did not know about God and sin, would I still go to hell?" "No," said the priest, "not if you did not know." "Then why," asked the Eskimo earnestly, "did you tell me?"

We become stuck like Edward Espe Brown trying to bake Pillsbury biscuits, trying to "look good" instead of valuing our own biscuits, awakening to our own life.

One thirty-year practitioner of Tibetan Buddhism notes:

With all my years of spiritual practice, there was some way I didn't know myself. I tried so often to meet the expectations of others. Who I was had become buried, invisible. We had a very social family. Everything outside was important. I was trained as a child to be socially skilled. This is how I approached spiritual life, trying to become someone special, to do it right. I took on all the legwork as the hostess, caregiver, and benefactor for the Western tours of my lamas, and arranged countless retreats and fund-raising events for over ten years. I invited everyone to stay with me. It was a busy and exciting time. Although I was connecting with the Tibetan spiritual richness, I gradually realized I was living someone else's life. Then there came a growing sadness and disenchantment, not with the Tibetans but with myself. Even though I felt I needed to help, I got sick. Then I started going off to meditate for longer and longer periods. At first I felt guilty, but I loved the solitude. I discovered I am more naturally introverted and artistic than I knew.

Then after a trip I took to Asia, I came home and found myself longing for an ordinary life. I started saying no to everything. I simply couldn't do it anymore. I moved out to the country and lived quietly, caring for my animals and my garden, playing the piano. Now I silently sponsor two monasteries instead of running around trying to be special. Nurturing the earth in a simple way is what comes out of me naturally. I didn't know who I was.

Ordinary perfection is being true to ourselves, to the way things are. Do we go into the garden wishing that the pansies were taller than the daffodils, or thinking that the roses would be fine if only they didn't have thorns? Do we go into a kindergarten and wish that the children would fit into some model of perfection we hold, or can we see that variety makes the beauty of gardens and humans, that our spiritual task is not to make perfection but to awaken to the perfection around us.

As one senior lama has said:

Perfection must be around here somewhere. Where is it? Is it the next experience or the one after that? My true prac-tice is patience, not wanting anything special or unusual to happen. As soon as I see striving and expecting, I know I've lost the great perfection.

The hardest thing I still have to pass through is the real-ization that there is no final perfect condition to rely on. It is all fundamentally insecure, changing. You don't learn this quickly—you have to let go into this ordinary perfection again and again.

There is a modesty in this ordinary human perfection. We need to acknowledge both our gifts and our foibles, whoever we are. Who among us has not struggled with his or her own human-ity? Instead of clinging to an inflated, superhuman view of per-fection, we learn to allow ourselves the space of kindness. There is beauty in the ordinary. We invite the heart to sit on the front porch and experience from a place of rest the inevitable comings and goings of emotions and events, the struggles and successes of the world.

One Sufi master expresses it this way:

My life is complicated and still I suffer a lot, but it doesn't mean anything. It is ephemeral, just a part of living. I also feel the suffering of the world very deeply. I do what I can. Yet it is also very clear that things are as they are, and to have any helpful impact my actions must come from the heart of peace. This is my goal: to show the peace in the midst of it all.

Beyond Praise and Blame

The Tao teaches that when we make good, we also make bad; when we make right, we also make wrong. Instead of judging, we might let "the weary heart rest." This is the freedom of the Tao.

> Do you want to improve the world?
> I don't think it can be done.
>
> If you tamper with it, you will ruin it.
> If you treat it like an object, you'll lose it.
>
> The master sees things as they are,
> without trying to control them.
> She lets them go their own way
> and resides at the center of the circle.
>
> (tr. Stephen Mitchell)

Within the mind of ordinary perfection, praise and blame, success and failure, pride and self-judgment are recognized as impostors, secondhand opinions about our experience. A tremendous relief arises when we finally step beyond praise and blame. In the resulting liberation of heart and action, many things become possible.

Here is one example of such a liberation. In parts of India where there is a scarcity of doctors, villages sometimes pool their money in order to send their youth to college and medical schools, to later return as healers to the community. In one poor mountain town there is a sign outside a doctor's office which reads: "Dr. V. S. Krishna, M.D. Failed, Calcutta Medical College." This meant that Dr. Krishna had attended medical school in Calcutta, but he had not passed his exams. Nevertheless he had returned home and opened an office, telling the truth about his lack of a degree and offering whatever medical knowledge he had gained. His office was a busy one.

Perhaps all of us are like Dr. Krishna—our human life

includes both considerable successes and failures. If we allow ourselves to be caught up by feelings of either shame or pride, we will
limit the scope of what we might do, who we might be.

Most spiritual teachers have found that becoming independent of praise and blame is a long process. We begin with only
moments. Then with practice we can gradually extend to hours
and days of being free from the judgment of others or ourselves.
We learn to let judgment rise and fall without getting caught in it.
We see how much bigger and more amazing life is than we had
believed. There comes a rest, a freedom when we experience the
dance of life without critical thoughts of how it should look. It's
like the man who was mailed this note by his furniture company:

Dear Mr. Jones:

What would your neighbors think if we had to send a truck to
your house to repossess the furniture that you still have not
finished paying for?

They got the following reply:

Dear Sirs:

I have discussed the matter with my neighbors to find out what
they would think. They all think it would be a dirty trick of a
mean company they would not want to patronize again either.

Sincerely yours,

Mr. Jones.

To live outside of praise and blame does not mean we will not
make mistakes. At seventy-six, Ruth Denison is one of the most
respected teachers of insight meditation in the West. In recent
years her husband, a lifelong dharma student, developed
Alzheimer's, to the extent that he would wander out of the house
not knowing where he was. For months Ruth regularly drove four
hours back and forth from her retreat center to her home, staying

up all hours to care for him. One day he left the stove unattended and part of the house burned.

During this period she was invited to Portland, Oregon, to give a lecture and lead a retreat. Arriving exhausted, she entered the room of 150 students gathered for the teachings. She began by encouraging them to feel their breath and body, to know directly their present experience. She talked about being mindful of what is going on. Then she told the story of her husband's Alzheimer's and the recent fire.

She continued to teach about awareness. Then she said, "Did I tell you about my husband and the fire?" and proceeded to tell the story all over again. She spoke further about attention and after some time said, "Oh, I have to tell you about my husband and the fire we had," and began for a third time to tell the story. Many in the room became frightened and upset for this woman, who, it appeared, was beginning to show signs of Alzheimer's as well.

Several people stood up to leave. Before they reached the door Ruth called out, "Wait! You meditation students there, where do you think you're going? I want you to look at your expectations. What were you expecting when you came?" Some moments passed as they stood, reflecting. Then she continued, "Tonight you have a chance to observe something special. You have a chance to see a senior dharma teacher fail. I don't even know what I have just said." They sat back down, and Ruth continued to teach: "Can you be awake to whatever is happening? That is your practice."

Fortunately Ruth's memory loss was only for that night and only due to exhaustion. As soon as she got some rest, her memory and energy came back full force. But that evening she had demonstrated true presence—the ability to stay with anything, even her own disorientation, and allow it to be held in awareness and compassion.

Becoming Eccentric

When the emotions are free and the heart can express itself without concern for the opinions of others, that freedom extends to every aspect of our character. If you were to meet Ruth Denison you might see her as an eccentric old woman. When we look honestly at the community of spiritual teachers, we find them in general to be an eccentric lot. Some are strangely hermitlike, some publicly flamboyant. Some are part of the spiritual jet set, the Dharma glitterati, while others are Dharma nerds. Some are slow and mindful, others passionate and excitable. There is no proper single model. Eccentricity means uniqueness, finding the freedom to be utterly one's own person. Even if outwardly we do not appear different, inwardly there is the fearless ability to be wholly the embodiment of yourself.

The painter Georges Braque once exhorted those around him, "It's up to us to be real strong eccentrics, and not to waver." One Zen master called this the culmination of Zen training, its fruition: "To be faithful to yourself and to life."

On one hand we center ourselves in Zen so that we are not lost in the power of greed, hatred, and ignorance. This is a purifying process of letting go until we let go fully. But then we need to return and be authentic, absolutely true to our own life.

Ajahn Sumedho, the Western monk who has established half a dozen monasteries in Thailand and the West, recalls his first term as an abbot.

I didn't really know what I was doing, nor how I was supposed to act. So I tried to be just like my teacher, and because I admired him so much, I tried to run the monastery in just the way he did. But it didn't work; it was a disaster because I'm not him. And then I realized that what people

*admired in him was that he was just himself. So I discov-
ered that's what I had to do, be myself.*

Because spiritual teachers are often charismatic and traditions are compelling, in the beginning spirituality can involve a lot
of imitation. This is natural for a time. But it can become rigid. If
we think "spiritual" means to be quiet and unruffled, we might
imitate this with blandness. On the other hand, if the master is
licentious and drunken, we can find communities of alcoholics,
disciples trying to show their wildness in exactly the same way.
These all become forms of spiritual materialism.

Unfortunately, the spiritual world can become as confining
and narrow-minded as the rest of our culture; it seems that almost
every religious or spiritual community has its unconscious "group
think," its "in-group" behavior. Sister Claire, an old Catholic nun,
sadly described how during her first years as a nun, "It wasn't my
inner life that mattered at all to the church, it was only my decorum and belief." And in a Hindu community where everyone
believed they had found the "best" way, a student who finally left
commented, "We were trying so hard to be Hindus we forgot to
be ourselves." As e. e. cummings put it, "To be nobody but yourself in a world which is doing its best to make you everybody else,
means to fight the hardest human battle ever and to never stop
fighting."

While emotional, physical, and mental freedom is not imita-
tive, it is also not its opposite, the acting out of unconscious needs
and fears. Like Ram Dass, who became the connoisseur of his
neuroses, we come to know ourselves as we are, but without indulgence or self-pity. When we are truly aware of our feelings while
not being bound by their energies, we can choose; no matter what
the circumstances, we are free to follow our wisdom. The person
who has tasted real liberation embraces the richness of life as a
whole.

We find this broad perspective in the wisest of human
tales, from the Ramayana to Shakespeare, from the Jataka Tales

to the Bible. There is a joy in this freedom like no other. Trudy Dixon, who edited *Zen Mind, Beginner's Mind,* offered this characterization of the freedom her teacher Suzuki Roshi represented:

> The qualities of his life are extraordinary—buoyancy, vigor, straightforwardness, simplicity, humility, serenity, joyousness, uncanny perspicacity . . . but in the end it is not the extraordinariness of the teacher which perplexes, intrigues, and deepens the student, it is the teacher's utter ordinariness. Because he is just himself, he is a mirror for his students. . . . In his presence we see our original face, and the extraordinariness we see is only our own true nature.

Happiness of Being

Japan's most beloved Zen poet, Ryokan, was known for being unpretentious and wise. Like St. Francis, he was a lover of simple things, of children and nature. In his poems he writes openly of his tears and loneliness during long winter nights, of his heart leaping with spring blossoms, of his losses and regrets and of the deep trust he has learned. His emotions flow freely, like the seasons. When people ask him about enlightenment, he offers them tea. When he goes to the village for alms food and to offer teachings, he usually ends up playing with the children. His happiness lies in being at peace with himself.

> Today's begging is finished: at the crossroads
> I wander by the side of the Buddhist Shrine
> Talking with some children.
> Last year, a foolish monk.
> This year, no change!
> (tr. John Stevens)

The emotional wisdom of the heart is simple. When we accept our human feelings, a remarkable transformation occurs. Tenderness and wisdom arise naturally and spontaneously. Where we once sought strength over others, now our strength becomes our own; where we once sought to defend ourselves, we laugh. Allowing room for our dependency and needs brings forth a hidden wholeness. Happiness and love come naturally in letting go of fear. They bubble up like spring water, they spread throughout our being.

Ajahn Jumnien, one of my teachers from the jungles of the Malay Peninsula, brings this spirit when he comes to teach in America. An orange-robed ball of vitality, with endless good humor and a shining heart, he speaks only a few words of English. When he is without a translator his teachings are very simple. "Empty, empty!" he will say. "Happy, happy!" He opens his arms as if embracing all the world and says again, "Empty, empty! Happy, happy!" He knows all things arise and vanish like a dream, they change, they cannot be possessed. Accepting this truth, he moves through the world gracefully and is happy.

One spiritual teacher tells the story of an African-American woman who participated in her yearlong training group. This woman had experienced a lifetime of trauma, poverty, abuse, the death of a parent, racism, illness, a divorce from a painful marriage, and single-parenting two children. These difficulties poured out of her soul in the course of the group, how she had struggled for years to educate herself, to fight for justice, to gradually find her way. The others in the group told their stories of difficulties as well, the pain and the challenges, the many ways they had struggled. Finally at the last meeting this woman announced, "After all I've been through, all the troubles I've lived through, I am going to do something really radical. I am going to be happy."

When we understand that freedom of the heart is a possibility for us too, we can awaken to our own happiness wherever we are.

14

HONORING FAMILY KARMA

A prophet is never heeded in his own country, and in his own home.
JESUS IN THE GOSPEL OF MATTHEW

*No matter how many communes and communities they make,
the family will always come back.*
MARGARET MEAD

It is one thing to offer a multitude of prayers for the sick and the poor, or to undertake loving kindness and compassion meditations for thousands of sentient beings everywhere. It is another to bring these same practices to our own family and our closest community.

Even the Buddha and Jesus encountered difficulties when they went back home after starting to preach. Jesus' ministry was dismissed without respect by His family. Then, when His mother and brothers came to the house where He was preaching, Jesus refused to let them in, pointing to His disciples and saying, "These are my true mother and brothers, those who do the will of God."

Similarly, when the Buddha returned home after his enlightenment, he was rebuked by his father for being an unseemly beggar. His father and stepmother demanded that he stop being a monk, change his clothes, and return to his princely duties. When the Buddha tried to teach his family, they dismissed his understanding as worthless. He had to perform a miracle—floating in the air while spouting both fire and water—to convince them that he had learned anything of value.

Like Jesus, Zen Master Basho warns: "You can't teach the truth in your native town. They only know you by your childhood names." As it happens, this may be the best reason to go home. Where better to fulfill a genuine practice of the heart, the mandala of the whole, than with one's family and neighbors? Because they see us unclouded by spiritual ideals, by image or reputation, they become the true testing ground of our practice. My daughter Caroline has remarked to me more than once when I have been angry or careless, eaten sloppily, or become upset, "Daaad, I thought you teach mindfulness!" or "Daaad, look what you're doing. What kind of a meditation teacher are you?" Sometimes when I'm having a hard time, she simply says, "Dad, I think it's time for you to go meditate."

As one Zen master puts it,

The role of a spiritual teacher can imprison us in the very task of enlightened helper: Bringing wisdom and compassion to others, we can lose our common human relations. Most of the people we know are in the role of students. We run the risk of isolation, of becoming a kind of sacred monster, without the counterweight of ordinary human connection—friends, family, and real relationships. Family provides this best of all.

One devotee laughingly stated of her husband, a well-known Hindu teacher, "My husband came home from his last visit in India in an amazing state. He was enlightened for six months, until he spent time with his mother." Another respected teacher of Raja Yoga used to emphasize what her guru taught her: "You are not the body, you are not the mind." She taught these truths and wrote about them for many years. As she aged, she determined not to be dependent on anyone. After having a series of strokes, she called her children together, reminded them, "I am not the body," and with their help took a large dose of morphine to end her life. Days later she awoke from a coma in the hospital, and when she returned home her family was understandably in great disarray. Not only had participating in the attempted suicide been a terribly hard trial, but the experience had brought up other long-held resentments. Her teaching of "You are not the body and mind" had made her a poor mother in many ways over the years. She spent her last year making amends and learning to tend to her family, and allowing them to tend her.

Family pain is common throughout our culture, and spiritual communities often draw those with a painful family history. Spiritual seekers may come for release, to heal, or to find a way to transcend the troubles they carry within. This is not true of the students alone. Most Western spiritual leaders, meditation teachers, monks, nuns, and clergy also carry deep family wounds. They too may have initially hoped that spiritual detachment and peace would release them from dealing with family pain.

But one Chinese Chan master cautions:

Don't confuse nonattachment and freedom with running away. Your idea of leaving your family and children to renounce the world is like running from your shadow. This is false emptiness. There is nowhere you can go that is any more or less empty than your own house. Enlightenment has been here from the start.

We cannot escape the fact of our family background and the wounds it inflicts. Nor can we impose our spiritual ideals on our family. One young woman who had become very involved in Buddhist practice returned to her parents' home. She struggled with their Christian Fundamentalism for a time, until she sorted things out. Then she sent a letter back to the monastery stating, "My parents hate me when I'm a Buddhist, but they love me when

I'm a Buddha." This is our task: to awaken the Buddha in facing our family karma.

When my father was dying of congestive heart failure, I went to be with him in the I.C.U. of the University of Pennsylvania Medical School. Because he was a biophysicist and had taught in medical schools, he was keenly aware of all the equipment monitoring his heart. He was terrified of dying, and especially of dying in his sleep without the nurses knowing it, so he dared not let himself sleep. He would fall asleep for three minutes, then startle awake and anxiously turn to the monitor to see if his heart was still working. This went on night after night.

Though brilliant, my father had also been violent-tempered and physically abusive. For everyone around him, he was a paranoid and difficult man. Now, without sleep for days, he was even more out of control. Still, over the years I had made my peace with him, and I loved him.

I sat with him and we talked. As he was very anxious and distracted, I tried to teach him meditation. We practiced breath awareness for calmness and tried a loving kindness meditation, with his grandchildren as the focus. It was useless. Fifteen minutes of practicing meditation could not undo seventy-five years of practicing paranoia. When I asked what he thought happens when you die, he answered, "Nothing." As a scientist he didn't believe in anything beyond the physical: Death was the end. I noted that the majority of the world believes in life after death, which is also validated by near-death research. I told him about my own out-of-body and past life experiences and even explained the stages of dying and what he might possibly experience. He was doubtful. "Just wait, you'll be surprised," I said. "And," I added, "if it happens, remember I told you so." He laughed.

Later in the evening most visitors had gone and I told my father I needed to sleep. "Don't go!" he pleaded. I sat with him for another hour as he repeatedly drifted into sleep and startled fearfully awake. "I can't sleep. Please, please don't go." I was happy to comply; I've learned to sit. Eleven, twelve, one, two A.M., I sat with him over a number of nights. There wasn't much to say. I held his hand. He was frightened. He didn't want to know about meditation. He didn't even want to talk. What mattered was that I sat there, not being afraid, not rejecting his fear and his pain, simply holding his hand. He died after several more days. I was grateful to have been able to sit with him during this extraordinary time.

Perhaps this is the best we can do: to help when we can; to witness each other with kindness; to offer our presence; to show the trust we have in life. Spiritual life is not about knowing much, but about loving much.

Most of us in spiritual life have to go through a large measure of family healing. To finally be able to sit at ease with my father was the result of many years of conscious work. My family pain had been covered over in my early monastic meditation, while I focused on being empty, peaceful, and wise. But it was there underneath, waiting, unconsciously influencing my whole way of being, and when I returned to family and to intimate relationships, the struggles all came back. It may well be that even if I had stayed in ascetic practice, they would have eventually returned.

To find myself still struggling with my emotions was hard. I needed the assistance of both meditation and therapy before I could acknowledge the deepest levels of fear, anger, judgment, and grief I carried. The therapist was essential as a compassionate witness, another being to help me face the images and fears I carried in my body, everything that I had not been able to face alone. I saw how much the old patterns had reinforced my small sense of self. In the face of pain in our family, my brothers and I had each become regularly depressed or angry, fearful, cynical, needy, or cautious. These deep wounds remain part of each of us to this day, but by opening to them, we began to lessen their power.

In the mandala of wholeness, our difficulties, including these generational problems, are carried until the pain of the past can be transformed. In his death poem Lama Chogyam Trungpa wrote about the value of the teachings he had offered to his students, and then reminded them, "I will be haunting you." Our family's patterns can likewise remain to haunt us even after years of spiritual practice. We may carry dependency, fear, self-criticism, unworthiness, anger, or depression as a family legacy. These early wounds need healing, whether in a therapeutic relationship or through the growing wisdom of our spiritual path. We need to find the freedom of our own spirit and discover that our family history is not who we are.

One Catholic nun told me:

There was plenty of pain and abuse in my family's past. Most of the biggest changes in my spiritual life came around shame. I grew up in an alcoholic family, from at least my grandfather on down, and the sense we had of ourselves was shame-based. When it arises strongly enough, none of my practices and prayers work; I just don't feel good about anything. I'll be praying and a voice comes: "You are a disgrace compared to what you should be. You are not using your gifts; you are not enough." Never enough! I used to be so caught and feel so terrible. But with good therapy and a great deal of inner work I've come to understand it. Now I see it as family cycles of shame that just arise. I know it for what it is. "Oh, it's another cycle of shame." I can even laugh at it now. This insight has meant more to healing my heart than years of struggling to be holy.

Tolerance Gives Birth to Intimacy

Traditional teachings focus so often on love and its transformative spirit that we can overlook a more basic and fundamental power, the tolerant heart.

After the ecstasy of spiritual awakening there is the day-to-day fulfillment in the laundry room of our sustained practice. One natural outcome of an awakening experience that sustains us during this time is an increase in our spirit of tolerance, in accepting what is. In this renewed and capacious tolerance, the heart's harmony can be found. Human differences are enormous: our rhythms, what our bodies like, our aesthetic sense, our emotions, our fears, the way we move and speak and love and rest. There are vast differences of race, culture, class, and values. Without tolerance there is no ground for relationship, no possibility of intimacy. Without tolerance, family life can be unbearable. Temperament and personality all differ dramatically. Without tolerance we would have a society of perpetual conflict, a world of sectarianism and tribalism, of warfare and genocide.

We don't have to like, let alone love those we tolerate. The truth is that even spiritual teachers do not always like one another; nor do they necessarily get along. Many respected Zen masters and swamis, ajahns and sheikhs, lamas and rabbis have powerful disagreements. Some have a distaste for one another's teaching or style. Yet the wise among them embody a genuine tolerance, knowing that another person's reasons may be invisible to us, that another person's way is as worthy of respect as our own.

Tolerance does not mean acceptance of what is harmful. Just as detachment and numbing can be spiritually misused to hide from our feelings, so tolerance can be misused if we avoid seeing the truth or fail to take a necessary stand. Tolerance does not mean turning a blind eye to abuse. To prevent further suffering, we may need to respond with great strength. But when our heart is connected with our actions, even this strength can be combined with compassion and understanding.

I saw this in the way Ajahn Chah handled the abbot of a branch monastery, a man named Ajahn Som who had been a street tough and petty thug before he ordained. Even as abbot he had a reputation of being harsh and difficult, and monks who returned from his temple often complained about him. One day I demanded of Ajahn Chah why someone like him was allowed to remain as an abbot. Ajahn Chah paused thoughtfully and said: Although he was a difficult fellow, Ajahn Som had founded this cave monastery through years of labor with his own hands in a remote, pristine forest. His spiritual dedication was slowly growing. It's true he might never be a picture-book monk, but if Ajahn

Chah were to take away his monastery, he would probably go back out on the street. Is that what I was recommending?

We so easily become judgmental of one another. Sometimes the closer we are to a person, the stronger our judgment and frustration can become. That is why family is one of the final frontiers of spiritual development.

One former Hindu swami told me:

After my years of yoga in India I came back to teach and marry and later I became head of a temple. My samadhi experiences showed me the bliss of all things. Over time I got busy and I started to lose it, to tell you the truth. I tried to meditate more to get it back. We had conflict in the temple. And in my marriage we fought, sometimes quite terribly. Some days I wondered if I should ever have tried to practice in this worldly life. Even meditation was not giving me much help.

One day I was visiting my family and taking care of my young nephew. It was a hard day for the swami and the three-year-old. We messed up the house. He threw a tantrum. Finally I took him in my arms and just held him. I sang Sanskrit melodies. And I realized that's all the world wants, to be held in spite of it all. The bliss and samadhi came back as soon as I opened my heart.

The birth of tolerance and acceptance is most truly won close to home. In my own home my wife and I are temperamental opposites, and we each come from difficult family backgrounds. She is quiet, an artist and writer, with a deep need for solitude, stillness, and interior life. I, though a meditator, am more extroverted, with a huge network of dharma friends, colleagues, and community members.

In our first years I dreamed about getting a large house in the country with lots of rooms for visiting friends. She, of course, had something smaller in mind. When I protested, she asked, "Didn't you just spend ten years living in a meditation center in the country, with a big library and kitchen? If that's what you want, why don't you just go back to your retreat center?"

With a lot of care and some good therapy, we made it through our stormy beginnings, got married, had a beautiful child. Still, some of our differences continued. One day we were walking through a Zen center garden with our baby daughter. Liana had recently given me Jean Shinoda Bolen's *Goddesses in Every Woman* after reading it herself so that we could talk about the different aspects of feminine energy and the parenting of a girl. I told her I enjoyed it, especially the chapters that described the strength of Artemis women and the grace and beauty of Aphrodite. Then I added that there was one goddess I didn't particularly connect with, Hestia, who has no temple. She is the goddess of hearth and home, ever-present but invisible.

When I said that, Liana looked at me stunned, threw the book on the ground, and broke into tears. "That's me. That goddess describes my life! I knew you never really loved me. I knew it." And she turned and strode away.

It took a few moments to feel the force of her words, to collect myself and turn back to her. Shocked by the truth in what she said, and by a flood of realizations, I could only reply, "You know, my dear, I'm sorry to say you're right. I do love you, but without knowing it, somehow I was still hoping that you would be different." For so long I had kept an unconscious hope, an idea of how she would change. And, of course, she felt it. It was only after being forced to see her reality instead of my own desires that I grew to love her for who she is. Together we created a home for Hestia. Now I go out to work with big groups and return home to a quiet and simple family life. I have come to be nourished and protected by my family and to love it as it is, and praise my wife's wisdom every day.

Family is a mirror. In our spouses, our lovers, our parents and children we find our needs and hopes and fears writ large. Intimate relations reach in and touch our history without anesthesia. The wounds we carry, the longings we have to be nourished are right on the table. They need to be respected.

That is why even in our own families, to say that we love one another underneath it all is not enough. We also need to be tolerant and respectful of one another. We extend the same large-hearted spirit to the members of our family that we practice in prayer or in the nonjudging awareness of our inner states.

A Catholic sister recalls how her years of prayer led her to this:

It has come to one main thing: a willingness to have an ongoing relationship with all good and evil, to allow myself to suffer consciously, to be the tolerant ground that holds the tears of the world, those far and those close around me. My spirituality does not pit itself against anger or passion or conflict anymore. That is garbage. Those teachings have done more harm than good. In the end there comes a realization of no blame. I vow nonviolence to everything. Do not torment, do not escalate pain in myself or outside myself—this has become one of my greatest prayers.

Tolerance and blamelessness grow when we see the remarkable and strange qualities in each of the lives we touch. Every person is singular and unique, expressing his or her own nature—even those who are difficult are living the best they know how.

Respectful Parenting

Such honorable appreciation between adults is also the basis for wise child-rearing. Another word for this tolerance is "respect." This is found in the story of a seven-year-old boy who went out to dinner with his parents and their friends. The waitress took his order last. "What would you like?" she asked. "I'd like a hot dog and french fries," he answered. His mother quickly interjected, "He'll have the meat loaf, mashed potatoes, and carrots, with milk to drink." As the waitress walked away she asked, "Do you want ketchup or mustard on your hot dog?" The boy turned to the table smiling and announced, "Do you know what? She thinks I'm real!"

Our children love respect. Even little ones want respect for their needs and respect for their fears. Our lovers, our parents, our coworkers, the animals and trees around us blossom with our respect. Offering respect is the foundation of parenting as a spiritual practice. Without awareness and respect we simply repeat what was done to us, acting in ways conditioned by our own upbringing. Without respect we will continue whatever cycles of wounding, shame, unworthiness, stress, or abandonment existed in our own past.

Without a spiritual perspective, our heart's natural caring in parenting can be overpowered by the speed and materialism of modern life, by the pervasive values of the media, by the accepted norms of stress and violence. Without a respectful attention, we allow the media and modern pressures to hurry our children to grow, forgetting to protect their dependency and vulnerability. We forget to trust that children naturally become independent in their own sweet time. Without attention to our hearts we become like the generation of parents who followed popular experts in refusing to feed or pick up crying children, even though every wise instinct and cellular impulse in their body called for them to hold and comfort their child in pain. With respect we can offer our children protection and wholehearted nurturance, while at the same time setting appropriate limits on behavior. Our spiritual teaching will be conveyed not just in our words but in the integrity of our daily life, how we demonstrate the deepest values of our heart.

It is never too late to offer this respect. When we become adults we can carry this respect back to our family. A woman who had trained as a Buddhist nun in the monasteries of Thailand and Burma spoke to me of her difficulties upon returning to visit her home. Her family lived in Detroit, in a working-class neighborhood. She had let go of much of the pain in her family's past, but even now they did not understand or accept her as a shaven-headed nun. And however hard she tried to teach them about the dharma, it only led to conflict and more frustration. The family evenings were usually given to drinking beer and watching TV. After each disagreeable weeklong visit home, she fled. I had a few suggestions for her. "Why don't you try going to your parents without your robes, and no teaching. Just be there as a family member and love them as they are. Maybe sit with them and sip a beer and watch the games on TV. Oh yes, and don't stay too long— three days at the most." So she tried it. Next time I saw her she was smiling. It worked.

One Sufi master says:

Being with family and close friends is different from all my other relationships. It's certainly not the same as holding the teacher role. With my family I just have to be, to let love and openness have its effect. I'm not ahead or in charge. I'm trying to accept them, to be who I am and be tolerant of their nature. There is in all this also an undeniable passion and Eros, a built-in charge between children, parents, and siblings, whether positive or negative. Even the conflicts become larger because of the depth at which we touch one another. What I try to do is tap into that place of the heart's connection, the essence beneath the story.

Thomas Merton described this kind of tolerance for others as learning to see "the secret beauty of their hearts" beneath all our expectations in regard to them. When we see the secret beauty of others' hearts, we connect from our true nature; we see the sacred spark that illuminates our life as well.

You Will Be Tested

In the commandments of the great Middle Eastern religions, Jewish, Christian, and Islamic, it is taught that "you must honor your mother and father." In Indian and Chinese traditions these teachings can be even stronger. "If you were to carry your parents on your back," says one text, "you could hardly repay them for giving you life." Whatever your tradition, this obligation remains, and its fulfillment is not necessarily simple.

Aging parents, unhappy teens, conflicts with siblings, money problems, family illness, addictions—all are part of accepting family life as an ongoing practice. These difficulties become even more burdensome in a society like ours, without much community, where aged people are shunted to old-age homes and where teens, isolated from their elders, often seek initiation in destructive ways. Underneath all these problems is the essential human need to be connected. Someone once said, "It is better to be wanted by the police than not wanted at all." For better or worse, family is the original source of this connection, offering both love and responsibility.

Family responsibilities never end. Many of us will find ourselves caring for parents through the slow decline of Alzheimer's, cancer, or stroke. Many others will be involved with difficult teens or family depression, or tending to marital conflicts or the divorces of our siblings, our children, ourselves. The sacrifices of a family are like those of any demanding monastery, offering exactly the same training in renunciation, patience, steadiness, and generosity.

Thus, when one middle-aged monk told me that monks had to self-discipline and sacrifice while a layman's life was by nature one of indulgence, I laughed. He went on, "You can eat when you want, dress as you choose, party, enjoy a succession of lovers, live a carefree life." I wondered whose lay life he was describing. Further conversation revealed that he had ordained at age twenty-one, so his vision of lay life was left over from his own teenage years. He didn't understand that marriage, work, parenting, citizenship are their own forms of discipline.

Zen teacher, poet, and father Gary Snyder writes:

All of us are apprenticed with the same teacher—reality. . . . It is as hard to get the children herded into the car pool and down the road to the bus as it is to chant sutras in the Buddha-hall on a cold morning. One is not better than the other; each can be quite boring; and they both have the virtuous quality of repetition. Repetition and its good results make the very activities of our life into the path.

The demands of family life call on our hearts and test our strength like almost nothing else. One teacher told me:

As a young Catholic I was inspired by the saints. I had always wanted to do things like work with Mother Teresa in India, but most of my life has not been so glamorous. After college I became a teacher in an elementary school. And then my mother had a stroke and I had to drop out of teaching and help her for two years: bathe her, care for her bedsores, cook, pay the bills, run the house. At times I wanted to complete these responsibilities and get back to my spiritual life. Then one morning it dawned on me—I was doing the work of Mother Teresa, and I was doing it in my own home.

At home or in the temple, it is the same. In one ancient account the Buddha found one of his monks sick and uncared-for because the other monks were busy with their meditations. The Buddha himself washed and tended the monk and then called the entire community membership together to castigate and instruct them. "If you do not care for each other as family, who else will do so? Monks, those who would attend to the Buddha, let them attend to the sick." Five hundred years later, Jesus said to His disciples, "In truth I tell you, insofar as you did this to one of the least of these brothers of mine, you did it to me." This is the love that knows we are one family, and all later loves in our lives will stem from this.

Robert Johnson, the Jungian analyst and author, tells a story about first going to India some years ago. Though he was warned about the chaos, the dirt, and the poverty, he said, "No one prepared me for the immense deep happiness of almost everyone in India." He described how in India one's sense of reality is expanded to include more of life, the suffering and the sublime coexisting together. For along with encountering enormous difficulties he was embraced by the immediate friendship of the Indian community as well. His friends showed him a new sense of what familial love can become.

If you want to make friends with an Indian, you edge up just beside him—this is always with somebody of your own sex; you never do it cross-sexually—and wait. If he consents to something with you, he won't go anywhere. He will just stand there, and after what seems like a terribly long period of time, somebody says something or somebody does something, and then you are probably friends for as long as the two of you wish or intend, likely for life.

In this way, in India I ended up with friends amazingly quickly. Then I got sick. I was in an Indian hospital—a nightmare. They explained to me it was a truly modern, Westernized hospital. They had one thermometer, which all of us patients had in succession, one after the other. I objected, and they said, "It's all right, because we rinse it off under the tap." Somehow we survived.

The point of the story was that one Indian friend who had taken me on as a blood brother—for what reason I'll never know, it's futile to ask—came and slept under my bed at night. He said, "I'm not going to have you there alone," so he or somebody assigned by him slept under my hospital bed every night. Now, if I go to the hospital in America I can't get anybody to sleep under my bed; it's just not possible. One day when my fever was 104, and I was slightly out of my head, Amba Shankar—that was his name—stood at the foot of my bed and told me the story of Baba.

Baba had a friend, and the friend was ill. It looked as if Baba's friend would die. So Baba came to him and said,

"I wish to die for you, and you have only to say the word and I will go and die so that you may live. This is my wish, this is my friendship, this is how it is." The friend agreed, so Baba went away and died and the friend lived.

Being told this story, which was like something out of *The Arabian Nights*, snapped me into focus, because Amba Shankar then said, "You say the word and I will go and die, and then you will be all right." I was speechless. I don't understand things like this. So I managed to say, "Amba, I don't think I'm that ill. Don't do anything rash now, please; I think we will both pull through." And as it happens, we did. But that man had offered me a priceless gift—his life.

When I heard Robert Johnson's story, it touched a longing to live again in such a connected way: to be held in the trust of the community and in the heart's friendship. Having lived in the old cultures of India and Asia, I knew the reality of this way, and how much of it has been lost in modern times.

But the essence of family connection cannot be lost. Do not doubt its power. It is this love of parents and children, brothers and sisters that brings the most amazing stories: the mother who miraculously lifts a car off her child's body, the disabled father who throws himself, wheelchair and all, into the swimming pool, to hang on to the side for hours in order to save his toddler son from drowning.

In Argentina the terrible military dictatorship of the 1970s tortured, killed, and "disappeared" tens of thousands of suspected opponents. Sebastian Rotella describes how desperate mothers began to protest in spite of the dangers, becoming famous as the Mothers of the Plaza de Mayo.

Twenty years ago the mothers went to the plaza in front of the presidential palace and confronted the bureaucracy of horror.

The mothers were fed up with futile visits to military

chaplains who wore army boots under their cassocks, and to the "complaint office" where the dictatorship denied inquiries about people whom for years it was systematically kidnapping, torturing, and killing.

When the women congregated at the plaza, police snapped at them to keep moving. So the fourteen mothers walked the plaza in slow circles. They kept coming back to protest, braving nightsticks, police dogs, and military spies who infiltrated the group and killed three leaders.

"They say the Mothers of the Plaza de Mayo were fearless," said Maria Adela Antokolez, now eighty-five, who moves with slow, tottering steps and enormous dignity, "but we were scared to death. We learned to walk with fear, to live with fear. We had an obligation to find our children."

The mothers still march every Thursday afternoon demanding justice. The ritual moves bystanders to tears and applause. The women are elderly and fragile now. They walk arm in arm, hunched beneath the white head scarves that have become an international symbol of the fight for human rights.

"We never found our children," Maria Adela said. "But in the plaza we went to school. We told our story fifty times. We cried together. It was our educational academy. The plaza saved us from the madhouse." At 3:25 the plaza would be as empty as a desert. And five minutes later the mothers would appear like plants growing out of the subway station, the side streets. The people would come up and ask, "Who are you? Teachers, pensioners? What are you protesting?" It spread by word of mouth. When Cortázar, our great writer, heard about it in Paris, he said, "The mothers are out, the military have already lost."

Stretching the Heart's Mercy

Facing the suffering in our family and community brings us a great task: to stay true to our deepest values and still remain open and vulnerable. Whatever hardens and closes our heart leaves us rigid, frightened, unresponsive. Through our grudges and fears we become increasingly territorial and defensive. How can we keep the heart open without losing our strength and our sense of justice?

To do this we must allow the heart to become strong in a new way. We turn toward the suffering of the world willingly, and let it stretch our compassion. In the inevitable pains, conflicts, and betrayal, we discover we can embrace the power of love. In the midst of difficulty, we can repeatedly stop and return to our heart, reconnect to our strength of compassion and our vulnerability.

One Sufi teacher says this of his prayer and meditation:

My main practice is stopping and listening to the heart. It's like a moment of Quaker silence. Even if I can't stand still, I stop inside, step out of the drama, recognize the pain, the busyness, and being lost. I breathe and return. With my family or students, I try to come back to my own heart before speaking, to hold or acknowledge what's needing attention in me. Then I include them in that space of heart. This makes a strong presence, a connection.

When times are tough and we can't do this alone, we may need another person to help us return to this truth. This is the basis for true spiritual friendship and fine therapy. One Zen master tells how he needed this in his first year of teaching. He had practiced for thirty years when he received formal transmission as a roshi. Months later he found himself becoming painfully lost and insecure, as he had been years earlier in his practice.

I went desperately to a senior Zen master in my lineage. I was afraid he would condemn my insecurity. Instead he took

233

me in and loved me and expressed total confidence in me.
He helped me hold my suffering and confusion with steadi-
ness and faith. My mind relaxed and my teaching was trans-
formed.

When we are confused or in pain, we often judge ourselves as
"not spiritual enough." But the awakened heart does not judge
anything—not our family or our love, nor our pain and confusion,
our passion or anger. "Terrible harm has been done by this misunderstanding," said one Catholic monk.

In mature spirituality we are willing to have a dialogue with
pain, with evil, to hold them in our prayers. In situations of
great pain, someone has to consciously suffer the impact, to
become the ground where the sorrows can be held and
reworked. These things can be carried with grace. But it
can't be faked. If you go to someone with 99 percent of good-
will and are still caught in 1 percent anger, all they feel is
the anger, and it pushes them from reconciliation. The heart
has to willingly hold the whole of suffering for it to be trans-
formed.

In Zen, holding the suffering sometimes takes the form of
"eating the blame." It is illustrated by the story of a cook who made
soup for the monks from a turtle offered by fishermen that morning. When the soup was ladled into the monks' bowls, the roshi
bellowed for the cook to come out. The turtle's head, which should
have been removed before serving, was floating in the master's
bowl. The cook bowed to the master, looked into the bowl, saw
the problem, and with a deft movement of chopsticks plucked the
turtle head out and ate it. Then he bowed to the master, the master bowed back, and the cook returned to the kitchen.

Eating the blame requires both strength and compassion. It is
like the divorcing parent who in the midst of messy litigation consciously gives away more than what is legally required so as to

spare his children the damage and suffering a protracted court battle would bring. "Even if it is unfair, I want this suffering to stop with me," said one father. "Let me sacrifice now so that it will not be passed on to my children."

The truth is that in spiritual life, our awareness of suffering actually increases over the years. We see and know more clearly the sorrows of the world. We can no longer hide from their occurrence. With this knowledge comes a deepening compassion.

No matter how extreme the circumstances, compassion is possible. Once on the train from Washington to Philadelphia, I found myself seated next to an African-American man who'd worked for the State Department in India but had quit to run a rehabilitation program for juvenile offenders in the District of Columbia. Most of the youths he worked with were gang members who had committed homicide.

One fourteen-year-old boy in his program had shot and killed an innocent teenager to prove himself to his gang. At the trial, the victim's mother sat impassively silent until the end, when the youth was convicted of the killing. After the verdict was announced, she stood up slowly and stared directly at him and stated, "I'm going to kill you." Then the youth was taken away to serve several years in the juvenile facility.

After the first half year the mother of the slain child went to visit his killer. He had been living on the streets before the killing, and she was the only visitor he'd had. For a time they talked, and when she left she gave him some money for cigarettes. Then she started step by step to visit him more regularly, bringing food and small gifts. Near the end of his three-year sentence she asked him what he would be doing when he got out. He was confused and very uncertain, so she offered to help set him up with a job at a friend's company. Then she inquired about where he would live, and since he had no family to return to, she offered him temporary use of the spare room in her home.

For eight months he lived there, ate her food, and worked at the job. Then one evening she called him into the living room to talk. She sat down opposite him and waited. Then she started, "Do you remember in the courtroom when I said I was going to kill you?" "I sure do," he replied. "I'll never forget that moment."

"Well, I did," she went on. "I did not want the boy who could kill my son for no reason to remain alive on this earth. I wanted him to die. That's why I started to visit you and bring you things. That's why I got you the job and let you live here in my house. That's how I set about changing you. And that old boy, he's gone. So now I want to ask you, since my son is gone, and that killer is gone, if you'll stay here. I've got room, and I'd like to adopt you if you let me." And she became the mother of her son's killer, the mother he never had.

Forgiveness and a Kind Intention

This story brings us back again to Nachiketa's journey and the forgiveness he begged for as his first boon from the Lord of Death. In the mandala of wholeness we are called to the practice of forgiveness. We must especially find a forgiving heart with family and those close to us. Only then can we bring it to the world. Whether we practice through Buddhist meditation, or as Jesus taught by "turning the other cheek," or by finding "the mercy of Allah," we must learn to forgive ourselves and others. Booker T. Washington said it simply: "Don't ever let them pull you down so low as to hate them." Forgiveness is the heart's capacity to release its grasp on the pains of the past and free itself to go on.

There is so much to learn about letting go and loving. Family becomes the ground for this wisdom to flower. I have heard countless grateful stories of a family member saying, "I finally called my mother and told her I loved her before she died," or, "After all these years of pain I finally reconciled with my brother." Forgiveness offers the heart's mercy that our hurt and fear have withheld for so long.

It is in tenderness and tolerance that our path is made whole. It is in reconciliation and love of those closest to us that the spirit of our human family grows, to widen and fully embrace our true family: all that lives. We awaken as a part of one another's family.

Ishi in Two Worlds is the remarkable account of the last remaining Yana Indian of California, who was befriended by the anthropologists Theodora and Alfred Kroeber. Ishi tells stories of the way of life of his people, never more to be seen on this earth. Yet one of the most moving stories was not told in the book. Among all the teaching songs and exquisite knowledge of nature revealed by Ishi to the Kroebers, there was a sacred song that he had been sworn never to teach to anyone outside the tribe. It was the song sung to the dying, used to sing his people back to their families, to their ancestral lands after death. No one else was allowed to know how to go there. Yet Ishi was alone at the end of his life, the last member of his tribe. It was then that he finally had to teach his last secret to the Kroebers, so they could sing him back to his people.

In the end, no matter how isolated or embattled our lives, we need one another as family, we need each other's hearts and songs to help one another find the way.

15

MANY BROTHERS
AND SISTERS:
The Gifts of Community

The jewel of community, of the Sangha, is to be held equal to the
Buddha and the Dharma. . . . Indeed, the whole of holy life is
fulfilled through spiritual friendship.

BUDDHA

Saints are what they are not because of their sanctity but because the
gift of sainthood makes it possible for them to admire everyone else.

THOMAS MERTON

You say you can't create something original? Don't worry about it.
Make a cup of clay so your brother can drink.

RUMI

The stories of Jesus and Buddha, of
shamans and sages, may initially emphasize their solitary quest,
alone in the desert or forest, seeking a holy understanding of our
human dilemma. But then the stories go on. Whoever steps
beyond individual self and connects with eternity is naturally
drawn back to community. This is how we express the heart's realization, by bringing it to maturity with others.

In Buddhism, the practitioner is offered sustenance from
what is called the Triple Treasure: Buddha, Dharma, and Sangha.
Sustenance comes from the Buddha because his awakening rep-

resents the potential for awakening in each being. The Dharma, which represents the eternal truth and the teachings that can bring liberation, is the second source of sustenance. The third and equal treasure, the Sangha, is the community of awakened beings and all who practice the dharma.

"Sangha" means spiritual community and it is treasured because without it awakening cannot be sustained. The Sangha carries the teachings and acknowledges that we cannot awaken alone. The world of spiritual prayer and practice is sustained through teachers, spiritual friends, and community. As we practice we become part of the process of nourishing the awakening of others. Every moment of compassion or understanding that we awaken spills from us to our families, our community, our world.

The community of the sacred is revered in Judaism as the minyan, the minimum number of Jews needed for a prayer service. It is the sacred communion of the Sufis, the satsang of Hinduism, and the holy Christian love, "whenever two or more are gathered in His name." However it may be expressed, true community is central to spiritual life.

From Isolation to Community

One old Hasidic rabbi asked his pupils how they could tell when the night had ended and the day had begun, for that is the time for certain holy prayers. "Is it," proposed one student, "when you can see an animal in the distance and tell whether it is a sheep or a dog?" "No," answered the rabbi. "Is it when you can clearly see the lines on your own palm?" "Is it when you can look at a tree in the distance and tell if it is a fig or a pear tree?" "No," answered the rabbi each time. "Then what is it?" the pupils demanded. "It is when you can look on the face of any man or woman and see that they are your sister or brother. Until then it is still night."

In the maturing of spiritual life, we move from the wisdom of transcendence—that spiritual illumination beyond the world—to the wisdom of immanence. We discover that the sacred is always

239

here. The natural cycles of spiritual life that carry us away to mystic solitude eventually return us to some form of community. Just in this way, the one who has sought and tamed the sacred ox in the Zen accounts must inevitably return with their gifts to the world.

This return can be difficult, especially because so much of the spirit of true community has been lost in our times, lost even to ourselves. Contemporary life is marked by atomization, where each individual is hurrying, spinning in his or her own direction. One can literally see the individualistic forces in modern society: each person in a car, houses with separate rooms for each person, offices where each works at a computer terminal, children raised in front of a television. Modern American individualism too often entails what Marian Wright Edelman calls "the sacrifice of our community and our children." How can we return to such a marketplace with, as the ox-herding story suggests, "gift-bestowing hands"? It is not easy.

Westerners who complete long periods of Buddhist or Hindu retreats generally experience confusion and isolation when they return. Retreatants and yogis often speak of the difficulties and conflicts they find as they reenter the sorrows and complexity of modern life. A key to bridging these worlds is spiritual friendship. A compassionate friendship is one of the most important gifts we can offer one another.

As one meditation teacher describes it:

After five years of retreat and some extraordinary meditation experiences, I went back to live in Seattle. My perspective was changed, truly different from those around me. At first the city seemed exciting, but also somewhat frantic. I didn't know how to put the inner and outer worlds together. Then I grew increasingly overwhelmed on my own. I felt lost and a little crazy. I really needed spiritual friends. When I found some they helped me through the difficult years. Remember this when times are tough. It's the most important thing I can say—don't forget spiritual friendship.

To sustain spiritual life, we need one another's eyes and hearts as surely as we need help creating food and shelter. This reflection and encouragement is no small thing. As Adrienne Rich says, "Truthfulness, honor, is not something that springs ablaze of itself, it has to be created between people."

Sangha and spiritual friendship appear in surprising forms. Over the years I have participated in a series of retreats for young men from the inner cities. Most of these youth are former gang members who are finding their way back from an environment of despair, racism, poverty, and violence. Invariably what begins their return is a friend, a mentor, a benefactor. Even for a moment, there had to be someone who saw their beauty, their possibility. It may have been a grandmother, a custodian at school, a teacher, or an uncle in the neighborhood. The experience of being truly seen and honored by another reminds us of who we are. We cannot underestimate the importance of the awakening we bring to one another.

It is not only street youth who need companionship on the path. Several monastics who run retreat centers spoke of how hungry their guests are for spiritual friendship, and how this makes the monks and nuns even more grateful for their own community. Community is a blessing.

A Western lama describes this aspect of practice:

In the three-year retreat we were thrown together in our tiny retreat compound, fifteen of us, as if we were married and dropped into a war zone. It was that intense. Living closely with others rounds off your rough edges; you can't fool yourself, because others see you more clearly than you allow yourself to see. It was a very bonding time. In a way, living collectively was as valuable as all of the other meditations. It brought alive the teachings of compassion moment to moment.

Now my main practice has become communion, to recognize the living spirit in everyone, in everything, not just in peaceful people. If you look in anybody's eyes, the light is shining there; also in every animal, every leaf, every flower and dewdrop, in every clod of earth. People are no more enlightened in the monasteries than out in the world. It's the same everywhere. Spirituality is not about the mountaintops. It is seeing the sacred, right here, celebrating and affirming perfection just now. Even our enemies show us how to awaken if we recognize the truth.

Community Is Also Difficult

Community, however important to a full human life, is not easy. Living with others evokes all kinds of difficulties. When we get close enough to one another to offer love and support in an intimate way, our old family patterns, our fears, our needs, our limitations show up as well. They're all right there in front of our nose. We may be able to avoid conflict in our prayer and meditation, but in community we might as well not try—conflict will come.

A few ancient accounts of spiritual community speak of harmony, "living together like milk and water, regarding each other with kindly eyes." But more frequently the ancient texts are filled with accounts of problems. Hasidic tales recount many conflicts among community members and between teachers and students. The early Christian stories tell of conflicts and struggles in the community, and the epistles of Paul are filled with advice on resolving these difficulties. The first seven volumes of the Buddhist scriptures, devoted entirely to the topic of spiritual community, spell out hundreds of tales of the conflicts, misdeeds, and difficulties that arose among the monks and nuns even while the Buddha was still alive. There was the Buddha's jealous cousin who tried to have the Buddha murdered. And then later a quarrel among the obstinate monks at Kosambi got so bad that they would not even listen to the Buddha. Finally he threw up his hands and left to live among the peaceable animals of the forest, leaving the monks for a time to work things out on their own.

One Hindu teacher describes her reluctance to engage in community.

> *After years in India I returned and became a well-known leader of yoga retreats. I would fly from one city to another. People kept saying, "Let's start a year-round yoga community," but I avoided that. Even when my friends got a big ashram, I kept going away to travel and teach. Finally it dawned on me I simply didn't want community, especially with me in the teacher role. It was too much responsibility, too hard to be close to all these people. I suppose it evoked the unhappiness of my family. I couldn't imagine being together without it being stifling and painful. I just wasn't ready.*

If we expect community relationships to be ideal, spiritual, friendly, and enlightened, we are seeking what we can't even expect of our own minds. To want the company of others without suffering is unrealistic. But if we avoid close relationships, we will also suffer. In a wise spiritual community we acknowledge our difficulties and choose to help one another anyway. Sometimes we will be the one to carry the blessings of spaciousness and love. Sometimes it is we who will carry conflict and trouble to the group. This too is a gift others can learn from. We play both roles in this plot, switching periodically.

If we go to spiritual community in search of perfect peace, we will inevitably meet failure. But if we understand community as a place to mature our practice of steadiness, patience, and compassion, to become conscious together with others, then we have the fertile soil of awakening. One Korean Zen master told students that their communal practice was like putting potatoes in a pot and spinning them around together long enough to rub off all the peels.

In community we become mirrors for one another. An older nun remembers:

In my second community there were only a dozen nuns. I liked all but two. One was lazy and the other was self-absorbed. After my first year I was in the kitchen complaining to a friend, who said, "You know these are really not bad people. What is it that gets to you?" I said, "One is lazy and the other takes too much care of herself," and she replied, "Well, you ought to be more lazy and take better care of yourself!"

Our spiritual formation—training—came collectively. We weren't given much time for private prayer and all our individual life as young women was almost entirely surrendered to a communal whole. This was a trial in many ways, and required a great trust because it sacrificed so many desires. It was not like solitary Christian and Buddhist training where you wrestle with yourself alone. For us community came first, and years later we would find the individual emerging from that communal world of prayer and dedication. To really let go into that training, to surrender to the difficulty as a gift, brought an ecstasy. It was a gift to be with other souls moving toward a great goal.

I still love it when I meet sisters who have gone through this collective awakening. You learn to join together on the level of the heart. To live a complete spiritual life we need to learn how to be with one another.

Such accounts do not mean we have to leave our job, home, or family to find a monastic community. We have the opportunity to learn about community all the time. There are others all around us who can highlight our prejudices, our fears, our attachments, and show us the way to an open heart.

One man, a military officer who was studying meditation in a class for stress reduction, recently found this out at the supermarket. It was a crowded evening, the lines were long, and the woman carrying a child in front of him had just one item but would not get into the express line. The officer, whose habit was impatience, began to get annoyed with her. It got worse when she got to the checkout stand and she and the clerk started cooing over the baby. The woman even handed the child to the clerk.

He began to tense up, his anger building at the thought of how selfish she was. But because he had just come from his class, he noticed what he was doing to himself and began to breathe more softly and relax. He even noticed that it was a cute baby. By the time he got to the clerk he had let go enough to say, "That was a cute boy." "Oh, thank you. That was my baby," she replied. "You see, my husband was in the air force but he died last year in a plane crash. Now my mother takes care of my boy and brings him in once a day so I can see him."

We judge each other so quickly, yet know so little about what another carries in his or her heart. To truly awaken to grace and sacred presence, we must offer to all the same respect we would give a great teacher. The sloppy, angry, inconvenient, hurried, difficult Buddhas around us can teach us steadiness, equanimity, and compassion. We are the grist for one another's mill.

A close friend, the psychiatrist and consciousness researcher Stan Grof, tells a story of one such teaching that took place soon after he arrived in the United States. Through his work at Johns Hopkins Medical School, Stan met with a psychiatrist of Native American origin, who offered to arrange a visit for Stan and several other staff members to his traditional peyote circle in Kansas.

When they arrived they were driven far out onto the plains to meet the Road Chief, the elder who runs the ceremonies for the Native American Church. Although the chief had previously agreed to include the visitors, the other Indians who saw these white men balked, and it took a good deal of persuasion to allow this unusual participation. The history of anti-Indian prejudice, the monumental losses of Indian culture, the genocide at the hands of white people were still painful, but because the Johns Hopkins doctors had come a long distance, they were finally permitted to join the circle. Still, one man clung stubbornly to his anger at the white men who had come to "steal" this last Indian treasure, their spiritual gold. All through the nightlong ceremony, his mood only amplified by the peyote and drumming, this angry man sat silently, glaring at Stan, who sat opposite him in the circle. By morning he had not softened, even after a whole night of prayers. It seemed as if this was how it would end—in an angry standoff.

Finally, on the last round of blessings, the host psychiatrist thanked the tribe for being willing to include these white healers in their midst, especially Stan, who was living in exile because the Communists were preventing his return to his native Czechoslovakia. All at once the angry man's face changed. He leapt to his feet, crossed the fire, and fell into Stan's lap sobbing. For many minutes he hugged Stan and the others nearby, apologizing for his misguided hatred.

As he wept, his story poured out. He had flown a bomber in the air force during World War II. In the last weeks of the war, as the Nazis withdrew, his plane had bombed and unnecessarily destroyed Pilsen, one of Czechoslovakia's most beautiful cities, even though Czechoslovakia had been anti-Nazi and forcibly occupied by Germany.

Now the tables had turned. Not only did Stan and the Czechs never steal Indian land, but he, a Patowatame Indian, had helped destroy Stan's homeland. He was the perpetrator and Stan's people were the victims. This realization was more than he could bear. He kept embracing Stan, begging forgiveness, apologizing for his behavior during the sacred ceremony. Then he paused to say what he had learned: "I see now that there can be no hope for the world if we carry hatred for deeds committed by our ancestors. I know now you are not my enemies but my brothers. All that happened long ago was in the time of our ancestors. Who knows— at that time I might have been on the other side. We are all children of the Great Spirit. Our Mother Earth is in trouble, and if we do not work together we will die."

Recognizing the Buddha in One Another

In Buddhist mythology it is said that each new era is served by a Buddha who offers a perfect form of teachings for that time. Maitreya, the Buddha of Love, is the name given to the Buddha who will next appear on earth. However, Zen Master Thich Nhat Hanh has stated that this next Buddha may not appear in the form of a single awakened individual. As our understanding of interdependence grows, he says, "The next Buddha may be the Sangha itself." That means that collectively we will be the ones helping one another awaken.

A cartoon in a San Francisco paper showed a man walking down the street with a signboard that proclaimed, "Jesus Is Coming!" Half a block behind was an Asian-looking fellow wearing a signboard that read, "Buddha Here Now!" In spiritual maturity we realize that both Buddha and Jesus are here now in everyone we meet, including the man carrying the first sign.

There is a traditional practice of meeting all beings as the Buddha, of seeing Christ in each of us. Rabbi Hillel called this simple understanding the summary of all the holy words: "Love God by loving your neighbor." It is expounded by Zen Master Dogen when he says, "To be enlightened is to be intimate with all things."

We have now come full circle; we are back to the art of bowing, of bringing respect to life as it is. This is a beginning and an advanced practice, for students and abbots, lamas, beginners and elders alike, to meet each being as our own brother and sister.

The foolishness of others, the frustration, blame, and conflict we encounter, the struggle and betrayal can all be met with a bow. They come to us as Mara came to the Buddha, to awaken us to compassion yet again. "The only devils in the world," said Mahatma Gandhi, "are the ones running around in our own hearts. This is where the battle must be fought."

When Ram Dass taught a series of classes on service several years ago in Oakland, participants wrestled with how it is possible to see the Divine in everyone they encounter. After some weeks one woman stood up and said she had been putting change into a homeless man's cup every day for several months, but that since the class had begun she'd come to realize she'd never really looked at him. Reflecting on this surprised her. "I discovered my big fear was that if I looked him in the eyes, by the next week he would be sleeping on my living room couch."

At first there is fear. If we open to one another fully, how can we not be overwhelmed by their suffering? It seems our heart cannot possibly be big enough to contain it all. Or we become afraid that we will have to give everything away, including ourselves. But this is not what is asked. What is asked is our compassionate attention, the inclusion in our heart of the joys and sorrows of our brothers and sisters. When we see the Buddha who lives within all beings, a wise and natural response will emerge.

Compassionate Listening

Compassionate listening is a key to transforming the world. In an act of peacemaking diplomacy, Gene Knudson-Hoffman and others from Quaker, Buddhist, and Jewish backgrounds have founded the Compassionate Listening Project. Committed to world peace, the project has sent teams to try to understand the most isolated and conflicted figures worldwide. They have visited Mu'ammar Qaddafi in Libya, listened to all sides of the warring parties in Central American revolutions, given their ear to the most fanatical factions in Asia and the Middle East. Their belief is that through a deep listening to the sorrows and predicaments of others, the conflicts will change.

The Tao calls this "listening with the heart so that we can find the Way." This listening compassion embraces our own struggles as well. We give too much away only if we forget that the circle of compassion also includes ourselves. With a wise compassion we discover what is right for others and for ourselves. We awaken our heart's amazing capacity to hold all that is human. We realize we ourselves are a part of all that lives. The compassionate heart grows strong from this truth.

Several years after the Los Angeles riots/insurrection of 1993, I joined together with Malidoma Somé, Luis Rodriguez, and Michael Meade to begin a series of multicultural retreats to address the difficult dialogue on race. In one retreat a hundred men from the black and Latino communities of Watts and East Los Angeles joined with white participants for teachings, story-telling, truth speaking, and healing rituals. The retreats drew on communal practices from the ancient traditions of West Africa, Native America, and the Buddhist elders to attempt to create a common ground for understanding. It was a fiery and passionate week.

One of the most heated moments came when a white man told how frightened he had become for his family when the Los Angeles riots/insurrection came within two miles of his home. He was so frightened that he had gone out and bought a gun for protection, he said. Several African-American men instantly bolted from their seats to confront him. "Who are you going to kill with that gun? You know you got it to shoot at black men!" one man said. Another shouted, "You talk about fear. If you want to be afraid, brother, you better look in the mirror. Look who invented the machine gun, the land mine. Look at the owners of gun factories. Look at who built nuclear weapons and then used them. Look at who shipped twenty million people to this country as slaves, who fought the biggest wars in the last thousand years, who colonized the world. You want to be afraid, look at white people. You better sell that gun, man."

Several white men rose to support the man with the gun and began shouting back about defense for individuals. Other black men argued louder. The tension was building. We wondered if we could keep the room from exploding.

Finally Ralph Steele, a six-foot-two African-American Buddhist teacher, stood up. In his voice we could hear the soft echoes of the South Carolina Gullah language of his childhood.

I live in rural New Mexico where everyone has guns for hunting and protection, but I don't have one. When I was in Vietnam I saw enough shooting to last a lifetime. We would go out on patrol or into the villages and every day somebody would get shot, sometimes your best friend. We would get to a new area and people there would move and some of the guys would get spooked and start shooting. Later we found we shot women and children. There were some human beings in our company who liked shooting other human beings, even women and children. We didn't know what to do with them. It was my life for two years.

You don't want a gun. It doesn't matter who you are, you don't want a gun. You don't want the dreams, the nightmares that come from using a gun. You don't even want the memory of a gun in your hand. You've got to live a lifetime with that.

Ralph finished speaking and stood quietly, looking around. All the other men sat down. He had spoken without anger or defensiveness, with a compassion bigger than all the anger and fear in the room. We were silent for a while.

By listening with the heart, by giving voice to the truth of compassion, one person can turn the energy of conflict back toward peace. In every relationship and community, there will be frustration, blame, grasping, anger, and betrayal. No matter who we are, nor how enlightened, these will come. It is here that our connection in community will help us. In emphasizing the Sangha as the Buddha, Thich Nhat Hanh reminds us that wisdom is held collectively. When we or our community are stuck and cannot find the blessings of compassion, someone bringing us true spiritual friendship can open the gates to heaven.

This is the power of the rabbi's table, the A.A. meeting, the Sufi Gathering of the Truth, the Buddhist Council. In our own community we draw on the Buddhist elders' ancient tradition of seeking consensus by meeting regularly in council. To this listening council we have added the Native American talking stick, and encouraged simplicity and unrehearsed truth. Then when difficult issues such as resolving conflicts between teachers, choosing staff, or setting new directions for our center arise, we meet in council. Whoever holds the talking stick is listened to without interruption. Then it is passed to others. In this way each person gets to speak his or her heart. Out of this respectful listening we find healing, consensus, and new direction. Over the years such heartfelt council has carried the wisdom of our collective experience more fully than any of us could have individually.

Even at a distance, spiritual friendship can support us. Jungian analyst James Hillman gives an account of Chinese dissident Liu Qing, who served eleven years in the notorious Weinan No. 2 prison. Liu was forced to sit on an eight-inch stool without moving for ten hours a day. If he moved or talked to other prisoners he was beaten. To end his suffering he needed only to sign a statement admitting mistakes in his thinking. Against all odds, he refused to sign. When asked later how he remained strong, Liu said he saw before him the faces of friends and family and knew he could not sign. His heart's connection with this community of beings would not permit betrayal of them.

The Gyari 14 is a group of young Tibetan nuns aged fourteen to twenty-one who were imprisoned and beaten by the Chinese Communist army for publicly reciting their chants and prayers. Yet even in prison they resolved to remain united in their determination to pray and sing freely. When they managed to smuggle out a tape of prayers sung in the prison, their sentences were doubled, yet they remained steadfast. They wrote, "We are grateful for the support of so many outside the prison and we will never forget." Most remarkably, they pray not for themselves but for the people of their country—and for their captors. In the documentary film made about their struggle, *A Prayer for the Enemy*, they speak through a smuggled letter: "We have been treated so terribly. What should we do? What can we do? We pray for the enemy."

In our own countryside, in our cities, hospitals, and jails, we find so many who need our prayers: the sick and the well, the prisoners and the guards. The prayers of these young nuns are joined with ours. We offer our blessings; we share our trust in the healing beyond all sorrows; we expand the circle of our heart.

The Heart's Intention

Becoming aware of intention is a key to awakening in moment-to-moment practice. In each situation that calls for our engagement, some inner intention will precede our response. Buddhist psychology teaches that intention is what makes the pattern of our karma. Karma, the cause and results of every action, comes from the heart's intentions that precede each action. When our intentions are kind, the karmic result is very different from when they are greedy or aggressive. If we are not aware, we will unconsciously act out of habit and fear. But if we attend to our intentions, we can notice if they spring from the body of fear or from our deliberate thoughtfulness and care.

Every tradition offers prayers and meditations for setting the heart's best intention. Sometimes the intentions are general. "May the words of my mouth and the dedications of my heart serve you, oh Lord." "May every activity be a prayer." "May my heart freely offer loving kindness and forgiveness." "I vow to bring awakening to every being I meet in thought, word, or deed." The Jewish tradition uses hundreds of prayers throughout the day, to foster a seamless gratitude and love of the heart.

Intentions can also be focused on one day or one situation. "May I remember my breath and center myself each time I encounter conflict today." "May I treat all those at work with kindness." "May I take the time this week to let my family know I love them."

In times of difficulty it is this repeated setting of our heart's compass that determines the result. Whether in a family disagreement or community conflict, before we speak and act, we can become aware of our deepest intention. Even the simplest words can have a vastly different effect depending on our intention. The phrase "What do you mean?" can sound accusing and judgmental or considerate and humble. Our hearts are like seismographs, picking up the tremors of intent.

Notice how this works in conversation. Do we speak from a subtle sense of control or self-righteousness, or do we really wish to listen, to learn? If we set our minds toward freedom, our good intentions will help us to let go of what blocks our openness. If we set our hearts toward compassion, we will reaffirm our love in spite of whatever difficulties we face.

Instead of inflaming a bad situation, we can seek ways of touching the good in another. Without denying pain and injustice, we can also look for the secret beauty of others. Our spiritual practice can be this simple: to see with eyes of compassion and act with our wisest intention. This often has a surprising effect. Nelson Mandela put it this way: "Thinking too well of people often allows them to behave better than they otherwise would."

Do not doubt the transformation that can be born out of such conscious attention. When Ananda, attendant and close friend of the Buddha, met a young outcaste woman at a village well, he politely asked her for water to drink, but she was ashamed and refused him, lest her untouchability contaminate his holiness. Ananda replied, "I ask not for caste but for water." Her life was transformed by this simple kindness, and she joyously and lovingly followed Ananda to the monastery. There the Buddha blessed her and bid her to take up the kindness Ananda had shown her and, by keeping that simple intention, to "let the actions of your life shine like the jewels of royalty."

It is in such small things that we fulfill the lessons of the heart. It is from our intentions that our life grows. It is in opening to one another that our path is made whole.

Community Is Serving the Beloved

Mother Teresa spoke of "seeing Christ in the poor and sick."
The poet Rumi longs for the Divine: "In the face of everything separate, I want to see only You." And when he remembers there is
nothing but God, he laughs and says, "Why struggle to open a door
between us when the whole wall is an illusion?" With every in-
and-out breath, with every mouthful of food, with every word we
voice, we express our interbeing with all that lives. Modern tech-
nology makes this visible in new ways, from the Internet to CNN.
Israeli prime minister Yitzak Shamir quipped, "Television has
made dictatorship impossible and democracy intolerable." We are
all in it together.

One Western lama recalls:

*After I had trained in India with my guru, a highly revered
Rinpoche, I developed such respect for the lineage, the
group of masters he represented. These men had carried the
pinnacle of Buddhist realization for centuries until he
brought it out of Tibet. On one of my last days with him I
was walking the three miles out to his cottage practicing
the taking and sending of compassion. All at once my
understanding of the lineage grew. It wasn't just the high
lamas, but it was the devoted tea ladies who fed the pilgrims
on the way to the lama from their roadside stands. It was
the old herders and the Tibetan traders who visited and supported him. It was the clothes washer pounding clothes
down by the river, the cook in his kitchen, the herbs that
grew in his garden. The world was serving my lama and he
was serving them.*

We exist in a mandala of wholeness amidst a sea of Buddhas,
visible whenever we open the eyes of love and wisdom.

When my friend and colleague Gil Fronsdal traveled to
Morocco as a young man, he went far out into the Sahara Desert.
There he and a companion were taken in by a Bedouin tribe, as

was the custom of these nomadic Arabs. For three days they were given lavish feasts and so much care and attention that Gil said, "It felt like we were kings." When the time came to leave they offered many thanks. "After I returned home I realized I had understood it wrong. It was they who were the royalty, they who showed us the true generosity of kings."

To serve the Beloved is to admire the ones before us, to see them as Buddha, to welcome them as Christ. One of my teachers, Ajahn Jumnien, talks about this in his role as abbot. He looks to admire the Buddha in everyone who comes to the temple. Most Thai men are ordained for some period of their life, and he receives each postulant with admiration. When a local boxing champ came to be ordained, Ajahn Jumnien asked if he would like to be his bodyguard. "I had no need for a bodyguard, but he guarded me with so much dignity, eventually he became a fine monk." Another man arrived boasting in an egotistical way about his prowess as a builder. Ajahn Jumnien smiled and said, "Excellent. We have needed a new meditation hall for some time now. I turn the whole project over to you." Our nobility blossoms when we are admired and respected.

Years ago Ram Dass went to his guru, Neem Karoli Baba, to ask, "How can I best be enlightened?" His guru answered, "Love people." When he asked about the most direct path to awakening, his guru answered, "Feed people. Love people and feed people. Serve the Divine in every form." Kabir, the Indian mystic, says, "There is only one thing that will satisfy my heart . . . to serve You with every breath."

Service is the expression of the awakened heart. But whom are we serving? It is ourselves. When someone asked Gandhi how he could so continually sacrifice himself for India, he replied, "I do this for myself alone." When we serve others we serve ourselves. The Upanishads call this "God feeding God."

A wise spiritual community must serve something larger than itself. If people gather in community primarily to alleviate their own isolation and loneliness, to have their needs fulfilled by others, they become like a group of needy children, and the community inevitably fails. But if their vision and creativity is in service to the sacred, to God, to the larger common good, there is a better chance for a healthy and wise community to grow.

A Sufi master speaks of this need:

When we founded our community we recognized that people came together for social needs, for financial and political needs. We did not want their needs to be the main point of our community. We came together to pray and serve God, to grow in a truly spiritual way, to express some things higher than ourselves. We wanted to imbue every part of life with a holiness, to bring this to shine in the world.

Past generations in America understood this in ways we have largely forgotten. Our history is filled with examples of communal care for one another, from barn raising to the sharing of food and seeds in times of hunger to churchgoing and spiritual partnership.

In times of disaster, like the Great Plains flood a few years ago, there is a remarkable outpouring of mutual aid, across every barrier of class and race. After life is "normal" again, people speak wistfully of wanting to keep the spirit that made everyone neighbors. We hold those pioneer and immigrant communities like a genetic memory, reminding us of what we can be to one another.

Serving one another is an expression of our sacred connection. It reawakens the oneness that has been lost, allows us to again look into the eyes of another and see the Divine that shines in all things. One senior Buddhist practitioner who regularly does hospice work remembers that she had a stronger connection to her dying patients than to almost anyone else in her life.

At first I thought it was because of their openness in the face of death. But then I realized it was mostly because I do several periods of loving kindness meditations for them daily. When you intentionally offer your loving wishes, your prayers and blessings for someone over and over, it changes your own heart. You become the love you offer.

We each are engaged in a multitude of acts of service to our brothers and sisters. Every time we stop at a red light, offer money to a cashier, say hello, wash the dishes, put out the trash cans, we serve our family, our community, and the earth. In each of our daily roles—as builder or merchant, gardener or artist, teacher, healer, secretary, or salesman—we can awaken compassion, we can find the spirit of Sangha and freedom.

"The scope of service," says the Indian master Meher Baba,

is not limited to heroic acts, great gestures, and huge donations to public institutions. They also serve who express their love in little things. A word that gives courage to a broken heart or a smile that brings hope in the midst of gloom is as much service as heroic sacrifice. A glance that wipes out bitterness from the heart is also service, although there may be no thought of service in it. When taken by themselves all these things seem to be small, but life is made up of many small things. If these small things were ignored, life would not only be unbeautiful, it would be unbearable.

Skillful Service Is Born of a Quiet Heart

Wise intention and skillful service need to be nourished by periods of quiet and prayer. Every great tradition includes some form of the Sabbath. In the West we inherited the blessing of the Christian and Jewish Sabbath. Muslims have Friday as their holy day, and likewise Hindus and Buddhists renew their vows of simplicity on full moon, new moon, and quarter moon days. When I was young, Massachusetts had Sabbath "Blue Laws" requiring all forms of business to stop on Sundays. But now, one generation later, we have twenty-four-hour supermarkets and twenty-four-hour banking, seven days a week; our consumer society has claimed the right to operate without constraint. This is a recipe for burnout.

A spirit of service to one another and to ourselves grows out of a different soil—out of moments of remembering, moments of prayer and blessing. If we pay attention to the cycle of our breath and the beating of our heart, there is a tiny and necessary pause between each. To beat for our whole life, the heart must restore itself in the stillness before each new beat. Spiritual maturity also requires such periods of Sabbath, where we step out of commercial time into that which is timeless.

We need to become the sanctuary we seek. This can begin with a Sabbath day or a daily period of meditation and prayer. Sometimes it may require creating regular periods of silence where we work. It can mean reassessing our lifestyle, moving toward voluntary simplicity, spending time in nature, attending periodic retreats. It may mean turning off CNN and turning on Mozart. In times of difficulty or conflict, it may mean taking a breath, settling the heart, listening silently to our deepest intention. In these moments we remember our heart's task on earth. A Christian contemplative teacher recalls:

I had lived many years in a small protected community. Then it came to me that it was time to go back to society to serve. I began an integration, going back and forth. I worked at an AIDS hospice and crisis center. Once a month I would return to my community, my heart longing for silence. I would stand in line when the gift of food was presented, and feel how each thing there, even the most ordinary, was held in a holy way. This is actually how it is all the time; this is the mystery of grace. I knew it wasn't just the prayer or meditation that was important. It was the silence, stopping and taking a breath, opening the heart, seeing that the whole planet, and everything on it, is holy. I want to bring this beauty with me to everyone I touch. So I return to silence regularly. I know if I can stop and remember this, life will fulfill its promise to me.

From moments of stillness, the most skillful way to love and serve becomes clear. By stopping to listen we connect with one another, and true community is born.

16

AWAKENING WITH
ALL BEINGS

The real work is becoming native in your heart, coming to understand
we really live here, that this is really the continent we're on, and that
our loyalties are here, to these mountains and rivers, to these plant
zones, to these creatures. The real work involves a loyalty that goes
back . . . billions of years. The real work is accepting
citizenship in the earth itself.
GARY SNYDER

Every morning I awaken torn between the desire to save
the world and the inclination to savor it.
E. B. WHITE

The mandala of awakening opens the
web of life so that we can directly feel our single-stranded breathing together with all that lives. In India this is called "seeing the
Jeweled Net of Indra," the net where each intersection holds the
reflective jewel of an individual woven together with and reflecting the other strands of existence. This deepening connection to
the natural world becomes an undeniable reality, bringing with it
both responsibility and joy. Chief Seattle said, "What is man without the animals? Without the beasts men would die of a great loneliness of spirit."

Similarly, we might ask, without the earth, how could we walk
and dance? Without mountains where could the snow reside,
where could the snow leopard keep its secret watching? All the

earth and its many beings must be included in our wide-hearted practice.

Practicing with Mountains and Rivers

After the Buddha saw the morning star and awakened under the Bodhi Tree, he went forth to teach. He chose to begin his teaching in the forest under the trees of the Deer Park of Sarnath, rather than in the City of Benares, six miles away. Moses led his people into the wilderness seeking not cities but a land of milk and honey. Jesus went alone into the same desert, and though he taught in the towns, he returned often to the shores of the sea, the olive groves, the fields and gardens; his words were woven with the lives of the shepherd and the fisherman, the lion, the lamb, and the lilies. All spiritual traditions include the natural world in their wisdom, both as a place of refuge and as a manifestation of sacred and natural law.

Catholic and Buddhist contemplatives still practice in mountains and forests. Ajahn Buddhadasa, who founded a great forest monastery, speaks of the natural world as our teacher.

The organs of our own bodies, arms, hands, lungs, kidneys function as a cooperative in order to survive. Humans and animals and trees and the earth are interwoven, integrated as a cooperative. The sun, moon, planets, and stars are a giant cooperative. Awakening beyond our self-interest, we find a natural ecology of mind and nature, fresh, open, joyful, where we are organically connected with all things.

Modern notions of an ecologically sound culture are not the first. One traditional Indian Buddhist teaching suggests that a person plant a tree for every five years of life, and one of the wisest rulers in world history, India's emperor Ashoka, created a vast kingdom governed by the principles of interconnection.

One day, grieving over a particularly bloody campaign to conquer the south of India, Ashoka saw a simple monk walk peacefully across the bloodstained battlefield. Watching this man, the emperor thought, "I who have everything am not as happy nor peaceful as this man who has nothing." Ashoka became the monk's disciple, and the dharma he learned transformed his land into a kingdom of righteousness. Armies were devoted to keeping peace rather than making war. Religious tolerance, moral responsibility, and renunciation were promoted. Vegetarianism was encouraged, wells were dug, forests were preserved, and laws were promulgated for the health and well-being of both the people and the land. Two-thousand-year-old stone pillars carrying Ashoka's edicts are still found all across India.

Unfortunately, wisdom, like the environment, must be continually nourished to flourish. After Ashoka the stance of many monks and nuns of Asia regarding their interconnection with the earth became passive, without much thought or care for the environment. In the tropical villages and forest monasteries of Southeast Asia, you would just throw your trash on the ground. This was workable when the trash was banana leaves, the indigenous wrappers, but it became a nightmare once plastics were introduced. Yet the teachings of most masters still focused almost entirely on the individual mind and did not encourage responsibility for the natural world around us.

But then the cutting of the forests of Thailand, Laos, and Burma became so widespread that monks had to become activists to save the last stands of wilderness from the loggers. They began to go out and ceremonially wrap their robes around ancient trees, ordaining them as abbots of the forest. Now monks have become champions of the forest, saviors of the environment. Similarly, in the West, there is a growing Christian ecological movement. Churches worldwide, led by the example of nuns and priests in Latin America, are beginning to include care for the holiness of the natural world as part of God's way.

The nuns of one convent describe how these concerns are growing:

For decades we were purposely isolated from the problems of the world. We still don't get involved in politics or all that passes for news.

But we did start to recycle in 1978. Then we stopped using pesticides in 1983. Now most of our food is organic. And we minimize the use of our cars and van. A care for the earth has slowly infiltrated into our actions and our prayers. We educate those who visit us. We have sisters who have become activists in Latin America. It's not like our prayers to God were separate, but now the endangered species, the rain forest, and the poor farmers are included in our sacred work as a part of ourselves.

Human and natural realms are not separate. Whether in contemplating the responsibility of our lifestyle for global warming or the pollution of our rivers or in considering the sources of our food, our eyes must open to this interdependence. When we shop in the supermarket we can reflect on the rain clouds that bring us this food, the moist soil in which it is grown, and the thousand human labors by which it reaches our table. Poet Alison Luterman writes:

Strawberries are too delicate to be picked by machine. The perfect ripe ones bruise at even too heavy a human touch. . . . Every strawberry you have ever eaten—every piece of fruit—has been picked by callused human hands. Every piece of toast with jelly represents someone's knees, someone's aching back and hips, someone with a bandana on her wrist to wipe away the sweat.

Spiritual life may initially be focused on self-transformation and wise human relationships. But a sense of selflessness must also lead us to our oneness with the mountains. One teacher of yoga reflects:

When I lived in India in the 1970s, one of my gurus taught yoga in a noisy, dirty, polluted city. We learned all about

inner purity, but he never mentioned the distress around us.
My second guru had an ashram in the country, and there too
we studied yoga, meditation, and powerful breathing prac-
tices to transcend the world. The environment was still left
to fend for itself. I was shocked to see how ecological aware-
ness and the yoga movement were such separate worlds. We
thought being vegetarian was enough. Now I take my yoga
retreats to pristine places and try to teach how the pure mind
and the purity of our rivers and our air are interconnected.
It's become necessary to live more carefully and have a
world-yoga, to consciously connect our bodies with the body
of the world.

Joanna Macy, a visionary Buddhist teacher and activist, points
out that for ecological transformation to take place a spiritual revolution is also needed, "a great turning of human consciousness."

Even our scientists can see that there is no technological
fix, no amount of computers, no magic bullet that can save
us from population explosion, deforestation, climate dis-
ruption, poison by pollution, and wholesale extinction of
plant and animal species. We are going to have to want different things, seek different pleasures, pursue different
goals than those that have been driving us and our global
economy.

Through spiritual awakening the values of consumerism are
revealed as increasingly shallow and false. Grasping and possess-
ing give way to love and integrity, an innermost desire to live in
harmony with all creation. There comes a longing to live more
simply for the sake of our own hearts, and a growing sense of
responsibility for the life of the earth.

But this transformation is not automatic. In every area of the
mandala of awakening we need consciously to face our conditioning and habits. One teacher speaks of her daily struggles with
this.

The sufferings of the world continue to be a wrenching dilemma for me. There is not a day that goes by that I'm not shocked by how much needs to be done. I have been teaching contemplative practice for thirty years, and I think inner awakening is where the root lies, in the possibility of transforming our own self-centered existence into something beautiful for the world. But sometimes it seems so slow. It's not like I expect it to change the human realm. In India and Nepal, in some of the poorest circumstances imaginable, I also saw the utter perfection of life and the living reality of freedom. I saw also, and still see, that there are millions of people hungry, poor, sick, and incredible numbers of beings in need. I do the things I can to help. I try to live simply. Each day I wonder, am I supporting the right causes, making the right choices? Am I doing enough?

To our sadness, the United States remains the largest manufacturer and supplier of weapons worldwide. And we know that the world is spending its wealth in the trillion-dollar arms market while only 10 percent of this spent annually could feed all our children, every hungry person on earth. We have seen that our growing groundwater pollution affects every one of us—an analysis of PCBs in New York State Mohawk Indian mothers' milk shows that our bodies have become part of the landfill. What are we to do?

Spiritual values do not require us to live as renunciates in monastic simplicity, nor to go back to the land. We also need spiritual leaders in politics, in medicine, in law, on Wall Street, in our police forces—in every area of life. The Buddhist story of Bodhisattva Vimilakirti tells how one enlightened being purposely chose to incarnate as a wealthy businessman to bring wisdom to the world of commerce. He then entered the hospitals as a patient to teach compassion to the doctors, and later the bars and brothels to carry the teachings to those within. No realm of human life was outside the range of his compassion.

Bringing blessings to all by entering life fully is a noble idea, but we can easily fool ourselves by saying we are following

Vimilakirti's example. The riches we enjoy in modern Western society come at great costs, which include the exploitation of other cultures, the economic colonization of much of the world, the ecological devastation of habitats and species. Every time we drive, we contribute to worldwide pollution and global warming. Every time we fly, our jet fuel is secured through the politics of power in the Middle East and the destruction of the caribou range in Alaska. Our desire to eat imported food as inexpensively as possible can have terrible consequences for the farmers and soil of Guatemala and Brazil.

In Ancient Greek the word for awakening is "alethe." Awakening's opposite is not evil or ignorance, but "lethe," sleep. Even after some experience of awakening, we can be asleep to the consequences of our modern way of living. Sadly, interdependence and ecological understanding are not explicitly taught in most traditional spiritual curricula. We have to educate ourselves to see the invisible costs of our actions, until our outer life is in harmony with our heart's true values.

To be honorable in these times we need to extend a "moral inventory" to our way of life. The Buddhist Eightfold Path includes Right Thought, Right Action, Right Speech, Right Livelihood. Is the way we are living—our work, our home, our finances, our travel, our level of consumption, our political and social participation—in harmony with our newly enlarged understanding of interconnection? In what direction does our care for the earth and our realization of interdependence ask that we move in our life? How might we change, not out of guilt but out of love? We begin our transformation by the very act of asking these questions.

Seeing with the Animals, Listening with the Rivers

At times we need to step out of our human-centered consciousness altogether. As part of this work to open our awareness of interbeing, environmental activist John Seed has developed a group meditation called the "Council of All Beings." These councils have been held all over the world. When participants gather in a place of natural beauty, each group member, for a day or longer, is asked to walk outside and connect his or her heart with the voice of a particular part of the earth, a particular mountain or river or plant or animal, a heron, a pine tree, a bison or columbine that seeks to be heard. Then after making masks or costumes to represent what they have chosen, the members of the group reconvene in council.

Each person speaks in the voice of his or her species or place. "I am a loon and speak for the waterfowl." "I am a mountain stream and speak for the rivers of the world." When all the species are introduced, they begin to bring their concerns to the council. Some members of the group—in their human role—are asked to sit in the center and listen.

"As a wild goose, I want to tell the council that my long migrations are hard now because the wetlands are disappearing. And the shells of my eggs are thin and brittle; they break before my young are ready to hatch. I fear there is poison in my bones." The council sits with this truth.

"Oh humans, I speak as river, bearer of life. Look at what I bear now that you've poured wastes and toxins into me. . . . I have become a carrier of sickness and death." The council continues to listen.

After all the other species have been given a voice, the humans speak. Usually they voice regrets and fears about human greed and the forces, now beyond their control, that they have unleashed. The sorrows of the earth that are expressed galvanize their concern for the fate of all species.

Then the humans are invited to ask for help from the vast world of nature. The nonhumans offer their wisdom and strengths: The mountain offers her steady peace, the hawk a far-seeing eye, the coyote a playful creativity, the wildflower a scent to call us back to beauty, the old pine her unflagging endurance.

As in this council, we can learn from nature wherever we are.

The plants, animals, and river valleys bring us wisdom and sustenance, they bring the Dharma to us. The great Zen teacher Master Dogen once said, "In every bamboo all the Buddhas exist." Yet if this bamboo Buddha were thoughtlessly transported from its native country to our backyard, it might soon become the scourge of our neighborhood if we did not respect its tenacious power as well as its beauty. Whether transporting bamboo or damming rivers, for us to live wisely in the natural world we must honor its power and integrity, and not imagine we can simply adjust it to our own ideas and convenience. The monks who live in the teak forest love the beauty and shade of its green canopy, but they also respect the strength of the tiger, the poison of the cobra, and the fevers of malaria the wilderness holds within. All are their teachers.

Grasses and Trees as Teachers

The Elders of the forest tradition tell us to spend time in the natural world. We begin to transform our spirit each time we go for a walk and smell the bay laurel after the rain, each time we pause to admire the quince in spring, the fire maple in autumn, today's certain shade of rose at twilight, the budding lily on our neighbor's porch, the last rustle of small animals into the astonishing silence at nightfall in the mountains. We renew our spiritual life each time we walk back into the wilderness of our world and sense the beauty that has given us birth and the untameable cycles vaster than all our plans. In this way, our care for the nonhuman world can grow, not out of duty but out of love, out of gratitude and reverence for the web of creation, an unceasing holiness.

Tending this earth, we become part of its awakening. As Ralph Waldo Emerson wrote, "To appreciate beauty and find the best in others; to leave the world a bit better, whether by a healthy child, a garden patch, a redeemed social condition, to know even one life has breathed easier because you have lived, this is to have succeeded." Caring for the natural world is one way we also tend to the human one.

The Prison Garden Project of Cathy Sneed has shown what remarkable blessings can emerge when we acknowledge our interconnection with all life. In 1984, out of concern for the soul death of local men stunted by imprisonment, she began a project to allow each of them to help plant a garden. In the San Francisco County Jail, men were invited to grow vegetables in a garden plot behind one of the prison buildings. Through fund-raising she was able to offer them seedlings and mulch, fertilizer and simple garden tools.

To be able to grow a garden with their own hands, to be responsible for its blossoming, to overcome insects and drought brought out the best in these thrown-away people. It awakened a connection to and caring for something outside of themselves. (Cathy tells about one macho giant saying, "Don't step on my babies.") The prison wardens were amazed by the change. The gardens became so important to those who cared for these patches that their lives began to revolve around them. In fact, when the time came for these men to be released from prison, some purposely recommitted petty crimes or violated their parole so that they could return to their gardens.

This led Cathy Sneed to the inevitable next step: a garden project for ex-prisoners, and community gardens for the disenfranchised in several Bay Area cities. The garden project itself became a kind of garden, one whose harvest was people. Being given the opportunity to plant created a community of people with increased care and concern for the earth. This was its great blessing. The care and intention of the gardeners blossomed in their hearts as well as in their garden patch.

We learn from the natural world a different relationship to time, one based on rhythms and cycles different from our usual plans. Some insects die within a single day. Some plants bloom once in a century. The mandala of awakening embraces these different time frames, and allows us to honor them in our life of practice. We become tenders of the cycle of life.

Native American elders teach that we must plan "unto the seventh generation." Anthropologist and systems theorist Gregory

Bateson gives a feel for what this means in the story he tells of New College at Oxford University, founded in the early 1600s. When the Great Hall was built there, its roof was supported by huge oak beams four feet in width. In recent years the caretakers discovered that the beams were severely weakened by dry rot. With this came a dilemma: how to find such beams in modern times?

Finally it occurred to one caretaker to speak to the college forester. The forester smiled at the question. "We've been wondering when you would call us. The builder of the Hall knew there would eventually be dry rot. So he instructed our predecessors to plant a grove of oak trees to replace them. Those trees are now three hundred fifty years old—just the right size for the beams."

With the sincere mind of attention, such considered action becomes a way of life. Our small steps and heartfelt concerns are held in a vast perspective. We know that we are part of a measureless whole. With a consciousness not restricted to our single human life, our breath can move easily, our heart can hold compassion for all living beings.

Acting on Behalf of All Beings

In the Buddhist tradition, a bodhisattva is a being dedicated to universal awakening, to bringing compassion and wisdom to all that lives, however long it takes. One expression of this is the vow not to enter the realm of Nirvana until the last blade of grass may also enter. Before every meditation, many practitioners worldwide recite the bodhisattva vows daily as a reminder of this intention. The vows begin in this way: "Living beings are numberless; I vow to serve until all are liberated. Ignorance and grasping is boundless; I vow to transform and uproot it all."

The vow to bring awakening and compassion to innumerable beings through eons of time is an overwhelming task. Every student who takes such a vow must wrestle with what it means, how it can be lived. Does it mean that I, this "small self," must travel the universe and save all beings? How can I measure my success; how can I begin?

Quite simply, the bodhisattva vows do not speak about an accomplishment, but a direction, a setting of intention. No matter what circumstances arise, whether birth or death, joy or sorrow, I commit my body, speech, and mind to the direction of compassion and awakening. In each new moment, I will plant seeds of kindness and liberation for myself and all living beings.

The bodhisattva vows are not a gauge but a compass, a guide for the heart to follow. They become the source for wise action, the direction from which all else follows. They become our legacy. As Martin Luther King Jr. put it, "I want you to say that I tried to love and serve humanity. . . . I just want to leave a committed life behind."

In the midst of the terrible tragedy facing the Tibetan people, the Dalai Lama has often spoken of how important it has been for him to rely on these vows. Over decades of difficulties, as a political and spiritual leader and a worldwide exemplar of nonviolence, he has had to make wrenching decisions for his nation and his people. He admits that sometimes he is not sure his decisions are the best ones, that sometimes he has made mistakes. "The only thing I can rely on," he explains, "is my sincere motivation." His heart's motivation is to foster compassion and liberation as best he can in each act. He takes refuge in the seed of intention behind his acts. By one's planting seeds of goodness, eventually something beautiful grows.

To serve all beings, we must remember one more essential truth—it is never too late to begin. When we see with wisdom, the heavy press of time, the responsibility for all things is transformed. We find perspective, a long view. We are not in charge. In our relationships, in our community, on this earth, we may not live to see all the changes we work for—we are the planters of seeds. When the seeds of our actions are caring and sincere, we can know that they will bear nourishing fruit for all beings. No matter what has passed, we can begin again. We can only begin now, where we are, and it is this now that becomes the seed for all that lies ahead. Our responsibility, our creativity is all that is asked. With such sincere motivation, we will naturally ask wise questions and offer true care, tending what we love with a far-reaching wisdom. This is the long-term tending of a farmer for his orchard, a parent for a child.

This broad perspective is that of the elder, the sage. It grows naturally out of a committed life of spiritual dedication. One meditation teacher says:

It's as if my spiritual life has been a slow horse. I started with a lot of ambitions. I tried to gallop in the beginning, doing extensive practice here and in Asia. I was going for enlightenment. I found ecstasy, yes, bliss, mystical states, incredible insight—it all came. But all it did was wake me up to what I had to do. To be a truly happy person I had to slow the horse down, get really down into earth and make my life actually follow my values. Then after lots more meditation and inner work, I took a hundred-eighty-degree turn toward the world. Increasingly I saw how the forests, the oceans, the pandas and the krill, the biosphere depend on me as I depend on them. I became a spiritual activist. I taught it, I wrote about it, I lived it. We had some success, but then again I had to slow the horse down because my ambition had come back in a new way.

Now I understand renunciation better. It's not about monasteries and renouncing life. We're put here to learn the lessons of this human life. It is the renunciation of greed and ambition, of the self-centered ethos of our time. We're not in charge here. We need to be patient, to let our actions come from a simple and pure heart, and from the circumstances in which we find ourselves. Everything good comes from that.

Appropriate Action, Appropriate Stillness

In the natural world we find the teaching of doing and non-doing. Trees bear fruit and fall dormant; otters, bears, and spotted trout sleep and wake; day alternates with night, and summer with winter. Often we feel that we must be making a continual effort to enact our bodhisattva intentions, or else we are failures or lazy. But the wider community of being tells us that without the winter-chill months of dormancy, there can be no apples. Stillness, nondoing, listening are as important and essential as action in the mandala of awakened life.

Thomas Merton cautions us:

> To allow oneself to be carried away by a multitude of conflicting concerns, to surrender to too many demands, to commit to too many projects, to want to help everyone in everything is itself to succumb to the violence of our times.

Sometimes it is necessary to march, sometimes it is necessary to sit, to pray. Each in turn can bring the heart and the world back to balance. For us to act wisely, our compassion must be balanced with equanimity, the ability to let things be as they are. Just as our passionate heart can be touched by the sorrows of the world, so too we must remember that it is not our responsibility to fix all the brokenness of the world—only to fix what we can. Otherwise we become grandiose, as if we were put here to be the savior of the humanity around us.

Compassion and equanimity come into harmony when we live in the reality of the present. It is very simple. Mindfulness and compassion are genuinely undertaken one step at a time, one person, one moment. Otherwise we become overwhelmed by all the problems that must be attended to: the dilemmas of our extended family and community, the injustice and suffering worldwide.

Compassion is most real in the particulars, in our response to the immediacy of this moment. Even in global situations it is this way. It is in the particulars that the mercy of the heart is extended. Whether it is our ailing next-door neighbor or the one-step-at-a-time building of a worldwide campaign to ban land mines or halt the destruction of rain forests, each day, each step is like breathing, a practice of expanding the heart. In these small steps our truth can blossom.

One meditation teacher says:

> *After thirty years of sitting, it seems like even fifty years of practice will be only a short while. Now I take the long view—over lifetimes. My commitment is simple. It is a dedication to the highest aspiration of enlightenment. Time is not a question. It's important that we teach the possibility of becoming utterly free and that we let every simple act every day be illuminated by this possibility, this truth.*

Every prayer and every conscious act contributes to the healing of the whole. Gandhi said:

> I believe in the essential unity of all that lives. Therefore I believe that if one person gains spiritually the whole world gains, and if one person falls, the world falls to that extent.

In the realm of action, not every gesture must be grand. Small acts are equally important, as can be seen in the story of an old man who was walking along a beach in Mexico after an unusually strong spring storm. The beach was covered with dying starfish tossed up by the waves, and the man was tossing them back in the water one by one. A visitor saw this and came up to him. "What are you doing?" "I'm trying to help these starfish," the old man replied. "But there are tens of thousands of them washed up along these beaches. Throwing a handful back doesn't matter," protested the visitor. "Matters to this one," the old man replied as he tossed another starfish into the ocean.

Bearing Witness for Justice

In one way, our most radical political act is a change of heart. If we want to overcome greed, racism, exploitation, and hatred, to end suffering and bring our lives into harmony with the earth, we must see that the fundamental crisis is in human consciousness. If the world is to be healed, it cannot happen by political and economic means alone. We have seen how the revolutionaries of one generation can turn into the oppressors of the next, and how political power can beget greed and delusion. We have to face the forces of separation, of greed, of hate directly, and learn to live peacefully, with a free heart. If we cannot do this, how can we expect it of others?

Wisdom tells us the human realm on earth has always included gain and loss, sorrow and joy, greed and generosity, ugliness and beauty. Even so, we cannot deny the cries of today. From a peaceful heart, we recognize a responsibility for alleviating suffering, no matter what the delusion is around us. We draw steadiness and courage from our prayers and meditation. Then we naturally respond. There comes a growing knowledge that we cannot be complicit with the outrages of the world. As William Faulkner put it:

> Some things you must always be unable to bear. Some things you must never stop refusing to bear. Injustice and outrage and dishonor and shame. No matter how young you are and how old you have got. Not for kudos and not for cash. Your picture in the paper nor money in the bank, neither. Just refuse to bear them.

Sometimes our most powerful response is to bear witness courageously, and this alone begins to create transformation. Buddhist teacher and activist Joanna Macy tells of conducting her despair and empowerment work in one of the cities closest to the Chernobyl nuclear reactor. The area around Chernobyl was once known not for the partial meltdown of its nuclear power plant but for its beautiful forests and mountains. For centuries the people living there walked in the mountains, picnicked, gathered mushrooms, fished, hunted, and cut firewood. Now, at home and at work, their windows and doors were sealed with tape, and they could not go outside or they would risk radiation poisoning. All they had left were pictures of the forest on the wall.

In meeting with community leaders Joanna pointedly asked how long it would be before they could return to their forests. One man answered, "Not in my great-grandchildren's lifetime, and not in THEIR great-grandchildren's lifetime!" It would be centuries. There was silence.

Then a woman stood up and angrily demanded to know why Joanna and her team were rubbing their faces in this sorrow. Joanna sat quietly. Finally one old man spoke: "At least we can say to our children that we told the truth." After further silence another woman said, "These visitors come and join together with us for a purpose: to bear witness to our suffering. Now they will return to their own communities and tell our story. They can go out in the world and let others know what happened. They must never let this poisoning of the earth happen in any other place, to anyone else's children." With that comment, personal bitterness was transformed into the work of the bodhisattva.

A respected psychologist I know works with the U.N. caring for newly arrived refugees who seek political asylum from dictatorships around the world. She sometimes finds it hard to sleep, to let go of the stories and images of torture she hears from refugees of Afghanistan, Uganda, Haiti, Guatemala, Burundi, Bosnia, and so many other countries. It becomes too much for the human heart to bear.

We talked about how because such sorrows cannot be borne alone, she decided to make a large altar where she works, putting there images of Kwan Yin, the Goddess of Compassion, plus Jesus, Buddha, and Mother Mary. Then she added the images of Haitian gods and an Arabic scroll of the Koran's passages of mercy, and images of the benevolent gods of Africa and Latin America. A few flowers or a piece of fruit are always present. Each day she calls on the gods and the ancestors of every lineage of earth. She prays that their great spirits will support her and those who bring their sufferings to her.

Now she feels that she need not carry her burden entirely by herself. The altar is a daily reminder not only of how she has dedicated her life, but of how the great forces of compassion throughout the world are dedicated along with her. The truth of interconnection brings us responsibility, but it also brings us companionship and solace. We do not work alone for change; the great powers of existence work with us.

As awakening deepens, reverence and prayer grow. An altar can be one expression of a concerned heart. The very ritual of turning to an altar is a profound act of rededication. Each time we bow we can reawaken to the reality that we are not alone. Each time we meditate or pray, chant or serve, we step beyond the small sense of self, we remember that all beings awaken together. Sometimes as a bodhisattva we must act decisively to stop suffering, to no longer allow it. Sometimes the highest response is to simply bear witness; sometimes our intention will bring success, at other times we must witness our failure.

One of the stories of the Buddha's life tells of the hostilities between the neighboring countries of Magadha and Kapilivatthu, where the Buddha's own Shakya clan lived.

When the Shakya people realized that the king of Magadha was planning to attack them, they implored the Buddha to step forward and make peace. The Buddha agreed. But although he offered many proposals for peace, the king of Magadha could not hear them. His mind would not stop burning, and finally he decided to attack.

So the Buddha went out by himself and sat in meditation under a dead tree by the side of the road leading to Kapilivatthu. The king of Magadha passed along the road with his army and saw the Buddha sitting under the dead tree in the full blast of the sun. So the king asked, "Why do you sit under this dead tree?" The Buddha answered the king, "I feel cool, even under this dead tree, because it is growing in my beautiful native country." This answer pierced the heart of the king. Recognizing the commitment and dedication the Shakyas felt for their land, he returned to his country with his army. Later, however, this same king was again incited to war, and this time his army destroyed Kapilivatthu. The Buddha stood by and watched.

Becoming the peace we seek can often transform a situation. But even in failure, we can follow our steadfast commitment to compassion. We can, like Martin Luther King Jr., stand up for the truth.

> I still believe that standing up for the truth is the greatest thing in the world. This is the end of life. The end of life is not to be happy. The end of life is not to achieve pleasure and avoid pain. The end of life is to do the will of God, come what may.

When we dedicate our lives to bearing witness to truth, our hearts become irrepressible. A Western photographer told me how he had seen this spirit in an old Tibetan nun who had been imprisoned and tortured by the Chinese army for fifteen years. After her release she fled to India, and he wanted to include her wizened face in his portraits of Tibetan elders. As he looked into the large camera lens, he could see her lips murmuring her prayers. When he asked her what had sustained her through these terrible ordeals, she said that no matter what happened she had never stopped saying prayers of compassion for all beings. In the midst of being tortured, she prayed for her torturers. When they saw her lips moving, they bound her mouth with tape. When they saw the tape moving, they put on more layers, but her prayers would not stop. And when she was free, still her prayers continued. No matter what happened, the nun prayed for the well-being of all. That was her true liberation, her unstoppable True Being shining through.

Our Gift to the Earth

Before we awaken, our joy is to use the things of this earth; after the grace of awakening, our joy is to serve the things of this earth. With the growth of wisdom our life becomes more and more a creative act, an act of service. The beauty of such an understanding is that it excludes no one. In the traditional culture of Bali there is no word for "artist," no particular group of "creative" people, no idea of those who serve and those who do not. Each person must offer his or her particular gift, and each act serves the gods. Sacred music, dance, painting, song, story, mystical trance, and prayer are blended with the cooking of a meal, the planting of crops, the driving of a cart. All is actively held worthy, all being is connected to the gods.

We each have gifts for the earth; we offer ourselves to the web of life all of the time. Often we don't honor the seeds of our own small contributions and recognize how they will bear fruit in the wide environment of all that lives. With awakening, we see that all our actions have consequences for the whole.

Seeing in such a way can make a difference in our lives. A perennial teaching story captures this truth. A man visited a huge stoneyard in Europe, where workmen continued to add to the towers of a nearby building, as they had for centuries. He asked one workman what he was doing. He replied wearily, "My job is to square off the stones and move them." When he asked a second fellow, "What are you doing?" he replied, "I am a stonecutter working so I can care for my wife and children and feed my family." A third man performing the identical labor looked up joyfully and answered, "I am building a great cathedral." When we can see that the earth is our cathedral, our eyes open to a secret happiness in all that we do. Each of the stonecutters was contributing to a great work; the only difference was that one knew this was so.

Whether we stand up politically or work in our schools, whether we meditate for a year or live for a year in a redwood tree—as the young woman named Julia "Butterfly" Hill did to stop the logging of the old-growth redwoods in Humboldt County—

we need to offer our voice, our way. It may be that our particular gifts manifest as caring for children, or in law, commerce, or music, in computer networking, or gardening. It is not a matter of what the building block is, but of allowing our unique and singular voice to move in harmony with a living purpose.

For if we are not able to remember our part in the cathedral, to offer our particular gifts, contribute our particular voice, our life becomes a great sorrow. Losing that vision, our spirits shrink and deaden. Even in the simplest tasks, we have this choice. I have seen certain toll takers on the Golden Gate Bridge evoke the spirit of St. Francis as they welcome each car to San Francisco. The expression of our gift need not be grand. Everyone who writes poetry does not need to publish ten volumes and win the National Book Award. The farmer in rural Asia who works his family's meager land for survival can plow with a song on his lips, can bring his inspired prayers to the mosque, can add his poetic voice to the village. He too is transforming the world.

One meditation teacher describes the impact of each small contribution as a "trim-tab effect." When an ocean liner is under way, its momentum is so great that it cannot be steered by moving its rudder. Instead, a series of adjustments is made in the flaps at the edge of the rudder—the trim tabs. These small changes begin to shift the direction of the ship until the rudder itself can be turned, and the ship takes another course. Like trim tabs, our deliberate actions, however small, can change the course of life around us. To use our life to move the world toward compassion and away from suffering is the only thing that matters.

Our gifts are blessings from the ancestors, the gods, the creative intelligence of life. If we are open, our gifts will choose us as much as we choose them. To begin we must only listen. If we quiet ourselves from the clamor and greed of modern consumer culture, we will find the intimate whisperings of what we are to do. That voice will tell us whether we are to start a garden project, write a letter for Amnesty International, comfort a crying child, or contribute a stone to the great cathedral, though we may never live to see its completion.

The Ojibway Indian saying reminds us: "Sometimes I go around pitying myself, and all the while I'm being carried by great winds across the sky." Whenever we awaken, we begin to feel ourselves being carried by these great winds, by the holy spirit, by the Tao, the Dharma, the sacred river of life. We realize we belong on this earth. Whoever we are is the right person; wherever we are is the right place to awaken, the place we have been given to serve.

With this understanding comes a natural ease and gratitude. We have been given so many blessings: the food of the earth, the dark of the starry sky, the warmth of friendship, the creativity of the arts, the turning of the seasons, the capacity for compassion. In these times we are asked to recognize the gifts of life on this beautiful earth, to protect it, celebrate it, and offer our own gifts as our blessings.

This is what you should do: Love the earth and sun and animals,
despise riches, give alms to everyone that asks,
stand up for the stupid and crazy,
devote your income and labor to others, hate tyrants,
argue not concerning God,
have patience and indulgence toward the people . . .
reexamine all you have been told in school or church or in any book,
dismiss what insults your very soul,
and your flesh shall become a great poem.
WALT WHITMAN

17

THE LAUGHTER
OF THE WISE

Since everything is none other
than exactly as it is
one may well just break out in laughter.
LONG CHEN PA

The end of all our exploring
Will be to arrive where we started
And know the place for the first time.
T. S. ELIOT

My friend James Baraz tells of traveling to India to be with the guru H. W. L. Poonja. Poonja was celebrated for his freedom of spirit, for the energy of awakening he transmitted to his disciples, and for his joyful laughter. James had completed twenty years of meditation practice and become a greatly beloved Buddhist teacher. Still wanting to grow, and yearning to touch more deeply the very heart of spiritual life, he went to India. After some days of dialogue with the master, James explained that his Buddhist training had offered wakefulness, compassion, and wisdom, but that nothing much had been taught about grace. He was perplexed. How could he know whether he was receiving the grace of the guru, how should he look for it, he asked. All the gathered disciples listened closely.

The master peered back at James and laughed, amused by the

question. "You teach in a community committed to spiritual life, you have a healthy family in beautiful California, you are in India surrounded by devoted brothers and sisters on the path. Now you are sitting, speaking with the master, and you ask where is the grace?" He laughed again. "You are neck-deep in grace!"

We are all neck-deep in grace. Whoever we are, we are held by the warmth of the sun and the shining embrace of the snow, nourished by the sweet waters of the rain, alive in the great mystery. Whatever our circumstances, we have the perfect capacity to awaken. With an open heart and open mind we discover a great stillness, a loving presence with things as they are. Resting in a simple awareness of the present, the heart becomes trustworthy. As we accept the stream of life, enlightenment and grace arise naturally. This is not attainment, but living wisdom.

As Suzuki Roshi says, "When we realize the everlasting truth of 'everything changes,' and find our composure in it, we find ourselves in Nirvana." Each moment of this awakening brings a sense of caring and natural responsiveness to tragedy and beauty alike. When strength is called for, it is there; when flexibility and surrender are called for, they are there as well. We are at ease with this amazing life.

Resting in Mystery

Inside the Great Mystery that is,
we don't really own anything.
What is this competition we feel then,
before we go, one at a time, through the same gate?
RUMI (tr. Moyne and Barks)

Within the mystery of life there is the infinite darkness of the night sky lit by distant orbs of fire, the cobbled skin of an orange that releases its fragrance to our touch, the unfathomable depths of the eyes of our lover. No creation story, no religious system can fully describe or explain this richness and depth. Mystery is so ever-present that no one can know for certain what will happen one hour from now.

From mystery's vantage there is no fixed path. In truth there is no path at all, for that would be to place it into the realm of space and time. Yet space and time too are a mystery—the past already disappeared, the future only imagined, and the present as fluid as water. To awaken is not to fix or hold but to love whatever is here. Knowing this truth releases our hearts from grasping. The mystery that gave us birth becomes a dance.

The Hindu sages call this dance "the lila," the eternal dance of life. Christian and Jewish mystics speak of it as the mind of God, a play of the Divine, while Buddhists describe birth and death as waves on the ocean of consciousness, arising for a short time and vanishing like a dream.

This truth is always with us. Whenever we have the experience of touching this timeless reality, we are healed. It may come when we are caught in fear or longing, love or jealousy, anger or success, lost in the melodrama of our life. Then in a moment we will hear a voice say, "Really caught by that one, wasn't I?" In that moment we laugh and are free.

This was the understanding communicated by Ram Dass when he first returned home after his major stroke. I called him and asked how he was doing. Still only able to speak slowly and hesitatingly, he replied, "It's been quite a trip." He explained that during the most agonizing weeks, he had relied on his prayers and his guru. Then he haltingly thanked me for the beautiful portrait of the sage Ramana Maharshi I had left in his rehab hospital room for inspiration, because Ramana taught mostly through silence. He kindly offered to give me a portrait of his guru, Neem Karoli Baba, in return. Then he said slowly, "It's . . . um . . . like . . . baseball cards . . . I'll give you one . . . um . . . Neem Karoli Baba . . . and . . . um . . . a Mickey Mantle . . . for one . . . Ramana Maharshi . . . and a Ted Williams." He laughed out loud, and I laughed in great relief, for in this moment, in spite of his massive injuries, I knew that underneath it all Ram Dass was all right.

The sage Hermes Trismegistus offers this meditation as a way to remember the timeless truth of this human life.

Perceive that you are not yet begotten, that you are in the womb, that you are young, that you are old, that you have died, that you are in the world beyond the grave. Grasp in your mind all this at once, all times and places, expanding it to all qualities and magnitudes together, and you can begin to see the play of the Divine.

The following poem offers a reminder in modern form.

REVERSE LIVING

Life is tough
It takes a lot of your time,
all your weekends,
and what do you get at the end of it?
Death, a great reward.
I think that the life cycle is all backwards.
You should die first, get it out of the way.
Then you live twenty years in an old-age home.
You are kicked out when you're too young.
You get a gold watch, you go to work.
You work forty years until you're
young enough to enjoy your retirement.
You go to college,
you party until you're ready for high school.
You become a little kid, you play,
you have no responsibilities,
you become a little boy or girl,
you go back into the womb,
you spend your last nine months floating.
And you finish off as a gleam in someone's eye.

Religion attempts to explain the mystery of our birth into this world; meditation and prayer attempt to open us to it. Wisdom celebrates this mystery, and compassion loves it all—the gleam in every single being's eye.

When I was in eighth grade my science teacher asked us, "If our vast solar system, from our giant sun to the farthest orbit of Pluto, were the size of this baseball in my hand, how big would the rest of our galaxy be?" "As big as a mountain," one student guessed. "As big as the city?" said another. "No," the teacher answered. "Compared to this baseball our galaxy is bigger than the whole country." Now our best telescopes can see a hundred billion such galaxies, and we have no idea what is beyond that.

Mystery surrounds us in a million different species of beetles, in the miracle of speech through which my thoughts vibrate the air into words, beat the drum in your ear, and spark images in your imagination. All this takes place through the mystery of consciousness itself. Science acknowledges it, meditation has opened to it, but no one can truly explain it.

"All is mind-made," begins the Buddha. Rabindranath Tagore elaborated, "Usually we think of the mind as a mirror receiving accurate impressions of the world outside, not realizing that the mind itself is the principal element of creation." How else to explain the double-blind studies of Randolf Byrd at the University of California Medical Center, which demonstrated that patients who were unknowingly prayed for recovered from their illnesses faster than those who were not. Consciousness is the source of experience, the play of mystery itself. Spiritual life opens us to the direct experience of this truth.

Buddhist teacher and hospice director Rodney Smith recalls the visit one morning of two grown children to their father, who was very ill and close to death. They had just learned that their father's youngest brother had been killed in an auto accident. Should they tell their father? After some consideration, they decided not to disturb his peaceful dying with this tragic news. They went together into their father's room to see how he was. After a few minutes the father said, "Don't you have something to tell me?" "What do you mean?" said his children. "About my brother who died." They were astonished. "How did you know?" "Oh, I've been talking to him all morning." Then they spent some last minutes together sharing their love, and shortly thereafter their father died.

At first such stories can reassure us about life beyond the body. But we must be careful not to explain away this mystery so easily. Our images of Christian heaven, the Hindu teachings of reincarnation, or the remarkably well-laid-out realms in *The Tibetan Book of the Dead* can mistakenly lead us to believe we understand the mystery of death. Yet when death taps us, it is still unknown.

Stephen Levine, who has done years of groundbreaking healing and hospice work, tells the story of a child with terminal cancer. As the young boy came closer and closer to death, he began to drift between worlds. Several times his respiration stopped. Returning from one of these near-death moments, he opened his shining eyes and when he could speak told Stephen about seeing a great light and entering a tunnel. So far this was not that unusual an account for Stephen to hear. But what the boy saw next was explained with some awe and excitement. "Then I saw Raphael, and he was trying to help me." It was not Raphael the archangel, but Raphael the Ninja Turtle, one of the benevolent wisdom figures among the Teenage Mutant Ninja Turtles that were popular at this time and important to this boy. This is who had come to lead him into the beyond.

Does this mean that we see only the illusions of our own mind at death? Or does it mean that the light that awaits us shines through whatever images we hold dear? We cannot know. Death remains a mystery. When one Zen master was asked what happens when you die, he answered, "I don't know." "But aren't you a Zen master?" continued the questioner. "Yes," he responded, "but not a dead one."

Thoreau understood this simplicity in his thoroughly American way. When someone asked him what he believed about death and the hereafter, he replied, "One world at a time."

The Wisdom of Not Knowing

Wisdom is not knowing but being. The Christian mystics instructed seekers to enter the Cloud of Unknowing with a trusting heart. The wise heart is not one that understands everything—it is the heart that can tolerate the truth of not knowing. Wisdom comes alive in the presence of the mystery, when the heart is open, sensitive, wholly receptive. Out of this simple presence, empathy, love, responsiveness, all good things are born.

A Hindu teacher describes how, as he grew older, he came to trust not in knowledge but in love.

> *I have let go of the need to know so much. What we can know is so small—the holiness around is so large. Now I trust in simplicity, simplicity and love.*

My teacher Ajahn Chah would often respond to people's questions, plans, and ideas with a smile and say, "Mai neh." The phrase means, "It is uncertain, isn't it?" He understood the wisdom of uncertainty, the truth of change, and was comfortable in their midst.

A Sufi master told me:

> *The most surprising thing about the process of spiritual opening is how unexpected it becomes. I had studied the sacred texts for years, but I never knew what was coming next. Powerful experiences would come; new possibilities beyond my knowing and beliefs would sweep over me. I learned that experience is never how we think it will be. Understanding this is real wisdom.*

The truth is, we don't know. Not the Pope, not the Chief Rebbe of Jerusalem, not even your mother can know what will happen tomorrow. And neither can we. We just don't know.

Korean Zen Master Seung Sahn trains his students to dwell in what he calls "don't know mind." He will demand of them: Who are you? Where is your mind? What is consciousness? Where did you come from? Each time the students will say, "I don't know." "Now keep this don't know mind!" he will say. Rest in it, trust it. As with the Cloud of Unknowing or the "unlearning" of the Tao, wisdom grows by opening to the truth of not knowing.

There is a natural pleasure when we speak with someone who doesn't know everything, who is open-minded, eager to listen. There is a delightful presence, receptiveness, and humility in such a mind. The Third Zen Patriarch puts it this way: "If you wish to know the truth, only cease to cherish opinions." In the oldest of Buddhist texts, the Sutta Nipata, the Buddha speaks of this, ending with a humorous poke at those who hold opinions:

> Seeing misery in views and opinions, without adopting any, I found inner peace and freedom. One who is free does not hold to views or dispute opinions. For a sage there is no higher, lower, nor equal, no places in which the mind can stick. But those who grasp after views and opinions only wander about the world annoying people.

For a long time I didn't understand this. After I had practiced in the monastery and began to offer retreats, I had many ideas. Much of my initial focus was teaching people Buddhist principles through which they could overcome greed, hatred, and delusion and develop mindfulness and understanding. I wanted people to understand their patterns of grasping, to rid themselves of greed, anger, hatred, and confusion, and I thought such insight would bring about transformation. As I matured, I began to see that it is much simpler than this.

Underneath all the wanting and grasping, underneath the need to understand is what we have called "the body of fear." At the root of suffering is a small heart, frightened to be here, afraid to trust the river of change, to let go in this changing world. This small unopened heart grasps and needs and struggles to control what is unpredictable and unpossessable. But we can never know what will happen. With wisdom we allow this not knowing to become a form of trust. We rest on what Buddhist elder Jocelyn King laughingly called "the Firm Ground of Emptiness." Chogyam Trungpa described this as giving up the ego's territory and trusting in groundlessness. St. John of the Cross described it this way: "If a man wishes to be sure of the road he treads on, he must close his eyes and walk in the dark."

Terry Dobson was one of the senior martial artists in the West. While studying aikido in Tokyo, Terry also trained under a Japanese master carpenter. For one whole year Terry was taught to sweep the shop, sharpen the tools, and observe. Then, when he was finally given his first pieces of wood to work with, he was blindfolded. For months he had to learn how to plane, smooth, and square a series of wood projects solely by his sense of touch. These months brought one of the most memorable experiences of his time in Japan, a patient learning with his body and his heart, which became part of his aikido practice as well as his carpentry.

Wisdom is not information, but an abiding presence, an intuitive, sensing opening of the body and heart. In wisdom the body of fear drops away and our heart comes to rest. Like love, wisdom needs no explanation. Like the Tao, it brings harmony and ease. We understand how the beloved Zen poet Ryokan could answer visitors' questions about enlightenment or the nature of good and evil by saying, "I have only the tranquillity of my hermitage to offer in reply."

The Practices of Wisdom

In the mandala of wholeness we have discovered the awakened heart's willingness to open to all the dimensions of life. But over the years what happens to the practices of prayer, contemplation, and devotion, the daily rituals of yoga, chanting, or meditation? In one way, nothing happens. We continue the same practices, often with even more care and dedication; they remain important ingredients in a sacred life. However, we do them in a radically different way.

With spiritual maturity the basis for these practices shifts away from ambition, idealism, and desire for self-transformation. It is as if the wind has changed, and a weather vane—still centered in the same spot—now points in a different direction: back to this moment. We are no longer striving after a spiritual destination, grasping for another world different from the one we have. We are home. And being home, we sweep the floor, make nourishing meals, and care for our guests. When we have realized the everlasting truths of life, what else is there to do but continue our practice?

If our practice was bowing, we continue to bow, awakened to a reverence for all of life. If our practice was prayer, we pray all the more out of love, for ourselves and all beings. If our practice was meditation or sacred dance, we sit or dance as the expression of our awakened heart.

Of course, we also need our continuing practice. We can still become lost, entangled, caught up in the difficulties of modern life. Our continuing practices cleanse us, steady us, remind us of what is true. Our daily practices help us stay balanced, attend to our body, keep our heart open, strengthen our ability to offer clear love. Our practice becomes like cleaning house. We do not just clean the house once and forget it. It is a regular task, and a pleasure to live in a clean house, to honor all who enter. But the house is not who we are, and no amount of ambitious cleaning will change the nature of our life. We practice to express our awakening, not to attain it.

One senior nun says:

When I look at the older sisters, what I most admire is their good hearts. They still serve and work and pray and teach like they did years ago as young girls, but now there's a different beauty about them. Then we were all full of ardor, wanting to become virtuous and worthy of God, waiting to find something special in this holy life. Now we pray because we have come to love prayer; we teach or work with a sim-

ple natural kindness and love. It has become a way of giving God's joy.

Frank Ostaseski, the director of the Zen Center Hospice of San Francisco for many years, tells this simple story of wisdom and trust:

The day before his death, John was in a waking coma. His face was full of tension, his head thrust far back, the muscles in his throat were tight and constricted. His breath was a struggle. Clearly this was another stage of dying, but to me something seemed stuck. A famous teacher with experience in these things told me that his spirit was trying to leave his body and that I should touch the top of his head to show the way. A physician told me to increase his morphine to relax his breathing. A body worker told me to hold certain acupressure points on his feet to relieve the tension. I tried them all, but nothing changed.

Instinctively I just wanted to wrap myself around him. I climbed into bed, cradling John in the curve of my arms. I remember rocking him back and forth, and as I did I began to sing sweet lullabies to him. Not the nursery rhyme variety, but the kind you make up as you go along. Words and sounds mixing together randomly, not making any sense—just "love sounds," I call them. Every parent has done this for a sick or frightened child.

As I sang softly in his ear and kissed his forehead, my hands knew what to do, though there was no goal in mind. My fingers caressed his throat, stroked his face, and then my opened hands circled his heart. We lost all sense of time. I could feel him sink into me, my body cushioning what was left of his bony form. Eventually his throat began to relax and his head came forward. His eyes opened. They looked relieved.

Afterward I wondered if I had done the right thing.

Maybe I should have followed the teacher's advice. Had I pulled him back from some near-death state? Stopped some process of release? I don't know really. I do know that the heart has to be soft before any of us can be free.

The Child of the Spirit

The spiritual journey has led us through many adventures, back to where we are now. Rumi and Nietzsche use three poetic images to describe this journey: the camel, the lion, and the child. These stages on the path are simply aspects of consciousness unfolding; at each moment we contain them all. Still, it is also helpful to sense them as progressive steps on the path.

The camel stands for our initial surrender, for dedication, the willingness to kneel, to carry our burdens honorably, to pass through desolation, to travel to far lands. In the camel stages of awakening we make ourselves available to the spirit through humility, prayer, repetition, and manual labor. Our respect for each difficult step brings us to a place of trust here on the earth. Our devotion brings healing; our patient heart nourishes compassion. The camel offers us the ground of simple dignity.

When we have discovered the heart's capacity to face any situation, the joys and sorrows of existence as they are, we awaken to freedom. Then the golden lion speaks with a roar. Out of the mouth of the lion comes the undaunted voice of truth, the liberation of the unbounded heart. The kingdom is ours. In this second stage we are no longer seekers; we have discovered beyond our small self the certainty of grace and a timeless whole.

It is said that the Buddha spoke with a lion's roar. A lion roars with its whole body, and even in a zoo the sound shocks all the other animals into silence. Even after twenty years such a voice cries out, "I am not a creature of the zoo." The lion, like a king or queen, lives in regal ease and untrammeled freedom of the heart. The royalty of the lion bestows blessings on all it touches.

In the last stage the lion gives way to the child, to an original innocence. This is the Child of the Spirit for whom all things are new. For this divine child there is wonder, ease, and a playful heart. The child is at home in the reality of the present, able to enjoy, to respond, to forgive, and to share the blessings of being alive.

Through the child, our journey brings us back to witness with amazement and love the natural unfolding of all that lives. The Buddha declares, "This world and the pure heart that perceives it are luminous." When we allow ourselves to open into innocence, all existence becomes sacred.

Thomas Merton described the moment when he opened his eyes in this way:

> Then it was as if I suddenly saw the secret beauty of their hearts, the depths of their hearts where neither sin nor desire can reach, the core of their reality, the person that each one is in God's eyes. If only they could see themselves as they really are. If only we could see each other that way all the time, there would be no war, no more hatred, no more cruelty, no more greed. . . . I suppose the big problem would be that we would fall down and worship each other.

The innocence of childlike wisdom is celebrated in every tradition. The Hindus acknowledge the childlike aspect of God in stories of Lord Krishna as the holy child who comes to play his flute among the milkmaids and the flowers. Christianity celebrates the birth of the Christ Child near the winter solstice, and offers the images of the infant Jesus in His mother's arms. The mystic Angelus Silesius teaches: "If in your heart you make a manger for His birth, then God will once again become a child on this earth." Each year in Thailand and Laos Buddhist followers pour water on the monks in the monastery, bathing each monk as if he were the newborn Baby Buddha.

Ajahn Chah spoke of entering this innocence simply by resting in our Original Mind. He taught that our Original Mind is always here—the silence between thoughts; our fundamental awareness, clear, unhindered, and pure. This is the openness before and after experience, so vast it embraces both suffering and joy with unbounded compassion. A Zen koan points us to this Original Mind when it says, "Show me your face before your parents were born."

Seeing with the Eyes of the Moment

In the innocent heart nothing can be repeated. When the Greek philosopher Heraclitus said we can never step in the same river twice, he also knew that we can never meet the same person twice, that to say the word "bread" can never do justice to its shape and texture, to the unique moment when this particular piece is softened with butter as we prepare to put it in our mouth. Rumi delights in this freshness.

> Lord, the air smells good today, straight from the mysteries
> within the inner courts of God.
> A grace like new clothes thrown across the garden,
> free medicine for everybody.
> The trees in their prayer, the birds in praise.

We cannot predict how this awareness of mystery will reawaken in us, or in what form. Long ago I lived with one of my first loves and her young children, Seth and Chani. When the children were three and five years old the Ringling Brothers circus came to town. As a treat I bought tickets for us, ringside seats, right in the center, two rows back.

The children liked the clowns and the tigers. Most of the other acts—the high wire, the jugglers, the contortionists, the trained horses—were too far away, too small to seem especially remarkable to a young child's eyes.

But then the elephants came out, with their feathered plumes and sequined riders. In formation, they circled the ring twice, coming right near us. Then they stopped while the ringmaster talked. All at once the big elephant just in front of us began to pee; a huge flood cascaded to the sand below, making a giant puddle. The children's eyes grew wide. And then the elephant began to poo. Large, bowling ball–sized spheres thudded to the ground, one at a time, *plop, plop, thwack*. Each was observed with increasing wonder and excitement.

When we got home, and for weeks after that, the children talked about going to the circus. And what they told and recounted over and over was the story of the elephant. That was the most amazing circus act of all.

It is life itself that is astonishing, each unique moment. Zen honors this mystery for its own sake—each thing in its turn. As Kodo Rishi teaches, "You don't eat in order to poo, you don't poo in order to make manure." With the same eyes of wisdom, we don't practice meditation or prayer to make some special reality. Eating, walking, speaking, seeing, breathing, defecating—each is amazing in itself.

This innocent heart, our Buddha Nature, the Child of the Spirit, the Holy One within is never degraded nor lost. It is never born and never dies. To see in this way is to see, as the Tao says, "with eyes unclouded by longing." When we awaken this innocent heart, we find our true home. At ease, we celebrate the simple marvels of every day.

Zen Master Dogen reminds us:

The life of one day is enough to rejoice. Even though you live for just one day, if you can be awakened, that one day is vastly superior to one endless life of sleep. . . . If this day in the lifetime of a hundred years is lost, will you ever touch it with your hands again?

The Laughter of the Wise

The ancient city of Kyoto is home to the most exquisite monasteries of Japan. Many people travel there on pilgrimage to experience the rock gardens, to bow in the temples, or to take tea by its sacred shrines. One day on a visit there the famed Zen poet Basho penned these lines:

> Even in Kyoto,
> Hearing the cuckoo's cry
> I long for Kyoto.

Our sacred longing is to return to where we are "and know the place for the first time." Then we are coming back to our own true nature. Sri Nisargadatta used to laugh and ask, "How can you not trust? You're on your way home." He went on, "When you worry about renouncing the world, it is a mistake. You need not renounce the world, only renounce striving and fear; you renounce the smaller pleasures for the greater pleasure of the Divine."

The *I Ching* says, "A revolution should gladden the hearts of the people." To give ourselves to awakening is a revolutionary act, a transformation of the world. Even amid the suffering of one's people, Mahaghosananda of Cambodia teaches, one can remain happy of heart. He explains that the aim of Buddhist practice is to awaken a benevolent and compassionate heart in spite of everything. If we can't be happy, what is the use of our practice? And only within the wisdom of the open, unperturbed heart can we hold all the forms of this world with tender compassion, knowing that they appear only once. We can rest in their undying source, in the timeless grace from which all arises and returns.

This holy wisdom is whispered by the Tibetans in the ear of one who is dying. "Remember the clear light, the pure clear light from which everything in the universe comes, to which everything returns, the original nature of your own mind. It is your own true nature; it is home."

It is sung as the prayer of oneness in Judaism, it is worshiped as the Holy Spirit of Christian love, it is celebrated as the eternal Brahman by the Hindus, and it is the essence of the Tao.

> If you don't realize the source
> you stumble in confusion and sorrow.
> When you realize where you come from
> you naturally become tolerant,
> disinterested, amused,
> kindhearted as a grandmother,
> dignified as a king.
> Immersed in the wonder of the Tao
> you can deal with whatever life brings,
> and then, when death comes, you are ready.
> (tr. Stephen Mitchell)

When we embody this truth, our life becomes a blessing. Compassion, understanding, a joyful freedom touch all we meet. A radiance of love pushes out of us like the green shoots through the cracks in cement. We become like ancient Chinese teapots. When a beloved teapot is used by a Chinese family for a hundred years or more, it is said, there is no need to put in tea. You just pour in water and the pot makes tea by itself.

Like the teapot, we ourselves become the source. Releasing ambition or fear, we return to our true home. Without imitation, we become just who we are. Our being is at ease; our heart opens. Joy and freedom of spirit fill our days.

A story that carries this spirit was told by a friend who attended the Dalai Lama's teachings on the Tibetan Wheel of Time in Madison Square Garden. Because these are among the highest Vajrayana practices, their introduction was accompanied by a complex and respectful ritual. Sand mandalas were painted. An elegant teaching throne was set up, covered with carpets and silk brocade. After the crowd of thousands was seated, a colorful assembly of lamas and monks intoned sacred chants, accompanied by the sounds of Tibetan bells, cymbals, and the great mountain horns. When the Dalai Lama entered, he walked down the carpet and climbed the steps to take the Dharma seat at the top of the throne. To make the seat comfortable, the organizers had placed mattresses at the top, covered by carpet and silk. When the Dalai Lama sat down on the throne, it bounced. A smile lit his face. He bounced again, and smiled more. Then, in front of thousands of students, before offering the highest teachings on the Wheel of Time and the creation of the world, the Dalai Lama bounced up and down as happily as a child.

In ending this book, I honor the wholeness that is your own true nature. May your journey lead you home. May you rest in grace, in natural compassion and a liberated heart. Whether in times of joy or sorrow, in ecstasy or in the laundry, may you be happy. May all who read the words of this book find freedom and joy. May your love bring benefit to all beings. And in the midst of it all, may you too remember to bounce.

And as to me, I know of nothing else but miracles.
WALT WHITMAN

ACKNOWLEDGMENTS

First, I offer a bow of true gratitude for the personal accounts of the nearly one hundred Zen masters, meditation teachers, lamas, nuns, monks, priests, rabbis, swamis, and their senior students whose stories appear in this book. Their stories, though altered for privacy, are all true. Because our interviews were undertaken with the promise of confidentiality (so they could speak freely), I cannot name them here, but their life-commitment to the spiritual journey shines through their words. Thank you all, dear and respected friends.

Next, my deep gratitude goes to Evelyn Sweeney, who at the age of eighty, labored for three years on these pages, transcribing, typing, and editing with tremendous care. Without Evelyn's unflagging dedication this book would not be in your hands.

Jane Hirshfield is the main editor of this volume and it is the best of blessings to work with her. She is a poet of the heart and a master editor with pen and sword, whose clear-eyed under-standing and love of the Way graces all these pages. Gassho.

Toni Burbank, my wise and delightful senior editor at Bantam, offered her thoughtful and generous counsel throughout. In these times it is a rare privilege to work with such an understanding and supportive mentor in the publishing world.

I must also acknowledge how much I have continued to learn from my teaching colleagues over the years; all sixteen members of the Spirit Rock Teachers Council, Ajahn Amaro, Guy Armstrong, James Baraz, Sylvia Boorstein, Eugene Cash, Deborah Chamberlin-Taylor, Sally Clough, Howard Cohn, Anna Douglas, Gil Fronsdal, Robert Hall, Phillip Moffitt, Wes Nisker, Mary Orr, John Travis, and Julie Wester. And my longtime colleagues, Stan and Christina Grof, Michael Meade, Malidoma Somé and Luis Rodriguez, Joseph Goldstein and Sharon Salzberg, Ram Dass and Stephen Levine, as well as a growing circle of teaching friends in every lineage.

And especially I give thanks to my beloved wife and daughter, Liana and Caroline. Their love and wisdom sustain me throughout.

Jack Kornfield
Spirit Rock Center
2000

PERMISSIONS

Grateful acknowledgment is made to the following publishers and authors for permission to reprint the fine material from their books:

From *Open Secret: Versions of Rumi,* translated by Coleman Barks. Reprinted by permission of Threshold Books, Aptos, California.

Gratitude to Robert Bly and Michael Meade for oral versions from which the stories of Baba Yaga and Princess Aris are drawn, and to Coleman Barks for the images of the camel, lion, and child in his book of Rumi translations called *Feeling the Shoulder of the Lion,* Threshold Books, Aptos, California, 1991.

From *New and Selected Poems* by Mary Oliver. Copyright © 1992 by Mary Oliver. Reprinted by permission of Beacon Press, Boston.

From *The Gold Cell* by Sharon Olds. Copyright © 1987 by Sharon Olds. Reprinted by permission of Alfred A. Knopf, a division of Random House, Inc.

From *Selected Poems of Rainer Maria Rilke,* edited and translated by Robert Bly. Copyright © 1981 by Robert Bly. Reprinted by permission of HarperCollins Publishers, Inc.

From *Teachings of the Buddha* by Jack Kornfield. Excerpts from "Fire Sermon," from Mahavagga, p. 42; from "The Eye of

304

INDEX

ABOUT THE AUTHOR

JACK KORNFIELD was trained as a Buddhist monk in Thailand, Burma, and India, and has taught meditation around the world since 1974. He is one of the key teachers to introduce Theravada Buddhist practice to the West. For many years his work has been focused on integrating and bringing alive the great Eastern spiritual teachings in a way that is accessible to Western students and Western society. He also holds a Ph.D. in clinical psychology. He is a husband and father, and a founding teacher of the Insight Meditation Society and Spirit Rock Center. His books include *Seeking the Heart of Wisdom; A Still Forest Pool; Stories of the Spirit, Stories of the Heart; Buddha's Little Instruction Book; A Path with Heart;* and *Teachings of the Buddha.*